DEDICATION

I think most people can go their whole lifetime without making a 911 call. I have made over 25 calls to 911. The kindness, speed and professionalism of paramedics is truly heroic. They arrive at people's homes and face dire situations, and they stay calm under the greatest pressure. Thank you, Gilbert Fire Department.

I have visited several Phoenix-area hospitals and spent over 250 days of my life in them. I am uniquely experienced to say the men and women nurses, technicians, therapists, and doctors are special people. Thank you to the medical professionals at Banner Baywood Medical Center, Banner Heart Hospital, Banner Gateway Medical Center, Banner Ocotillo Medical Center and Mercy Gilbert Hospital.

ACKNOWLEDGEMENT

To John Lechtenberger, my high school English teacher and the editor of this book. I enjoyed our many discussions about the book and all the other topics over the last few months. Thank you for reminding me that with writing, less is often more. Your wonderful contributions were beyond measure.

To Savanna Harper, for all your hard work proofreading the manuscript. Your attention to detail was appreciated. I enjoyed taking the journey through the book with you.

Thank you to Celia Nabor and Seth Hudman for reading the manuscript and giving me your thoughtful advice.

FOREWORD

I received a telephone call from the author, Stephen Biles, in January 2024 after his mother, Shirley Biles passed away. I had treated Shirley many years previously but, even so, my memory of her and her devoted husband, Don, was quite clear to me. They would travel the 131 miles from Safford, Arizona, to Tucson, Arizona, every month or so in the 1980s and 1990s to consult with me. I remember her as a personable, friendly woman who struggled with challenging mental health issues. In spite of this she remained strong and persevered in the face of her illness. This was no simple task as it is common for those such afflicted to give in to the dark side of their emotions. Her husband, Don, would always be there by her side to support her, even when she was at her worst.

When Stephen contacted me, we discussed her emotional struggles and treatment during those years she worked with me. Stephen was 14 years old when I first began treating his mother and I never had the occasion to meet him in person though I remember his parents often speaking of him as proud parents do. I was pleased to learn from Stephen that Shirley had ultimately overcome her struggles with mental illness and was able to go on to lead a productive life. Unfortunately, she developed several medical issues later in life which she endured bravely and stoically until the time of her passing in 2022.

When Stephen told me that he had authored a book about his relationship with his mother I was eager to read it. He sent me a copy of the manuscript which I read over the following days. I found the story entertaining, compelling and moving, all the more so as it brought back memories of my work with Shirley and her devoted husband, Don.

As I read the book, I witnessed a strong family facing multiple challenges over a period of more than four decades. Shirley and Stephen faced these challenges head on without feeling sorry for themselves or blaming others. During those years they found support with their love of dogs, and this led Stephen to start a thriving and growing business caring for these wonderful animal companions.

This is a story of perseverance and courage in the face of great mental and physical adversity. It is the story of a mother and son each supporting the other as they faced often overwhelming challenges in their lives. It is the story of a mother's devotion to her son and her son's devotion to his mother. The book shows strong family bonds that are always admirable but not always evident in society these days.

This is a book that can be enjoyed by any person who is a part of a family that has been, as all families are, touched by adversity in one way or another and who steadfastly struggles to overcome such adversity. It teaches strength, perseverance and an indomitable human spirit.

I thank Stephen for giving me the opportunity to write this foreword to his inspiring book.

Daniel J. Fredman, M.D.
Diplomate in Psychiatry
American Board of Psychiatry and Neurology

PREFACE

I decided to write the story of Shirley Biles, my mother, because I had a front row seat to her last 49 years of amazing fortitude. She was an ordinary housewife and mother, but that was the only thing ordinary about her. She had an indomitable spirit when it came to living and loving her family.

I first saw mom's grace and strength when I was a young boy growing up with Perthes' Disease, a rare hip disease for young children. It took three years for me to recover, roughly the age of five to eight years old.

A little later in life, I saw mental illness not only take over her life, but the lives of everyone close to her. In 1979, I was about 11 years old; that was when her illness began in earnest. Her symptoms and perseverance continued for the next 20 years.

In 2000, I was 32 years old when her husband of 45 years passed away, I saw a true miracle. My dad was her sole provider for all her adult life. He was her caretaker during the last 20 years of his life. Those years can best be characterized as a mental-illness stupor for my mom. Yet, instead of seeing a complete collapse in my mother like everyone expected, I witnessed an epic rebirth, reminiscent of the Phoenix. This amazing recovery continued for the next 17 years.

I finally was a witness to her amazing final act. It was a life of strength, grace and perseverance that built into an indomitable spirit that was on full display during the final five years of her life.

I wrote this book to give hope to people suffering from mental illness and their families. Also, to help educate on the growing dangers of diet, diabetes and its ultimate ending--metabolic syndrome and its various related diseases such as heart and kidney disease. Finally, I hope the book inspires people to be like my mom. A selfless, loving champion of her family who instilled important qualities in her son at a young age--such as perseverance, patience, and grit.

Writing this book was both easy and incredibly difficult. I was a primary source for most of the very personal narrative. I reached out for help to her two sisters, Beverly and Virginia when it came to life before I was born. I also had a treasure trove of personal letters mom saved all her life. The hard part was returning to her medical records, returning to the physical locations of her life, and returning to my social media posts, but the most difficult was returning to my memories. The process was bittersweet. I loved mom dearly and loved our life together. Remembering all the many good times was rewarding. Remembering all the tough times was painful, but those memories reinforced to me her incredible spirit as she confronted her most difficult moments of life and death with courage and the kindest smile.

PART 1
THE PERSEVERANCE

"You may encounter many defeats, but you must not be defeated. In fact, it may be necessary to encounter the defeats, so you can know who you are, what you can rise from, how you can still come out of it."

-    *Maya Angelou*

CHAPTER 1
Into the Abyss
(1980-1993)

"Whoever fights monsters should see to it that in the process he does not become a monster. And if you gaze long enough into an abyss, the abyss will gaze back into you."

- *Friedrich Nietzsche*

Police cars started pulling up to my house at 124 Ironwood. A terrible anticipation began to build as the officers started getting out of their cars. Cricket Forstrom, a close friend of the family, was at the house. She told me, *"Stephen, don't look."* It was all a blur, I was twelve years old, but I remember several officers coming to the front door, maybe six.

Mom knew they were there for her. She said, *"Devil, what have you done?"* As she spoke to dad. She didn't go easily or quietly. They put a straitjacket on her as she resisted with almost superhuman strength. It took every one of the officers to get her under control. I yelled to her, *"Don't fight them, mom!"*

After they had the straitjacket on her, she would not oblige them with walking. She fell to the ground, and they had to carry her to the patrol car. Throughout the process, she continually let dad know what a bad man he was for doing this to her. Dad was in tears and devastated. He walked along her side as they were carrying her. She looked straight at dad and told him in a clear, calm voice— *"I'll never forgive you Don, look what you did to me."*

The delivery of mom to healthcare professionals was a culmination of a long, painful process that had its origins as the 1970s turned into the 1980s.

As the 1980s loomed, all my friends, the community of Morenci, and mostly my family were heading into a dark place. The neighboring town of Clifton was ravaged with the flood of the century, as the San Francisco River crested in a most violent way. Our copper mining community of Morenci was heading towards a famous workers' strike at the mine that was a fixture in the state news and even national news. It was surreal as helicopters were often flying over our tiny town way out in the eastern mountains of Arizona. The Governor was involved. The National Guard rolled into town with armored vehicles as a show of force towards the strikers. The community was deeply divided over the strike--it was neighbor against neighbor, friend against friend, family member against family member. As our closely knit community was imploding at every level—closer to home, things were not right with mom.

As mom entered the 1980s, several factors converged to cause a mental breakdown. The converging factors included: 1) nearing the end of her "nest" as a mother; 2) hormonal changes in her mid-40s; 3) lonely in her marriage; and finally, 4) the death of her father.

First, mom was a homemaker devoted to her family as her full-time job and her overriding purpose in life, it was all she ever knew. One of her biggest challenges as a mother came with her final child, me. I was a boy who grew up with a disability and all the challenges that went along with raising a disabled child. Rearing the final kid in the nest brought on mixed feelings. On the one hand, finishing the job of raising her four kids that started in 1956 and the finish line of 1986 was now on the horizon. It would be 30 years of her life devoted to raising a family. Of course, grandchildren were starting to join the family with many more to come. Grandkids were usually a helpful transition with mothers so devoted to their children.

Second, her manic episodes were a clear cycle, almost seasonal. As the late 70s turned into the early 80s, they became more intense and beyond our ability as a family to contain or manage. As we occasionally suspected, it was related to her mid-life age of 44. Perhaps hormonal changes contributed to behavior changes. As the manic cycle picked up steam, it usually resulted in less and less sleep and increasingly obsessive behavior and extreme delusions. Experts believe manic-depression episodes are amplified in most menopausal women.

Third, mom was lonely in her marriage. All the kids were almost gone, but her husband Don was already gone most of the time. He was an alcoholic. He spent most of his free time away from work at the local bars in town. Often not coming home until 9, 10, or 11 at night. When he did come home, he was drunk to various degrees—at times mild, but often so drunk he could barely walk. It was mom's job to wait for his arrival whenever that may be and cook a nice meal. Occasionally, it was heating up a nice meal already prepared, but it was often making a meal from scratch at his unknown arrival. Every so often, he was so drunk he couldn't even stand or stay awake. It was mom's duty to get him to bed if she could and take his clothes off. This happened frequently. Occasionally he'd pass out just inside the front door on a couch or chair and not wake up until morning. Every so often, he'd pass out in his truck outside the house after somehow making it home.

I witnessed this pattern for most of my adolescent years. Dad's workday would end at about 4 pm. It was a rare treat for him to be home at 6 pm or so. I would monitor his arrival from my bed to gauge his state of drunkenness and make sure things were going okay. One night he might be singing or telling some compelling story from work. I knew I could go to bed when he was friendly or happy. Another night, he might be belligerent, and I knew I had to monitor and possibly intervene to make sure he didn't cross any lines. Every morning, it was mom's job to get him up, lucid, and ready for another day of work. Mom not only had this difficult life at home, but also, she had to live with the gossip and lifestyle dad lived. He was a good-looking man who played pool, drank whisky, and generally had a good time with the men and women that would frequent the bars. It was an endless cycle of a lonely life for mom.

Fourth, my mother's dad Orvel died on June 9, 1981. I think life became too much to bear for her and it all started to spin out of control. She wasn't particularly close to her dad, but she did love him. The loss of a parent is a major turning point for all of us. Mom was combating multiple life transitions simultaneously and her biological predisposition was not equipped to handle it. I believe a lot of people are biologically predisposed to mental illness, but sometimes it doesn't surface because it often needs a catalyst, a perfect storm, a major life event of depression...and the result would become a mental breakdown.

Between 1980 and 1985, mom had about six severe manic episodes brought on by the conditions mentioned above. In the early days of her illness, it seemed to come with a fury, and then would abate and she would return to a tenuous, but agitated stability. Later, the episodes were so severe, she required in-patient hospitalization. During these episodes, she exhibited a commanding presence. She was obsessed with right and wrong, good and evil, God and the Devil. Her behavior was erratic, dangerous, and often hurtful.

When mom was manic, she took on a persona of power and strength. She dominated everything and everyone around her. Her dominance took both physical and mental forms. She would physically intimidate those who got in her way. Her wit and mental strength were also tough to beat or overcome. She accomplished amazing feats of planning and organization. She had seemingly unending endurance. To be in a manic state often feels good to a lot of people, it's empowering.

Mom studied the Bible a lot during this time in her life. There were certain things she was trying to get to the bottom of – such as the true name of God. The study of numerology and its importance in the world. Who was good and evil on Earth and in her immediate presence. Who needed to be protected and who needed to be watched. My sister Kristy, her husband George, and mom held regular Bible study meetings. When mom would get on a roll, she would be compelling. Plus, she was mom, there must be something to what she was saying.

12

One person above all others was her ongoing villain, her representation of evil and wrong in the world; he was often the Devil on Earth—that person was dad. She believed he epitomized everything wrong with her family, her life, and the world in general.

An example of how she would talk to him was something like this... *"Who would have ever thought the Devil himself was right in my house, Don Biles. Why are you here, Devil?"* Dad would plead with her to stop. Occasionally when he would least expect it, he might get a swift punch to the stomach. *"YES, Don Biles is the Devil, always was, always will be. Truth, Verified."* I could see her mind working, her silent whispers to herself. It seemed as if she was having multiple conversations with different people. One part of her would ask a rhetorical question or make a comment. Then another part of her would confirm that proclamation as true with the *"Truth, verified"* comment that would often conclude many of her statements.

I would carefully monitor the interactions between mom and dad all the time. On occasion, dad would have to yell at me for help. She might whack him with whatever she might be using as her banging instrument at the time. It was particularly scary when she was wielding a knife. I held a lot of influence with mom, so she would listen to me to stop hurting dad. Every now and then, I would have to get in the middle of them and just tell dad to *"get away, don't talk, don't interact, you are just making it worse, go into the other room."* I remember a time when dad tried to go into the kitchen and get some order with the banging of the pots and pans and I would hear him yell after getting hit in the head with a pot. Coming back into the room bleeding on his forehead, showing me. My response was often... *"Stay out of there, stay away from her, you can't stop it, you can't control it!"* Every so often, if I would go too far in his defense, she might say to me, *"You're falling under the influence of the Devil, Don Biles. Truth, verified."* She would tell the Devil to *"Be gone and quit influencing my son, he's the chosen one."*

13

Other people, often the friends of dad, were also villains in her mind. One day, long-time friends Carl and Cricket Forstrom came to visit my parents at their Ironwood house. At the time, Carl was President of the Morenci Mining Operation with several thousand workers under his control. Mom happened to be in the front yard at the time spraying water on the walls and windows of the house, as she would often do as a way of cleansing the house of evil. As her long-time friends approached the gate of her yard, they exchanged pleasantries, and then she turned the water hose on them and kept spraying them until they ran off down the street. As she was spraying them, she told them what she thought of them and how they had better not come back.

As her manic episode grew and strengthened, she would chant and bang on pots and pans for hours. She would seem to be in a hypnotic state and continue through the night in a rhythmic fashion. Her chants were clever and even spoken in rhyme as she would vary her vocal style with different tones and different speeds of her chant.

During her mild, manic times, she was busy going through every family picture she could find and cutting dad out of the pictures from the first twenty-five years of their marriage. She threw away many family treasures during this period and would often organize and store everything out in plain sight on the coffee tables, the dining room table, and the countertops. There would be stacks and stacks of arranged house goods in her orderly manner.

Another common theme was the true name of God. Was it Jehovah or was it Yahweh? *"I think it's Jehovah. Truth, verified."* Then a chant of Jehovah would commence for a long time, varying her pronunciation, and tone as she was chanting. Dad might walk into the chant, and she would turn her attention to him. *"Yes, Jehovah is God. But we also know the name of the Devil. It's Don Biles. Truth, verified."* Her chant would turn into a rhythmic focus of *"The Devil, Don Biles…Devil Don, Don the Devil. What's the matter, Devil?"* It would go on and on with repetitions of her latest chant. She would frequently keep time with the chant as she would bang a pot or pan against the wall and often dance along with the rhythm she created.

One particularly traumatic manic episode occurred during a family camping trip to the Apache Indian Reservation, where we would camp along the Black River. The campsite we visited was known as "Stove". The location had been a family favorite for years, dating back to fishing trips my dad would go on with his dad. We would camp, and then hike down the mountain to the river. On this one occasion, we traveled to the remote Black River location with the family dogs, cats and even birds in tow. As mentioned, her domineering personality allowed her to do whatever she thought she needed to do; everyone else had to go along with it. There was no denying her. She had an important reason for everything she did.

While at Stove, she began to formulate a terrible conclusion. Stove was the site of an unspeakable massacre. Worse than the Nazi ovens. She believed this to be true because the discolored red rocks were really discolored from blood. She was compelling as she told emotional stories of what she thought happened, upset and determined to uproot the evil. It was hard for everyone to understand what they were witnessing. Mom was the loving, family matriarch and it was heartbreaking to see her go down this terribly, delusional path.

I could see her mind working and at times there would be a flurry of whispering. It was a conversation she was having with herself. At times, it would be friendly and on occasion it would be angry. Then, in a different voice, she would respond to the whispering with a normal voice. It would be a full-blown back-and-forth conversation with raging hallucinations and delusions. We pleaded with her to stop, but we were not in control, she was. I would lie in my bed terrified and knowing that none of us were in control of the situation, not even mom. Her manic delusions were in control. It's a bit of a blur all these years later, but she seemingly went days and days without sleep. Her chanting was non-stop as she continued religious themes and brought in different people and places to her diatribe. Usually, her body was in motion during the chants, in a rhythmic dance.

She would go on spending sprees at the local Phelps Dodge Mercantile. Randomly, she would buy me a $1,000 worth of presents charging everything on store credit. All of it would have to be returned, we lived on a modest family budget. Dad would get a call from the store manager advising him to come get her.

It's hard to explain fully the terror I experienced during this time. It was a never-ending time of fear without any hope for the future. I remember thinking dad was not up to this challenge and I needed help. The help mostly never came, but there was one occasion I called my sister Kristy, pleading with her to come home to help. I felt alone and that my world was coming to an end. Kristy lived in Gunnison, Colorado, at the time. She made the drive down to help for a few days during a particularly rough manic time.

My life was held captive by her mental illness. I never had any vices like dad. I never smoked, did drugs, or drank any alcohol. I tried my favorite team sport, football, in the fall of 1982. I loved football, it was my favorite. Yet life at home got to be too much for me to continue playing. I quit the freshman football team three-quarters of the way through the season. I was ashamed of my decision at the time and still feel wistful about it. I called coach Padilla to let him know my decision and why I was making it. I think I had a hard time being in groups and just needed to be alone. No one could understand.

My diversions were playing tennis against a backboard, playing video games, and going to school. Those were the times of relief from my life at home. Solitude and reclusiveness were comfortable places for me—it was where I could find peace and comfort.

Even in my places of peace and comfort, it was unpredictable what might happen with mom. I remember one day while I was sitting in class as a high school freshman, I was sitting towards the back of the class with a view to the hallway. I looked out one time, and I was dumbfounded to see mom walking down the hallway with purpose and drive. She was undoubtedly looking for me. Needless to say, non-students weren't allowed to walk around the hallways during school hours. I just thought to myself, oh my God! I hoped she'd go home. My school day finished, and I was thankful there were no incidents with her. I saw her at home later and pleaded with her not to go to school again.

When mom was delivered in her straitjacket by the deputies to the local Morenci Hospital that first time, they had the authority because of her violent resistance to inject her with Haldol—a strong first-generation antipsychotic. This drug is usually the drug of choice in these first contact physically restrained patients. The drug calmed her down and mellowed her out. She desperately needed it as she had been going strong 24/7 for many days. The next step was to transport her to the Palo Verde Hospital in Tucson for a formal commitment hearing, which was the procedure for all involuntary admittances. I was not involved, but I remember sitting by myself in a waiting room outside the hearing. I was about 13. Admittance was confirmed through the testimony of my dad, statements from the sheriff's office, and the medical professionals involved.

As I was sitting in that waiting room, I thought to myself, was this necessary? There were so many times when she would stabilize and return to an agitated calm for a few months. Deep down, I knew it had to happen. Mom had to get help and she was not going to do it voluntarily. There were plenty of later hospitalizations that she went voluntarily, often because I told her she needed to go. It would happen because of our bond and connection. As a 13- or 14-year-old child, I could tell her, *"Mom, you need to go back to the hospital and get help"*, she would trust me and agree to go voluntarily.

My feelings when mom was gone and out of the house were despair and relief at the same time. I did not have any power or ability to help her. I wanted mom back; I wanted my life back. I wanted things to be normal again; yet I did feel relief that the time of terror was over, and I hoped she would get better in the hospital.

Mom was usually an inpatient at Palo Verde Behavioral Hospital. Those hospitalizations were usually a few weeks long, at times several weeks. Her experiences in the hospital were not known by anybody. Typically, patients go through time periods of treatment experiments to find the right combination and right dosage of medications for stability. Different medications were tried while she went through regular psychotherapy. She would live in a dormitory environment. Dad and I delivered clothes and personal effects to her. On occasion, she might have a roommate or have regular interaction with several of the other patients. My recollection was that she sadly didn't get visits from family often, even from dad and me. She was truly on her own with no guarantee that she would ever return. There was a stigma associated with patients who have mental illnesses. It was a family shame, and no one wanted to acknowledge it or actively take part in her recovery because it was commonly believed she would not recover or ever have a normal life. To have severe mental illness in the 1980s or before was a sad fate for her and the family.

Mom took on a rebellious personality in the hospital. She picked up smoking. I remember visiting her in the hospital one time in Tucson. She was resentful towards my dad, for not only putting her in the hospital, but more importantly, contributing to her breakdown in the first place. She would tell dad in no uncertain terms, he was a bad man and the source of all the problems in her life, as she puffed on her cigarette and blew the smoke in his face every few seconds and pranced around. Before that time, she had never smoked. She also let him in on an affair she was having with another patient, Charlie. All of this was well-calculated revenge she was seeking on dad. Mom felt empowered by telling him this as she had suspected or possibly had known of infidelity by dad through their 25 years of marriage. He had his nightly visits to the local bar and would often not return home until 6-8 hours after he left his job. Her intention was to wound him, and that was accomplished. She didn't even care that she was telling him in front of me. I never heard or knew of anything conclusive either way about infidelity. Yet there was an environment of mistrust on this topic.

In a small town, everyone knew about everyone's business. It was hard on me as a young teen. It was no different with mom's mental health. Some kids would tease me and tell me my mom was crazy. With dad, it was hard as well, as he was well-known in town.

With mom gone, dad had the responsibility of cooking and cleaning in the house. For the most part, he did a good job. He tried to curb his bar room drinking and tried to do most of his drinking at home, but this would only be a pattern for a little while after mom was gone. He would go back to his bar room drinking and try to cut that time short to get home to help with dinner. Dad was depressed and probably felt guilty for committing mom to the mental hospital and maybe guilty for contributing to her mental illness itself. He still had times when he drank hard on the weekends, drowning himself in pity. He would often get peer reinforcement that he was an angel for "tolerating" mom's mental illness. He came from a generation where mentally ill people would often get permanently institutionalized.

I would call mom at the hospital and talk to her from time to time. I was able to tell quickly on the call if she was making progress or not. She would ask if I was eating okay. Once she started to feel better, she would be more aware of her situation and feel bad that she wasn't home taking care of me.

Both of my diversions—tennis and video games—were activities that taught me patience and perseverance. As a kid who was lost in the world, I needed that outlet. I got good at both diversions. They became my identity. Practicing tennis against the backboard for hours by myself or playing the video game, "Make Trax' at the Dairy Queen and getting a new high score.

Mom was diagnosed with paranoid schizophrenia with a mood disorder; therefore, she was treated as a schizophrenic for many years. Her main medications she was treated with, and which gradually brought her stability, were the antipsychotic Haldol during the times of extreme mania and Mellaril on a more regular basis. She was also given Lithium. Both Haldol and Mellaril were first-generation antipsychotics developed in the 1950s and 1960s. Haldol was a go-to for patients who were exhibiting extreme psychosis.

The side effects of Lithium were confusion, poor memory, slow heartbeat, stiffness in arms and legs, trouble breathing and weight gain. The side effects of Mellaril were dizziness, drowsiness, depression, blurred vision, and nausea to name a few. Mom would go on to take these two drugs daily for the next 20 years. They controlled the manic beast inside of mom.

Mom was becoming a grandmother many times over during her years of severe mental illness. It was a cruel fate to a woman who devoted every fiber in her body towards her children and was not able to enjoy growing old with grandchildren as an essential part of her life. Both of my sisters Kathy and Kristy were having children during this time. Mom's mania would often get in the way and cause my sisters trepidation and caution towards their mom, especially involving their young children.

There were definitely incidents with mom and the grandchildren. I remember a time when she started to make her way out of town with Lisa and Lori, two of her grandchildren, in the car without the knowledge of her mother. I am sure this time left permanent marks on my sisters who kept a healthy distance between their children and their mother. There were a few exceptions now and then, but it was sad that mental illness constricted the relationships between grandma and grandchildren.

Somewhere around 1985, mom's body chemistry finally stabilized by the numerous inpatient visits to Palo Verde and their attempts to work out the right pharmaceutical formula for her. Thank goodness they did it. After five tough roller coaster years for mom and her family, she was medically stabilized for the rest of her life, she was about 49 years old at the time. The medications would take their toll on her, but it was a small price to pay for manic stability. The drugs largely altered her personality with their many side effects. Words such as zombie, lifeless, sleepy, emotionless, and numb were used to describe her after the manic stabilization.

It was terribly embarrassing for mom to live in the same small town where she had so many incidents of public, manic episodes. She remembered what she did when she was sick. When she wasn't ill, she carried herself with the greatest amount of class and dignity. I felt the worst for mom, not me or dad. She couldn't help what was happening to her.

As for me, I finished high school. I was finally able to look forward to my future. I had ambitions to go to college and to play college tennis.

Mom was able to participate in my life towards the end of my high school years and into my college years under close supervision from dad. She would go to tennis matches and watch me from the truck with dad. She attended my graduation and baccalaureate ceremonies and was my proud, loving mother whom I loved and adored.

Before my senior year, dad knew how important tennis was to me and my future. He sold his beloved camper to help pay for my tennis camp in the summer of 1985 in San Diego. It was the only way we could afford it. He would get off work and travel wherever I traveled. He was my biggest fan and supporter.

When it was time for college in Tucson, my parents helped as much as possible. They helped me get set up with an apartment near the Pima Community College campus. I was able to try out for the tennis team, and I earned a scholarship that helped with a lot of the college expenses. My parents did not have any money saved to help me get through college, so everything I could do on my own would be helpful. Make no mistake, my parents helped a lot financially and undoubtedly sacrificed more than I will ever know.

Going to school at Pima Community College in 1986-1988 was an enjoyable time for me. It was my first taste of true independence and no responsibilities except my own future. I played two years of tennis on a scholarship. I came to the realization that my skills had reached their peak at that level of competition. I knew I had to focus on the backup plan, good old education. As with most things in my life, I approached them with a silent, but determined chip on my shoulder when it came to proving myself. I shared an apartment with Daniel Lopez during my first year, and I was by myself the second year in Tucson. After I graduated from high school and prior to my first semester in college, my parents and I went car shopping and found a great 1978 black Camaro with T-top roof panels. The car was 8 years old, but I was a lucky guy to have such a cool car, undoubtedly a financial hardship for my parents as well.

I would return home not every weekend, but probably every other weekend. I was only 17 when I left for college, so it was a healthy dose of homesickness, and I knew how happy it made mom and dad for me to return home to Morenci. I would return home for all the holidays and semester breaks to spend a lot of time with my parents.

Summers were especially good as I would come home and work as a summer student with Phelps Dodge and teach tennis. This allowed me to save money for the high costs of college and living on my own. Every summer in 1987, 88 and 89, I returned home as a summer student. The best part of the summers was that I stayed at home again in Morenci. These were good times for mom and me. She was all about caring for her kids. Now, I was there in the house again needing care. I would live in my bedroom built out of the garage at our Ironwood house.

During these returns home, I was mom's coach, and we would work on losing weight. We walked around town every day from our house, and we took our dog Prince around with us off-leash. We would walk a little farther every day until we eventually began walking for as long as five miles per day. The highlight of each day was to walk up to the hospital and get an "official" weight on their scale and then we logged it back at the house. The staff at the hospital started to get accustomed to seeing us in the mornings asking to use their scale. This was one of my earliest efforts to put mom on a routine, and she showed me in those early days how devoted she could be to a program.

I was her encouraging coach and drill sergeant all in one. She trusted me implicitly and would do what I thought was best. She began to show how well she could diet and log her results. She became determined, through my guidance, to change herself for the better. She weighed about 185 pounds at this time in 1986-1987, morbidly obese for a 5'1", 50-year-old woman. Slowly, we got results. She lost a lot of weight, and we would talk about her progress, even when I would go back to college.

I was busy during my summer breaks at home in Morenci. I would wake up early in the morning, before work and play tennis with several of the men who were managers for the company. They had a morning tennis club that got competitive. I was far better than all of them, but they enjoyed the challenge of playing against me, and it was good for my young work career to become acquainted.

After tennis, I would have my time with mom to do our exercise. Then it was off to work, coming home for a nice lunch that mom would prepare for dad and me, like the old days when the family lived on Mariposa Street. After work, I would give tennis lessons and usually do some more exercises with mom. I would emphasize the need to control her eating along with vigorous exercise. I had a motivating effect on her, and I could see the real purpose and happiness returning to her.

In the fall of 1988, I started school at Arizona State University, after transferring from Pima Community College. I had an apartment in Mesa. My sister Donna was newly married to her husband Dan, and they had a daughter, Danielle, earlier that year. Donna and Dan bought a house in Mesa. The bottom floor of the house was undeveloped, and my sister asked dad for help, as he was handy with construction projects.

On one occasion, my parents were visiting Donna at her house, and I came over to visit. Mom tried to stand up and walk but was unable. She said she couldn't move her legs. As her coach/drill sergeant, I strongly encouraged her to walk, and she was unable to. She seemed to be having a mental illness episode after years of relative stability. Except this time, it was different. She wasn't manic; she was depressed. Her medication regimen was not working.

The depression began to spiral downward from that point onward. We talked to her about seeing a doctor and going into a hospital to help get to the bottom of things. She agreed that it was a good idea, but just asked that it not be Palo Verde. That hospital in Tucson was associated with a lot of bad memories, more than any of us will ever know. We found a behavioral health hospital in the Phoenix area called Charter. They had several around Phoenix and around the country.

Her behavior and mood were different this time around; she was not domineering and strong. This time around, she was weak and defeated. As bad as the manic episodes were, this episode of depression was much more concerning. She was talking about her many failures in life. She was even questioning why she should go on with life... *"What was the point"*, she proclaimed.

After her voluntary admittance to Charter Behavioral Hospital, I visited her on one occasion. Her depression continued, she again talked about purpose and questioned why she should go on with life. I had extensive talks with her about why she had a purpose. I told her... *"Because you are mom and the center of my world. I need your help and encouragement to make it through college. Don't you want to see me graduate? I try so hard to make you proud. Your daughters need you, especially Donna with the new baby. We all look to you for guidance, love and support. We need our mom. We will always need our mom."*

Mom continued treatment with psychotherapy and a new stronger drug. The primary antipsychotic medication she was taking from about 1984 to 1988 was called Mellaril. It was known as a low-potency first-generation antipsychotic. Haldol was a high-potency, strong antipsychotic that was given to mom during her most psychotic states, but not as an ongoing daily treatment. During her hospitalization in 1988, she was transitioned to a medium-potency antipsychotic called Moban. A little stronger than Mellaril. The human mind is incredibly complicated, and some antipsychotic drugs work differently from person to person, and on occasion, a certain drug works especially well with a person in combination with another drug. These were the difficult experiments that go on during inpatient hospitalizations.

The doctors at Charter finally felt mom should go home, and they had a regimen of drugs for her to take. Moban was now her primary antipsychotic. She continued taking Lithium as well. A new drug was added called Cogentin. This drug helped with symptoms of Parkinson's syndrome, which was a common side effect of Moban. It was often characterized by serious shaking in her hands and feet.

Mom went home stable, and the new drugs seemed to be helping. She didn't have that dark streak of depression any longer. She was often not very lucid. Her cognition was often dubious. She was neither highly manic nor deeply depressed, she was just kind of there. We all happily took this altered state instead of those terrible extremes.

After mom returned home to Morenci in a seemingly stable mental state, I refocused on myself and getting my bachelor's degree in business from Arizona State University. I had two years to go, as all my credits from Pima College transferred successfully. I took a lot of liberal arts courses to make my curriculum more interesting. I really wasn't enjoying the business courses that much, and I suffered academically. I was on and off academic probation throughout my 2 ½ years at ASU.

My passion was politics as my grandmother (we called her Maymo) shared and gave me a lot of political articles about my granddad, Sonny Biles. He was a famous and successful state legislator representing Morenci and the larger copper industry at a time when copper was the largest and most powerful industry in the state. He held positions of leadership and authority in the House of Representatives throughout his 18 years in office. When he wasn't working in the legislature, he had a "day job" as a supervisor back in the Morenci mine.

I didn't particularly enjoy the curriculum with ASU business, but I persevered. That was just what mom taught me by word and by deed. I didn't share my academic struggles with my parents, as they were so proud and heavily invested in me to complete the degree and to graduate from college and to start a successful career.

I continued to visit my parents back in Morenci often – again, not every week, but probably every other week. I knew my visits were medicine for mom. Let's face it, I was a Mama's Boy, and enjoyed seeing her (and dad). In the summers of 1989 and 1990, I returned home to live with my parents in Morenci. The year 1989 was my final summer as a Phelps Dodge summer student. In 1990, I put my entrepreneur hat on and devoted all my efforts to giving tennis lessons for a profit to help save money for the next college year. I didn't quite finish college on time in four years, it took 4 ½ years.

In December of 1991, I participated in the ASU graduation ceremony. Mom, dad and sister Donna all attended. They were all beaming with pride as I was the first in the family to graduate from college. I gave them a tour around campus. It was an odd December day in Tempe, it snowed a little bit.

Around this time, my Maymo invited me over to meet an old friend of hers and my granddad's who was still working in the

Arizona House of Representative. She was a contemporary of his in the 50s and 60s as she got elected out of Globe and was also a stalwart supporter of the copper Industry like my granddad. I was captivated by this 90-year-old woman, Polly Rosenbaum. She was wise, and I immediately felt a connection to her and wanted to know how I could work in the legislature with her.

Politics and learning about my granddad were my new passion in life. I didn't get to know him as he passed when I was only 5. Working with Polly gave me the best chance I'd ever have of feeling his presence and his spirit in the halls of the Arizona House of Representatives. Polly explained the application process to me as an intern and put in a good word. I secured the internship for the 40th legislative session starting in January 1991. It was a full-time job for about 5 months, and I also took a few courses from ASU concurrently. I loved working as Polly's personal assistant, my best and favorite job. I got an apartment near the capitol, not the greatest part of town, but I made it work. I dressed up in a required suit and tie every day. I got to work early every morning and ate at the capitol cafeteria. I worked with an excellent group of interns. It was a wonderful experience.

It was also an incredibly interesting time to work in the capitol as there was a huge scandal, known as ASCAM. Several legislators for whom I worked with daily were implicated in this sting operation targeted to uncover corruption. Of course, Polly was a Beacon of Integrity. She had been one of my greatest inspirations. At 90, she had lived alone for over 40 years after her husband died. She never took an elevator to her office. I had to try my best to keep up with this incredible dynamo, as she ran up and down the stairs. The job was truly a dream come true.

As summer came in 1991, the legislative session had already ended, and I was looking to return home for the summer as I was indecisive about my future. I really didn't want to pursue a career in business or in my family company, Phelps Dodge. I talked to

Polly and asked her what she thought about an internship in Washington, DC with Senator Dennis DeConcini. She thought it was a wonderful idea. As a prominent member of the Arizona Democratic Party, she knew people like Senator DeConcini personally. Everyone thought the world of Polly, so a good word on an application helped me secure the internship in Washington from August to December of 1991.

I got to live my dream in politics a little longer and put off the drudgery of a job in business. Financially, my dream came at a big cost for my parents. The DC Internship was a college-credit, unpaid program. My parents would have to somehow subsidize my costly life in Washington for five months. I returned home during that summer and opened my tennis lessons again and made a decent amount of money to help with the costs.

When I arrived in Washington, DC to get settled in, I played a basketball game with some of the staff of Senator DeConcini. I made an awkward movement and felt great pain in my lower left leg. I looked around instinctively because it felt like I got shot in the leg. As it turned out, I tore my Achilles' tendon. A lot of people thought it would be best for me to return home. I had only been there less than a week; surgery and rehabilitation would be difficult. I was not going to quit, no matter what. I went to see a doctor, and he scheduled me for surgery at Arlington Hospital in Virginia, a few miles from where I lived. I didn't even have a bed or furniture in my room yet. I remember how difficult it was to stand in my condition with nothing to grab for leverage.

On the day of surgery, I called a taxi to pick me up and take me to the hospital. I didn't know anyone, so the taxi was my only way. I was getting prepped for surgery by myself on the other side of the country. I remember when I was getting carted to surgery with the anesthesia slowly starting to work, they handed me a phone and it was mom on the line. She told me, *"I love you and I'm thinking about you. I wish I was there and I'm praying for a perfect surgery."* That was the last thing I remember as I slowly slipped unconscious. Her call meant the world to me, it was unexpected and perfectly timed. My parents must have called the hospital asking when I would be going into surgery.

   Letter from mom dated September 12, 1991, shortly after my surgery.

Dear Stephen,

How are you feeling? Hope the pain isn't too bad. Sure, was nice to hear from you. That doctor was nice to let me talk to you.

I put $350 in your account yesterday. Daddy said to put that much in. That was nice, huh.

I was sick yesterday from about 4:30 to about 8:00 or so. Vomiting and diarrhea at the same time. Think it is related to the illness I have every so often. My eyes had been bothering me for a couple of days too! So, we missed Megan's birthday party. Feel really bad about it. They went to an MHS football game after the party. They had ordered pizza; Kathy had a cake made and bought ice cream.

Told Kathy I'd like to make her birthday dinner. Got T-bone steaks, we'll cook out and make ice cream. I feel fine this morning. Daddy fixed boiled eggs for me and him last night. I fixed toast last night.

Feels like Fall here this morning, nice and cool.

The pictures you took were really good. Thanks for sending them.

Baby (or rather Stinky) is getting fat and pretty. She's been sleeping by my head for the past few nights. Callie got on our bed the last few nights, but not last night.

I hope your birthday card will get there in time. Do you get the balance of your checking account on that banking machine? Well, I guess I better close for now. Take care.

Love you,

Mama and Daddy

After surgery, I was on crutches and a leg cast for a couple of months. This was a true test of my toughness. I had to walk about a mile to a metro station near my rented room and take it into DC for work each day. It was hard putting on my clothes – suit and tie again with my leg cast. It was even harder making that walk every day in the cool fall/winter weather of Washington. When I struggled just to put my clothes on and to walk, it opened my eyes to things I hadn't often noticed in everyday life. I would occasionally see blind men and women by themselves somehow learning to navigate the complicated metro stations as they commute to work and don't ask for any pity or any help. I figured I could make it too; I was determined not to give up. It was the chance of a lifetime, and I was going to make it to the finish line no matter what.

I loved the experience of living in DC. I even applied for several jobs to stay there after my internship was over. Unfortunately (or maybe fortunately), the country was in a recession and jobs were scarce. I was often unhappy with the life that followed the next several years and wondered how things would have turned out differently if I had landed a job in DC and stayed there to build a political career.

My four months in Washington were the longest time that I had ever been away from seeing mom before or for the rest of her life. It was a good time for her because she was stable and happy. It was an exciting time for me. My 1991 year of political internships was a happy, satisfying time for me. I was disappointed I couldn't continue those dreams, but my experiences were priceless.

The year 1992 was a good one for mom. Not only was I back from Washington, DC looking for a job in Morenci, but also Kathy and her family were living right down the street from my parent's house. She was surrounded by her family. I lived in the familiar garage room that I had lived in during my high school years and the summers during my college years.

I had considerable mixed feelings at this time. I wanted to do something other than work for the family company. My granddad worked 40+ years for Phelps Dodge, and dad was just finishing up 40+ years with Phelps Dodge. I loved the company and loved the town, but I wanted to do something different. The recession and job shortage I experienced in Washington were still raging even in the job-secure town of Morenci. I was looking for some sort of professional position in the company after graduating from ASU. Weeks went by and then months went by, and no positions came up.

In the meantime, I was playing tennis with a lot of my students through the years. Tennis season was coming up, and that was something I could put my energy into. Mom and I sat around the house watching soap operas and going out to exercise and we stayed on top of her health. I remember this time because it was one of the few times, I really got into following several daytime soap story lines. I was bored and disappointed with my fate, but I wasn't going to settle on just any labor job that came up.

After several months of no activity and seeing his big investment sitting home and watching soap operas all day with mom, my dad finally had enough. He walked into the office of the head of the company, Tim Snider. He knew Tim and they both liked and respected each other. Dad told Tim, *"It's a rotten shame my son, a third-generation Biles man, goes off and gets a college degree from Arizona State and goes through the company's summer student program for three years but can't get a job now."* As dad repeated this story to me, he said Tim started to scrabble for a booklet that showed all the available jobs in the company. Tim mentioned many open jobs in the field and my dad cut him off and said, *"Piss on those jobs Tim"*. Dad said, *"I worked labor all my life, and there was nothing wrong with it, but the principle of it demands he get a professional job in an office somewhere in this huge operation."* About two weeks later, I was interviewed and hired in the supply chain management office.

With a job in hand, I could now get my own company house. I got my first new car as well a few weeks later. I had been driving my parent's old car. It was still a huge letdown from the excitement and passion I had for politics. I made the best out of it, and I put my energy into building something great in Morenci, a championship tennis program built from the ground up. It was a way I could use a lot of the sales and entrepreneur skills I knew I possessed and use them to build something that meant a lot to me, Morenci tennis.

As I was coming into the company, dad was moving out of the company after 45 years of dedication and hard work. It was a storybook ending to his career, as his only son was starting his career simultaneously as he left the stage. I was only in the company for a couple of months when he had his retirement banquet. The company does nice retirement parties for the employees who put a lot of time into the company and really made their mark. My sister Kathy and I were both at his table of honor, as we were both company employees, my brother-in-law Craig was also at the event and a member of company management. Mom proudly sat by his side as well. He was roasted by a couple of his friends and colleagues. All in all, a nice and honorable exit for him.

Dad had not really planned for life after the company. He did a little bit of consulting for a year or so and then was a full-time retiree as mom and dad moved from Morenci. He had always lived in a company house. Once you exit the company, the cold hard facts hit you that now, you're not part of the working family and it feels more like a mining camp. Dad lived in one of the nicer mid-level leadership houses that was highly sought after. He would not be allowed to remain. So, he looked around Safford and found the perfect house to live in. It was a fixer-upper on Relation Street that would be his retirement passion.

As my parents moved from Morenci it was 1993. Mom was 56 years old. About 41 of those years, she lived in Morenci. Her 15 years before Morenci was a challenging time—she was born during the worst years of the Great Depression and grew up during World War II and post-war recovery.

CHAPTER 2
Birth & Childhood
(1936 – 1955)

"Have the courage to start, the perseverance to continue and the kindness to make it all beautiful."

- *Maxime Lagacé*

Shirley Ellen Park was born in Globe, Arizona, on November 2, 1936, to Bernice and Orvel Park in the middle of the Great Depression. Shirley was named after the famous child actor Shirley Temple. Her middle name was given to honor her step-grandmother Ellen. Bernice's dad and stepmother lived in Globe; so, they stayed close for the first year after Shirley was born.

The family moved to Clifton, Arizona, in 1937 looking for work. Bernice's dad was a mine inspector and had a lot of influence with the local mines. He likely helped Orvel get his foot in the door at Phelps Dodge Mining Company.

Shirley was a healthy, plump baby until one day, she ate a bean when her mother wasn't looking. Little Shirley began to lose weight drastically and after starting to walk, she regressed back to crawling. Shirley's mother took her to the doctor, but that didn't help. Finally, one day, she tried a healthy dose of laxatives and baby Shirley passed a bean that was sprouting. She got healthy again shortly thereafter.

Growing up with Hispanic neighbors in Clifton, Shirley's first few words were Spanish. Agua (water) was her first word. In 1939, Shirley had a sister named Beverly. She was born in the neighboring town of Morenci.

After a couple of years at the mine, Orvel left his job and moved the family to Phoenix. Orvel's father was a state highway patrolman in the Phoenix area. Orvel likely moved to Phoenix to connect with a friend who could help with employment opportunities. They were in Phoenix for almost a year.

In 1941, Orvel got a job with Phelps Dodge again and the family moved back to Eastern Arizona. There was not any immediate company housing, so they lived in the primitive, unincorporated town of Franklin, just north of Duncan. It was about 36 miles away from the copper mine in Morenci. Their house was next to the railroad track going through town.

In January 2023, I visited Franklin and found it to be tiny and primitive. As I drove through the area, many of the residents were living in abject poverty and many were off the grid. I'm sure that 80 years ago, the financial and cultural environment was even more austere. Mom was about five years old at the time she lived there.

From 1942-1944, the family moved into a company home in Stargo, a section of the Morenci townsite. Shirley's youngest sister Virginia was born in 1944. Shirley was now 8 years old.

In 1944, the family moved out of Stargo and back out to the country to a town called York, a small valley about 16 miles from Morenci. The young couple and their three girls lived in York the longest of all their places of residence. It was seven years at the York house and farm 1944 until 1951.

Their home was close to the Gila River, where the kids liked to play, but only with adult supervision. For about 7 years, Shirley took a school bus to Duncan for 17 miles one way. She was about 7 years old (2nd grade) when she moved to York to about 14 years old (Freshman in high school).

During this period in York, the family was stable as Orvel had regular work at the mine. The one exception was during a long labor strike. Shirley's dad made ends meet by selling strawberries to a fruit stand along the road for 4 and 1/2 months. They had no other income to help them get by and no savings.

The family attended the Seventh Day Adventist Church for many years when living in York. Shirley taught Beverly how to harmonize with her; and they sang the song "Ivory Palaces" in church before the congregation. The preacher would visit the house regularly. Beverly was 9 and Shirley was 12 at the time. Here are the words of the song Shirley and Beverly sang according to my Aunt Bev.

1 My Lord has garments so wondrous fine,
and myrrh their texture fills;
its fragrance reached to this heart of mine,
with joy my being thrills.

Refrain:
Out of the ivory palaces
into a world of woe,
only his great eternal love
made my Savior go.

2 His life had also its sorrows sore,
for aloes had a part;
and when I think of the cross he bore,
my eyes with teardrops start. [Refrain]

3 His garments, too, were in cassia dipped,
with healing in a touch;
each time my feet in some sin have slipped,
he took me from its clutch. [Refrain]

4 In garments glorious he will come,
to open wide the door;

and I shall enter my heavenly home,
to dwell forevermore. [Refrain]

All their food was grown in the yard. Water came from a ground well and was stored in a water tank. Milk and butter came from the family cow, Bossy. Shirley's mother milked the cow twice a day. Eggs came from the chickens and occasionally the chickens were butchered for meat. Meat also came from rabbits and ducks in the yard. Occasionally, a pig would get butchered in the neighborhood, with several families sharing the meat. Once a month or so, a few basic groceries would be purchased from the Phelps Dodge Mercantile in Clifton.

Bossy didn't like the children. Every so often, she would chase them off when they came near. She would give birth to a calf now and then. The kids would pet the calves, as they were all animal lovers. Bossy once attacked Virginia aggressively and scared all the girls.

Meals consisted of a salad with dinner, and they ate vegetables from the garden—corn, tomatoes, cucumbers and strawberries. Occasionally, the family had potatoes and gravy. Also, hot chilies were a regular part of their meals. They had some sort of meat with every meal. One of the family favorites was biscuits for breakfast when everyone had time. Shirley's mother was a good cook, but she never taught any of the girls.

The two younger sisters, Beverly and Virginia, loved living in the country, but Shirley was fond of the town. The girls had two bikes, a regular girl's bike that was shared by Shirley and Beverly and a smaller bike for younger kids that Virginia used.

Shirley and Beverly belonged to 4-H. They learned important skills such as sewing and cooking. It allowed the girls some social interaction as well.

The girls had four dogs growing up in York--Pal, Snuffy, Jiggs and Lassie. Shirley and all the girls loved them dearly. At one point, Shirley's father took Lassie out of the home to get rid of her. He took her to the Duncan townsite area and dropped her off unceremoniously. What he didn't realize was that Lassie found the girls at school. They went home and begged him to find Lassie and bring her home. Over 10 years and two different homes later, Shirley's mom and dad still had Lassie.

Shirley grew up without electricity in the house until 1949. She was 13 years old. Before that, kerosine lamps were used for lighting. An ice box was used instead of a refrigerator. Blocks of ice would be purchased from the Clifton Icehouse to keep food cold in the ice box. Later, they upgraded to butane appliances including a stove, heater and refrigerator.

Shirley grew up using a washtub for bathing. The water needed to be heated on the stove. Her dad built a shower in the shed, but only with cold water. The laundry was done with an old wringer washer. They had outhouses they used for all their years in York and Franklin.

Shirley was a good student. She frequently made the honor roll and missed very few days of class leading up to her Eighth-Grade graduation. In May of 1950 according to her report card, she was 5 feet 3 inches tall and 106 pounds.

On May 18, 1950, Duncan Elementary School held Shirley's 8th grade graduation ceremony. The graduation program included several performances by students including a reading of a poem, some instrumental performances and a student duet. The big performance was the vocal solo by Shirley Park. She sang the song "I Love a Little Cottage".

I love a little church-house, On a friendly little hill;
I love a little school- house, With a flowering windowsill,

I love a little cottage as it stands nearby a wood;
I love them all so dearly, And I'll tell you why I should:

Because the little church-house Is a beacon on the hill.
Because the little schoolhouse Is a guidepost, if you will.

Because the little cottage, Where the toilers homeward plod,
Is another of the builders, that keep building men for God!

I love a little cottage, As it stands nearby a wood;
I love it, oh, so dearly and ill tell you why I should:

Because the little cottage, Where the toilers homeward plod,
Is another of the builders, that keep building men for God!

Mom kept the Copper Era news clipping of her 8th Grade graduation in her special and personal belongings all her life. A clipping that was near and dear to her heart for over 70 years.

When Shirley was 14, she had a date before a school dance in Duncan. The boy lived in the area near the York house. Her sisters remember how embarrassed Shirley was to bring people to their house because in her mind, it was so primitive. The boy liked her regardless.

In 1951, the family moved to Morenci. Shirley was finally in a comfortable environment living in a more populated town where she could be more socially active. It was a dream come true for her. She was popular and made friends easily, girlfriends and boyfriends.

When the family moved to Linden Street, big sister Shirley got her own room. Mom and dad got a smaller room, and the sisters Beverly and Virginia shared a room. Shirley and Beverly liked to sew, and both made a little extra money babysitting. Shirley had a way with hair and frequently gave her sisters haircuts. Shirley's best friend in high school was Carol. The two of them were active in school and around town throughout their high school years.

Academics were a bit challenging in the first couple of years at Morenci High School after transferring from Duncan. It was probably a bit of cultural shock for her, and perhaps the nonacademic distractions. Fortunately, she finished strong in her junior and senior years with a lot of As and Bs in her mostly business class schedule.

In March of 1954, Shirley began to prepare for life after high school. She reached out to her Grandma Maddy who lived in Phoenix. She asked her if she could live with her while taking a business course. This is what her grandmother said on March 31, 1954.

Dear Shirley,
Sure, I will be glad to have you and your friend come. You should know you are always welcome. Maybe all the rest of your folks can come. It's late, so I will do our visiting in person.

Love to all,
Grandmother

After graduating high school and near the end of her summer, Shirley got this letter finalizing plans to move to Phoenix on August 14, 1954.

Dear Shirley,

I hope you are coming to stay with us and take a business course. We have helped all our children in different ways, and this will be helping Orvel a little. I am sure we can get along fine. We have that empty bedroom which will be yours unless you have a girlfriend and want twin beds.

We buy our beef at about .45cents per lb., and hamburger at .35cents wholesale. We have some vegetables we put up and fruit. We will have a REAL bumper crop next year, and we eat so little. I have beans, black-eyed peas and corn and will soon plant beets, radishes, lettuce, Swiss chard, mustard and winter peas.

I will be proud to have my lovely, sweet granddaughter with me. Of course, if you do come, we will want to make Mildred a very short visit and a longer one with mother. We have our chickens and eggs, which helps.

> *Love to all,*
> *Grandmother & Mother*

Shirley went off to Phoenix, enrolled at Lamson Business College and lived with her Grandmother Maddy. Her social life was fantastic. This letter was from a Phoenix friend named Susie. In the letter, Susie talks about work, school and of course a whole lot about boys. Throughout the letter, Susie mentions six different boys that she socialized with and one of the boys sent his regards to Shirley. There was every reason to believe that Shirley was just as socially active. Susie refers to flying to Sedona for a wedding. She was likely an affluent friend who had access to an aircraft for a short trip from Phoenix to Sedona. Not many people now or then fly around in a private plane. This letter was sent just five days after Shirley's wedding on August 4, 1955.

> *Dear Shirley,*
> *I've started to write a letter to you several times, but never seem quite able to finish it. Just too busy to get a letter off in the evening and it's difficult to finish a letter at work. You know how it goes down here, busy one moment & nothing to do the next. Al and I have been busy writing out contracts. Boy does it make me nervous when I type anything legal—no erasers, you know.*

Wayne took me out to lunch Saturday afternoon and then home. Was I ever grateful for the ride in this weather. Don't know of anything I dislike more than riding the bus. Anyways, we had an awfully nice time. He certainly is a nice person. Once you can get him talking, you find he has an awful lot to say. Bashful, I guess.

Bill told me to be sure to say hello for him. His house should be finished shortly. Now the office crew tells me it's got aqua colored walls in every room. Bill says he's having 3 housewarmings when it's finished. First, for all their relatives, second for all his business acquaintances and fellow salt miners and third for all the pretty girls and drunks he knows. He says you can include yourself in whichever category you prefer.

You really aught to be glad you're in Morenci this month. The weather here is really the scroungiest! Humid? Boy, I'll tell you! Bob left for Yuma again this morning. He vows he's driving up here this weekend to take me out, but I'd have to see it to believe it. Wouldn't much like being in Yuma at this time of year myself. He didn't know he was going until yesterday, so last night we went out to dinner, goofy-golfing and then got a coke. We really did have a swell time, as always. Of course, neither one of us were very happy with the current situation, but there is virtually nothing I can do about it. And since Bob can't or won't change the deal, guess I'll have to stick it out the way it is. Most likely everything will eventually work out for the best. I certainly hope so.

On Friday night Roger and I are going with another couple to the show. Saturday night I'm supposed to have a date with Bob...Sunday night Roger and I are going on a hayrack ride and watermelon bust. We sure have a terrific time together and he's just the sweetest, most honest, and undoubtably the most considerate fellow I've ever gone out with. Seems funny to think he thinks the sun rises and sets on me and I'm stuck on Bob and Bob doesn't know what he really wants. "The eternal triangle"?

So far, I've been spending money just as fast as I got it. But this morning I gave Mother $20 to deposit into my savings account. Really do want to get a nice sized pile stashed away to fall back on. Don't know what exactly I'm saving for, but no doubt the money will seem like a windfall if I need it one of these days.

Next weekend, Bob, Charlie and I will fly up to Sedona for their sister's wedding. I imagine we will make quite the weekend of it. Wish Bob and I could make their wedding a double header!

Well gal, can't think of any phenomenal news at present, but hope this will suffice for the minute. Maybe I'll have more news in my next letter. Please write soon, I really enjoy hearing from you.

Love, Susie

It appears Susie did not know her friend Shirley was getting married since no reference was made. Mom saved the letter all her life, for almost 70 years. Did she save it as a memento of her life in Phoenix—remembering the good times, or perhaps a wistful memory of a different life she gave up with her return to Morenci?

School went just fine and after four months in Phoenix, she returned home to the family house on Linden in Morenci. Undoubtedly, catching up with her best friend in high school, Carol. They were planning their time together and right at the top of the list was the big Christmas Eve dance at the Apache Grove Dance Hall.

Back in the 1950s and 60s, the place to be in Greenlee County was the Apache Grove Bar & Dance Hall. It was a well-known country honky-tonk bar known by all the big stars of that era. You name it, Hank Williams, Johnny Cash, and Patsy Cline performed at the Bar as they made stops along the way between Nashville and the West Coast.

On December 24, 1954, it wasn't Johnny or Patsy headlining, it was time for the annual Christmas Eve Dance. The dance was the big event for all the local towns of Morenci, Duncan and Clifton. A young airman by the name of Donald Biles was on leave from Davis-Monthan Air Force base in Tucson; and he went home to see his family in Morenci and to go to the dance. Shirley was also at the dance with her best friend Carol. She was home from her first semester at Lamson College in Phoenix. Shirley and Carol were mingling in the crowd. Their gaze was fixed on the young man standing a few feet in front of them. It was Donald. Carol said, *"Are you thinking what I'm thinking?"* Shirley nodded, *"Yes, very handsome!"*

A few minutes later, Shirley visited the powder room. When she returned to the party, the handsome young airman fatefully approached and asked her to dance. From that moment on, the two were inseparable all night--one jitterbug after another. No one will ever know how the connection happened so quickly after the two girls commented on Donald. Perhaps while Shirley was in the powder room, Carol was doing some matchmaking. In any case, it was the moment that changed both of their lives forever and the beginning of a great legacy.

At the end of the evening, Don asked Shirley's parents, who attended the dance, if he could drive their daughter home. They approved. The two had one more date at the New Year's Eve Dance a week later. Then, they went their separate ways back to Tucson and Phoenix in the new year of 1955. Throughout the winter and spring, they corresponded through love letters.

On July 30, 1955, they were married. They began their new life together. Carol was the matron of honor and Uncle Gene was the best man and my dad's brother-in-law.

Grandma Maddy checked in and wrote on August 27, 1955...

Hi Old Married Woman, sorry I haven't written, I do hate to write letters. Say Shirley, I just got covers for the pillows. I can send you the pillows you slept on. Do you want them? Do you listen to Armstrong, or do you have a radio? Let me know. I  *am sure Don is a good Boy and I feel sure you will be very happy.*

May God Bless you both, Love Grandmother

On December 28 of 1955, another friend from her Phoenix days was checking in with Shirley, now married about five months.

Dear Shirley,

Gee I was so glad to get your card with your address on it. I have been wondering about you.

How do you like married life? I bet you and Carol are having fun. Also, are you working or what? Write to me when you have time and tell me all about yourself. What kind of wedding you had and everything. This letter is going to be very short because I am writing to you on my break at work. Things here are just about the same. The male situation is pretty good, but I am still after a dream which I will probably never get. Oh, by the way I have that picture of you in my billfold and everybody at work who sees it thinks you are real darling. Well, I have got to go mail this.
Love, Char

I will never know if mom had regrets for choosing the life of rural Arizona over the big city. The answer was probably yes, but that was typical of most who make major life decisions like marriage at such a young age.

Ironically, Shirley would once again return to the big city in the future. As for now, she was married and anxious to get on to the next stage of her life, a family.

CHAPTER 3
Marriage & Family
(1955-1980)

"Life is not easy for any of us. But what of that? We must have perseverance and above all confidence in ourselves. We must believe that we are gifted for something, and that this thing must be attained."

- *Marie Curie*

After Shirley and Don got married, they began to build their family. Raising children was the most important purpose in Shirley's life. In the 2010s, I conducted video interviews with mom asking her questions about each of her  daughters, and especially recollecting the birth of each of them. In her mid to late 70s during the interviews, I could see the sparkle in her eye and great love in her voice as she talked about her pride and joy, her children. She talked with great passion and with amazing detail. The video interviews were meant as the gift of a lifetime for each of the children, from mom in her own words. It started with Kathy.

On September 16, 1956, Kathy was born.

"Kathy was my first born. She was a sweet, sweet baby. A smart little girl and beautiful inside and out. And I love her dearly."

"Well, I got up and got Daddy off to work, and I started having pains. I called the hospital, and the doctor told me to come to the hospital. So, I got there about 9 o'clock."

Did you call the ambulance?

"No, I drove. (Laugh). Dr. Hookrine was my doctor, he was a German doctor. I had to have an enema, which I disliked. Then, I guess they called Daddy, and he came to the hospital. They did all the things they do when a woman is in labor."

How long were you in labor?

"I'm not sure, but I don't think it was very long. Probably about four or five hours and then I gave birth to Kathy."

Do you remember when they brought her in?

"I saw her when I gave birth to her, and they held her up and spanked her. I was real happy because I wanted a little girl." (Happy laugh)

Did Kathy like to share?

"No, Kathy didn't like to share" (laugh). Even when she was a little girl, Maymo saw to it that they each had candy and all that stuff. She looked at hers in her drawer, and nobody touched it. Or else, she would get mad."

Was Kristy scared of her?

"Probably a little bit. Kathy new exactly how much candy she had stored."

"She loved to eat. When she was a baby, she ate her bowl of cereal without stopping and she loved everything I fed her."

"She had a clarinet, and she was first in band, first chair...always first. Her academics, well, she was real smart in school. When she graduated from high school, she was seventh in her class."

"Kathy has retired now. She worked for many years; she was a hard worker. She even worked on the school board in Bagdad. I was really proud of her, and I am really proud of her. She's retired now after all those years, and I hope she will be happy on her retirement. I love her dearly."

A few days after Mom's first child, she received a letter from Aunt Lucile on September 22, 1956.

"Dear Shirley & Don, I received the good news from Mother on Sunday about that little baby girl of yours and I'm very happy for both of you. The name you pick I like very well. I almost named Joyce Katherine as I like that name. Is your baby's name Katherine or Kathy? The middle name is cute too. I hope you didn't have a difficult delivery."

The next video narrative from mom was on her second born. On November 3, 1957, Kristy was born. In an interview on October 31, 2015, mom was asked about the birth of Kristy and other memorable times. The picture shows mom pregnant with Kristy, holding Kathy with her dad and grandpa.

"It was my birthday, November 2. Maymo and Granddad and Daddy and I went down to the Coronado Inn and ate dinner. And I started to have some pains in my stomach. (Laughs) So I said, I may be going to the hospital. So, we left and when we got home, it was about 8 and Daddy went to bed. So, I was having some pains about 9 o' clock, and I said...I woke Daddy up...and I said, I think we better go to the hospital. (Laughs). I was having pains...".

As she told the story, she was visibly reliving it as you could see the distress on her face and deep breaths.

52

"We got there (the hospital), and I told Daddy, you better find a nurse. I thought I was going to have her before he got back. (Laughs). So, the nurse came and took care of everything, and they couldn't get the doctor because he was at a party in Stargo. And so...they finally got him, and she was born at 1:30 AM."

"Well, Daddy's favorite singer was June Christie. And I was kind of looking for a name that would go with her sister Kathy. So, I decided that we would name her Kristy...and that was in the back of my mind (the name Kristy). And Daddy didn't have anything to say about it. So, I decided to name her Kristy Ellen for me because my name is Shirley Ellen and my grandmother's name was Ellen."

"Well, Kathy and Kristy had their bedroom, and they slept in twin beds. And Kathy would say, Kristy? Can I get in bed with you? (Giggle). I'm scared. And Kristy agreed...and they would talk and have a good time. Kristy was popular all her life, even now...because she likes people, and she's real sweet."

"When she was in the eighth grade, I went to class visitation and Ms. Galusky was her teacher and she said, Kristy made her happy from just looking at her because Kristy was always smiling. Kristy was in the band, and she did real well and was in the concert band and second chair. We always went to her concerts. And she was Vice President of the Junior Class."

"Kristy calls me every night, and I look forward to her phone call. She's a...uplifting and...she's selfless, she gives good vibes. And a...I don't know what I would do without Kristy."

On January 5, 1976, mom got a letter from her Aunt Mildred regarding Kristy's wedding. Mom's first child to get married.

"Your mom had sent us the newspaper clipping about Kristy and George's wedding, so we were glad to hear about it from the mother of the bride. It must've been a very lovely wedding and as you said, a very meaningful one. Also, that must have been a great amount of work. I can't imagine you making all those dresses. I

think that would have killed me off. I know you hated to let Kristy go--what a beautiful bride she made, but we would never have recognized her as the little girl we saw 4 1/2 years ago at her grandparents' home. Remember you've gained a son now. He looks and sounds like a fine young man, and they should be happy."

It was truly incredible work for mom to create all the dresses for the wedding. A true work of art. Mom thought of George as a new son, just as Aunt Mildred referred to him. She loved him dearly, and he loved her in return.

Continuing with mom's narration of each of her daughters, her third child was Donna. On May 1, 1962, Donna was born. Leading up to Donna's birthday in 2012, I interviewed mom on video and here is what she said.

"Happy Birthday Donna! 50 years, my goodness. Seems just like yesterday when you were born. I had to wait overnight for the doctors and slept there and it wasn't until 3pm the next day until you were born. The doctors gave me several kinds of medications to induce labor and the nurse said they were taught not to give it, but he (the doctor) gave it anyways and I saw stars! Then you were born. (Giggle) You looked like a little chipmunk with fat cheeks."

"Well Donna, you were an excellent child, but I had to spank you one time. You got out of the yard, and you were only about three. And Grandma had said that you just don't ever want to let the kids get out of the yard. You have to spank them and that's what she did to me. (Laugh) But you got out of the yard and walked over to the Fay's house to play with Mike and DeeDee, and I went to look for you and couldn't believe you had walked all the way over there across the way. And like Grandma said, you have to spank them, so I spanked you for getting out of the yard, you were only three years old."

"One of your favorite things that you liked to do, you liked to go to Maymo and Granddad's house. But Granddad bought you little cans of beer. You just loved that beer. You always did. (Laugh).

He would tell stories about the green tailed horse up on the mountain and you would drink your beer."

"I will never forget when you fell during tennis practice. You were supposed to be running backwards and you did, and you fell and well, I just didn't know how serious it was, but it was pretty serious. I stayed with you at the hospital all night sitting in a chair, and you woke up in the night and I felt so bad. But it turned out alright."

"I was really happy when you decided to go to Apollo college. You excelled and got a 93.7 grade point average. And you got a good job."

In the Winter of 1967-68, the family was going through tough times as the miners, including dad, were on strike with Phelps Dodge. Dad's only means of making money for his family of three girls and wife was to sell turquoise jewelry. Mom's Aunt Lucille says in early 1968...

"Sorry to hear Don had to have an appendectomy. I guess that wouldn't be too much fun. Glad he's doing so well in making and selling his bolo ties. I am not surprised though as he is very artistic and does beautiful work."

But there was some good news that came in early 1968 as written by Aunt Lucille in a letter to mom...

"Your mother was down again, and although none of us saw her, she did call Evelyn. She did tell Evelyn your good news. We were all pleased, but laughed and said, see what happens, the strike just lasted too long, ha-ha, Hope it's a boy. We are glad the strike is over; it is hard to imagine just how much grief and hardship that caused many people."

I was born later that year on September 20, 1968, in the Morenci Hospital. Mom was 32 and still hoping for a boy before it was too late for her. She got her wish.

I think most of us have some of our fondest memories of our mom when we were young. I am no different, from my earliest memories when I was about 4 to 12 years old, those were my wonder years. One of my earliest, distinct memories of mom and dad was a memory of them hugging and sobbing together as they heard my Granddad, Sonny Biles, had passed away. It was the sort of memory that I have never forgotten. The grief and pain were extreme. It was a shared, grief-stricken sadness—something I had never seen before or after.

I remember going to school at Longfellow Grade School, kindergarten through fourth grade. My teachers were Ms. Witted in kindergarten, Ms. Jackson in the first grade, Ms. Waldorf in the second grade, Ms. Olney in the third grade, and Ms. Calderon in the fourth grade. It's funny how I can remember those teachers, but not a single professor at Arizona State University from my last bachelor's degree in history in 2014.

When I was four, people would comment that I walked funny or had a limp. My parents took me to see an orthopedic doctor in Tucson and he determined I had Perthes' Disease. It was a rare hip disease that caused one of my legs to grow and form differently than the other leg. The solution would be a long commitment to wearing a metal leg brace and special 4–6-inch platform shoe for three years. This would help align my legs and hips back into proper proportion.

It was a terrible blow for my family to see me disabled and in a leg brace, my sisters all cried. Through mom's kindness and strength, I set off to conquer this obstacle with determination and patience. I resolved myself to strictly follow what mom and doctor told me to do. No walking without my leg brace or with crutches. I understood that if I did this, I would be normal again in a few years. This was the life event that shaped and prepared me for the challenges ahead and the achievements ahead.

On December 7, 1974, mom received a letter from her Aunt Mildred that touched on the spirit of that time.

"We are so delighted that little Stephen is doing so well. It was great news to hear he is able to climb "his tree", fences and up and down the bank below your house. Sounds like he's not going to let the fact he has to wear a brace for a while get him down. Was Oct. his last check up? I know it's something to have to take him clear to Tucson, but I'm sure you're thankful you found a doctor you can trust. We hope and pray little Stephen's hip will continue to improve until it's back to normal. I know with four children you've been very busy getting ready for Christmas, and that it will be a wonderful time for you."

These were my formative years as I was experiencing life as a disabled child. I lived at 140 Mariposa, the end of the street, that was home. The bus stop to go to school was at the beginning of the street. It was a long walk, especially for a small kid with a leg brace. I remember at times mom would give me a ride and drop me off at the bus stop. Other times, as I got older, I would walk to the bus stop. And there were other times when I would get a ride all the way to the school on rare occasions from mom. I think mom tried her best for me to have a normal childhood, she resisted her nature to be overprotective. I remember my bus driver; her name was Ms. Dodd. On the bus, I would have to sit in a certain way with my leg brace angling out into the walkway, it wouldn't fit in the school bus seats. Kids would have to step over my brace to get to their seats.

My teachers would often keep me in the class during recess because they didn't want me to get hurt on their watch as I would often be running around trying to do all the normal things kids did on a playground. I would take a step and swing my other leg around and was able to get around fairly well. I was even able to run with that pattern of—step and swing my leg brace, step and swing.

I had the most wonderful backyard that dad created largely for all the kids and grandkids, but mostly for me. I had an extended area that was fenced off that included swings and a seesaw. I had a pool room with a pool table, and of course my tree and the treehouse that dad had built, it was a masterpiece.

When my day was done, I would ask mom for help to take my pants off and leg brace off. Once the brace was off, I had to keep weight off my right leg with crutches or hopping. It was such a relief every day to take off the brace and shoe.

Until I was 8 years old, I always needed help from mom putting on my pants and taking them off. The leather belts on the brace were tight, and often pinched and hurt. The big shoe was uncomfortable and awkward to wear. I can honestly say, I never put weight on my right leg for three years. I never cried or complained...mom would not have it. I never felt defeated or disheartened. I did my best and held my head high, like mom told me to do.

Taking my brace off was a thoughtful process, as it meant the end of the day for me. Putting it back on was so much effort. I would never wear shorts, as I liked how pants would hide the brace.

Going to the bathroom was hard and awkward with the leg brace. Kids knew when I was in a stall, as my leg brace would be sticking out. I couldn't ride a bike either because I wasn't able to bend my knee; so, I wasn't able to peddle. All I could do was to sit

on a bike and brush my good leg along the ground and hold my brace leg up in the air so it wouldn't drag. The constant voice of encouragement was coming from mom. She taught me to be strong and persevere...to handle myself with dignity and grace and to never feel sorry for myself. This too shall pass; it will just take time.

The bus and sometimes mom would drop me off at Longfellow Grade School. It was a steep incline up to the school. On occasion, I struggled and looked back at the bottom of the hill and saw mom watching me. She was not upset or running up the hill to help. She was just smiling and encouraging me so that I could do it. I knew I could make it because mom told me I could make it.

I remember the endless doctor appointments, mom and me. She was my advocate, my protector and my coach. We frequently made visits to the Morenci Hospital to get current X-rays to send to Tucson. Usually, the hospital would send X-rays and occasionally we would take them with us for the doctor to view at my appointment. He would put up the new X-ray and the most recent and show the comparison.

Taking trips to Tucson with mom and dad to see the doctor was a big deal. It would usually be a visit to the orthopedic doctor, Dr. Willingham, and then a visit to the brace and shoe doctor to get an adjustment per the doctor's order. My parents would make it a fun trip every time. We would go to my favorite restaurant at the time, Hardee's. They would make my favorite--plain hamburger patty and French fries. On occasion, when I was extra lucky, we might go to Farrell's Ice Cream Parlor.

Growing up with a large metal brace and platform shoe made me the subject of teasing by the other kids. They called me "big foot" and other hurtful names. I would occasionally be the monster they would run away from on the playground. I remember one time; I walked around for Halloween, and someone asked if I was dressed up as a little crippled boy? I generally took it all in stride. Again, mom never let any anger or sorrow show, she just gave me quiet encouragement and a loving smile.

I was frequently a daredevil with my friends. It was probably a way I tried to fit in but also stick out. I would jump off mountains in the neighborhood or occasionally, I would jump off houses—I was the kid that would take on the greatest challenge, even though my metal brace did not allow my leg to bend. I recall a time walking home from the bus stop, I jumped off a hill that was higher than anyone else would dare jump off. I did it but I hurt myself badly as the shock of the jump and landing on my stiff leg brace caused me considerable pain. I cried and my friends had to carry me home. When they got me home, it was off to the hospital with mom.

I remember another occasion when I was playing at the Brookes house across the street. I was jumping over the chain-link fence, which was no easy task with a leg brace on. My wrist got caught in a protruding piece of metal and ripped my hand wide open. Surprisingly, I was unaware that I had ripped it open until one of my friends alerted me to my bleeding hand. My friends rushed me across the street to mom. She wrapped my hand in a towel and drove me to the hospital to get stitches.

The Brookes kids were close friends—Eric, Kelly and Kyle and their parents, Cliff and Judy. Judy and mom would visit at each other house and have tea and a Danish. Later, I remember, when the Brookes got divorced and Judy moved to York Valley, mom would take me to visits to see Eric and she would visit with Judy.

Our next-door neighbors were the Tomlins; we shared a driveway. I don't recall that they ever had children. Occasionally I would be sent over by mom to ask them for a cup of sugar or flour.

We used to play hide and seek in the neighborhood. Kids of all ages would join the game; the base was the light pole across the street by the Brookes' house. I remember hearing mom call for me to come home when it was getting late. I would call back to tell her, I'm coming.

From an early age, I liked to make money. Mom encouraged me to be enterprising as I would come up with various ideas and schemes to make money. One of my most regular ideas was to go door to door selling greeting cards. I would knock on doors and show people a catalog of several types of greeting cards. Holiday cards were the best sellers. I would take orders, collect funds and then send off my orders to Olympia, the company that made the cards. The packs of greeting cards would get delivered in a couple of weeks by mail, then I would rush off to deliver the cards to my customers. Mom was one of my best customers, she would encourage my hustle. She was an avid writer; so, the cards came in handy.

I remember going to the Phelps Dodge Mercantile to grocery shop with mom. Inevitably, a trip to "town" would involve a stop by the Morenci Variety, a local dime store, where I might get some candy and maybe Estes Drug store as well to drop off some film or pick up something there. She might need to stop by Pine's or Buffo's to shop and maybe drop off a letter at the post office. Mom had the highest standards for her kids and herself. She was beautiful and would dress up when going into town.

I would usually take the bus to a nearby bus stop down on Sunflower for lunch each day. I just had to walk up the drain to my house where dad and I would eat together. Mom would have to be regimented with lunch. She would make me peanut butter crackers, macaroni or spaghetti or a hamburger patty with French fries. We would have a relatively small window of about 30-40 minutes to eat lunch together. Mom would set up a couple of TV trays in the living room for dad and me. Dick Van Dyke and Andy Griffith were on TV. Before the end of Andy Griffith, I knew it was time to get back to school.

Dad would drop me off at the bottom of the road leading up to Longfellow School. Occasionally, he would give me a ride all the way up the hill and drop me off right by the gate, but he would usually drop me off at the bottom where I would take an overpass with a long stairway up to the school. He would let me shift the gears from home all the way to my drop-off.

The Tomlins moved away and were replaced by the Smith family. In a lot of ways, they were direct opposites of my family. They didn't keep their yard tidy, dressed a little ragged, and it wouldn't be unusual for a tire to be randomly laying on the roof. The Smiths had a couple of older boys about the same age as my sisters–Joby and Benny. My sisters didn't like them at all and considered them strange. My dad had some confrontations with the boys and their dad as he didn't like the way they acted around his daughters. They had a younger brother named Bobby, who was my age. Mom's kitchen sink window was facing towards the Smith house as she felt she needed to keep an eye on them.

On January 5, 1976, mom received a letter from her Aunt Mildred pleased to hear about my progress.

"We both said good-good when we read about Stephen's progress. It's terrific news that he will probably be able to discard his brace in about six months! Great, and I know he will appreciate not having to wear his big shoe too. We know it's been quite an ordeal for him and all of you, but we hope and pray that his hip will completely mend in time. You said the knob is filling in, we wondered what bone is still disintegrating – is it the socket that the knob fits into? He sounds like a wonderful little boy. Give him a big hug for us."

I remember a special trip to San Diego with my auntie, uncle and cousin Cindy. Because of dad's large family and modest earnings, we could never afford to go on fancy vacations. So, my auntie and uncle, who lived in Scottsdale, would from time to time take us kids on trips with them. In San Diego, we saw it all—the San Diego Zoo, the Wild Animal Park and Sea World. We went to the beach and even went to Mexico across the border to Tijuana. This trip was memorable for a lot of reasons. Of course, the biggest excitement was to experience so many new things, but also it came shortly after my leg brace was removed permanently, and I had a new liberation of movement. I remember running and jumping everywhere we went. I had fun memories of my auntie and uncle and their great kindness. I collected thousands of seashells on the beach and took them home as collections.

It was a great time for me after getting my brace off. I remember how nice it was to walk around and not have people looking at me and feeling sorry for me. I could be just another kid and not be watched and pitied. With the brace gone, I could ride bikes now, play football, and run and jump without the clanky, heavy brace slowing me down. It was a glorious time for me and the family, especially mom and dad. They got me to the finish line of recovery and had endless hopes and dreams for me to obtain.

As I was getting my brace off, mom was becoming a grandmother...first Lisa, then Lori from her second daughter Kristy. Then came Bill and Megan from her first daughter Kathy. Mom loved being a grandmother. She probably had her closest connection with her first grandchild, Lisa. Mom saw her a lot as she was growing up. That wasn't the case with all the other grandchildren either because they didn't live close, or the daughters were concerned about mom's mental illness.

Becoming a grandmother was a special treat for a woman who had devoted her entire life to motherhood. She adored her grandchildren.

I moved on from Longfellow Grade School to Fairbanks Elementary School for grades 5th through 8th. I made several new friends outside of my neighborhood. Tom Vaughn was my best friend for years. Probably from 2nd grade to about 7th grade, we were inseparable. We would ride bikes all over town and do daredevil things that kids would do.

As I got into the 6th, 7th and 8th, my friendship with Tom started to fade as they do from time to time with kids. I started to gravitate towards the athletic boys who played a lot of football and basketball. Hector Salazar was one of those boys, along with Bobby Castaneda, Daniel Lopez, Steve Brannon, Timmy Miller, Johnny Loya to name a few. It was good times finishing up our years at Fairbanks, playing inter-mural basketball and team football for the first time, as we played other schools in the area. We were good. I was a starting wide receiver and made several touchdowns in my pre-high school career.

As I was transitioning into junior high, mom was transitioning into her mid-40s. It was a time of independence as she began working as a secretary and making money for the first time since she was 18. She bought her own car, a new Buick Regal.

It was probably a time of deep reflection for her as well. She could see the end of raising her family. She was often lonely and unhappy in her marriage. Her female reproductive chemistry was changing, leading to weight gain, depression and anxiety. Then her father died. It was a perfect storm triggering a mental illness episode. That episode led to five years of intense mental illness leading to several hospitalizations. Her mania was stabilized in 1985, but a flair up of intense depression befell her in 1988, leading to another hospitalization and further experimentation with medications.

She was again stabilized but this time even more listless. Her life was mundane. She didn't drive anymore; she didn't grocery shop; she didn't work; she didn't diet or exercise. Ten years after her brief interlude to independence, she was completely and irrevocably dependent on dad. She was just existing.

CHAPTER 4
The Lost Years
(1993-2000)

"Not only so, but we also glory in our sufferings, because we know that suffering produces perseverance; perseverance, character; and character, hope."

- Paul, Letter to the Romans, 5:3-4

Advancing ahead past mom's mental breakdown, hospitalization and stabilization, my parents' new home on Relation Street in Safford was a big transition in life, to say the least. It was 1993 and both had lived all or most of their lives in Morenci. Mom had lived in Morenci since she was 15 and dad since he was a small baby. They had never owned a home because they always lived in company-provided housing and paid rent. It was 45 years of hard work for Phelps Dodge; the only company dad had ever worked for. Dad (and mom) certainly earned a happy, restful retirement.

Dad was 61 and mom was 57 as they began their new life in Safford. Their home was 1,300 square feet and was originally built in the 1950s. The purchase price of their home was $60,000. It had a big, raw undeveloped yard. Both the house and especially the yard needed a lot of work, just the sort of challenge dad needed in retirement.

In 1993, my sisters and I surprised my parents with a puppy wiener dog. They named her Jennifer. It was for mom's birthday, and it was their first dog in several years since taking care of Kathy's wiener dog, Sunshine, in Morenci. Jennifer was a wonderful addition to the family, both mom and dad adored her. She was an important companion to both. As dad began his monumental renovation of the yard, it was Jennifer who became his "assistant" and regular companion. Jennifer was drawn to mom like a magnet, like all dogs. She made sure to spend equal time in mom's lap and in the yard with dad. It was competitive between Jennifer and the cats— Fatty and Stinky— on who could gain the prominent lap position. Every so often they would figure out how to position all three

of themselves on her lap. When night came, Jennifer would burrow deep under the blankets in my parent's bed. She was a little hot potato, we called her.

Dad loved her so much; he would let her sit on the arm rest of his recliner during meals and feed her bites of his food right off his fork. He would tell her slow...and she would bite the food off his

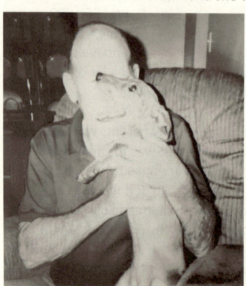

fork oh so delicately.

His favorite trick of all was to ask her to yawn. He would hold her up right by his face and say, *"She's yawning.".* Jennifer would oblige with a slow, long yawn, but then at the end of her yawn, she abruptly bit down on his nose. It was all part of the act; they had a wonderful time together.

On July 7, 1993, mom and dad got a letter from Aunt Virginia, it captured the time and mood in mom's life.

Dear Shirley & Don,

I'm happy that you and Don have found your home. It will be work but fun getting it fixed like you want it. When Bernice said you had a glassed-in room, I thought that's where I'd do my sewing and you can have indoor plants like your mom said.

Remember I love all of you.

Aunt Virginia

Now with a faithful assistant in Jennifer, dad was in his element fixing up the house and more importantly the yard. Mom was assistant number 2 for him. The yard was raw, with lots of boulders and dirt humps and random holes. Dad's vision was a structured, level yard with sidewalks, lots of grass, flower beds and plants. He had a block wall built all around the yard in the back and a wrought iron fence in the front. He planted tall hedges between the neighbor's house and ours for privacy. The transformation was so amazing that a local newspaper, The Eastern Arizona Courier and the City of Safford, nominated dad and his home for the Pride of Safford Award. The city official wanted to do an interview with him and a photo op with the mayor. The story would be a big write-up in the newspaper. After thinking about it, dad declined as he told them he didn't make the yard for them, he did it for his family. It was unfortunate dad didn't allow the article. At the same time, it was typical of dad, and it made me smile then and still makes me smile today.

As my parents were beginning their new life in Safford, I was beginning my new life back in Morenci. I lived in a duplex house near the old school I attended as a child, Longfellow School which had been converted into the company fitness center. My first job was in materials management. I had the title of materials analyst and was later promoted to buyer. I had a new car, a new house, and a new life. As mentioned, it was with considerable reticence that I started this new life. I loved Morenci as a child and as a place to visit, but it was not the place I wanted to be as an adult. Phelps Dodge was not the ideal company for a business guy to really advance and make a significant mark in the company. It was a company of engineers. Also, it was not the best place for a bachelor. However, I made the best out of it by pouring out my passion for tennis into the community. As I lived in Morenci, I was just an hour from my parents. It was nice that I could easily visit, which I liked to do frequently. It was good for both of my parents, particularly mom when I visited. They loved it.

I had an entrepreneurial spirit from a young age and into my career with Phelps Dodge. One thing I can say about the company, I had opportunities to be creative and express unique ideas and concepts that occasionally led to brand-new jobs and opportunities. Early in my career at PD, I developed a vendor performance system called STOPS which meant Supplier Tracking On-time Performance System. My slogan for the STOPS program was "At Phelps Dodge Morenci, poor delivery STOPS." I went on to transfer to the Maintenance Division where I created a new job and department known as contractor management. I had a lot of independence, visibility and challenge in my work years at Morenci. However, professionally and personally, I craved more, something uniquely my own and something truly great.

Every weekend, I visited my parents in Safford. I used the excuse of needing my clothes cleaned and ironed. I just liked to see them as much as they liked seeing me. I also knew it was good therapy for mom to have a greater purpose, and taking care of my clothes every week was something she did with love and passion. It was a topic of conversation leading up to the weekend about whether she had the clothes done yet. I would typically show up on a Friday and bring in a big hamper full of new dirty clothes. She would say with a smile— *"When do you need them?"*

Every so often, I would need them before the end of the weekend, but usually it wouldn't be until the following week. I would have a lot of dirty clothes from work and extensive gym and tennis clothing. I would tell mom— *"I need your help."* I would take my huge hamper of clothes and set it in her laundry room. She would tell me— *"look in the closet, I did all your clothes from last week this morning."* She would not only wash my clothes but iron each item with care and precision.

An even bigger passion for mom was making me some home-cooked meals during my weekend in Safford. Her specialty and my favorite were tacos. I would call their house and often dad would answer. I would tell him, *"I'm on the straight stretch, on my way for a visit this weekend, could you put mom on?"* I would ask mom, *"Do you think you could make me some tacos tonight?"* That would bring on instant laughter because that's what I would say every time I visited. She would say, *"Of course, I could make you some tacos, I have the meat thawing out already, how many do you think you want?"*, she would say with a bit of giggle. I would say the same thing every time, *"Three hard and three soft."* As I was referring to the crispness of the taco shells. Through the course of the weekend, I would usually have some of my other favorites of chicken fried steak and fried potatoes. At times using hamburger and sometimes using cube steak. Dad would typically have some steaks ready to cook out as well. At some point in the weekend, he would grill the steaks. It was a time to sit outside together and talk about my job. Also, he would talk about his latest plans in the yard.

One of the first steps during any visit to Safford would be to receive a tour from dad on some newly completed projects in the yard. I think he would time something amazing with my visits so he could show it off. His work was spectacular. My parents would want to hear all about my job and the people I was working with, especially dad. He knew everyone at the Morenci branch and would like to hear my stories at work. I could see him beaming with pride.

This was the era of video rentals. We would make the weekend a big event for the three of us. I would visit a local video store and bring home the latest popular movie for all of us to enjoy. I would buy popcorn and snacks and we would all thoroughly enjoy the movies.

The weekend would usually culminate with the final round of a golf tournament on Sunday and/or an NBA basketball game. Again, we would chit-chat about work in the background. I was not pushing fitness as much during this time, and it really showed with mom's weight as it started reaching higher levels. Nonetheless, she was stable with her moods, no mania and no depression. After mom got all the loads of laundry done by Sunday, I would have a final home-cooked meal at lunch and then head back to Morenci. Some of the clothes would remain that still needed ironing. We would invariably part on...thank you for getting my clothes done. Please get to work on the remaining clothes, I'm counting on you, with a shared smile.

My passion in Morenci, which grew into an obsession, was tennis. I played tennis in high school and gave lessons while I was going to college. Tennis was a big financial help to me as it assisted me through college. Once I was in Morenci to stay, I started doing several different projects to build tennis up in the community. I coached the high school team. At times as a paid assistant, but often as a volunteer. The players on the team were often my personal students from years of tennis lessons with me.

I developed a competitive tennis league for all the kids to play, it was like Little League baseball. The leagues started at 5 years old and went up all the way to 18-year-olds. At its peak, there were about 200 kids in the league, and I had about 50 volunteers who coached and administrated the league. It even grew to neighboring cities of Clifton, Duncan and Safford. At any one time, there may be several head-to-head team competitions going on in the different cities. All of it was administrated by me and my senior team from walkie-talkie communication.

During this era, the high school team won five straight state championships, a feat never done before or after in any Morenci High School sport. To prepare the top players for high school competition in Phoenix, there were all-star teams from the leagues selected. They would go to Phoenix and play in tournaments against the top big-city competition. This helped the growth and confidence of the players as they made it to the high school level. They were seasoned competitors with no fear of the big-city kids.

Tennis was often an overlooked sport in high school athletics, and I'll admit, I often had a chip on my shoulder on how tennis was treated. Yet in Morenci, during the 1990s, tennis was truly a powerhouse among the sports. Looking back, it was one of my finest achievements in life. There is nothing left but memories, but the memories are special.

During their retirement years in Safford, dad did everything for mom. It got excessive as she didn't participate or take the lead in anything, except maybe cooking. He handled the bills; he handled the grocery shopping. He'd usually stop by a neighborhood grocery store called Sal's—it was owned by an older Italian man and his sons. Dad developed a friendship with the family. Mom stayed in the house most all the time. The only trip she would go on would be a once-every-other-week drive to the dump, a place where people could discard their junk or waste. Dad was working the yard and filling his pickup truck with waste and garbage. He did not visit any local bars. He thankfully gave up that lifestyle in Morenci. Occasionally, he would share a 6 pack with a neighbor and longtime friend, Longo Figueroa. My parents lived a secluded life at their little house on Relations, just waiting and hoping for the family to visit.

Dad personally managed mom's medications. He would prepare them and visually make sure they were taken every morning and night. It was understandable he was careful with the medications; it was absolutely the key to 5+ years of mood stability. They would make their routine trips to Tucson and see mom's psychiatrist, Dr. Fredman.

The mid-90s were the time of two new medical problems for mom—Diabetes and Glaucoma. At the time, Glaucoma was seen as the more serious, imminent threat to mom's health. However, long term, Diabetes, like it is for millions of Americans each year, was a slow deadly ticking time bomb, and the beginning of her metabolic syndrome.

Metabolic syndrome is a cluster of conditions that increase the risk of heart disease, stroke, and diabetes. It includes high blood pressure, high blood sugar, excessive body fat around the waist, and abnormal cholesterol levels. The syndrome increases a person's risk for heart attack and stroke.

Mom's diagnosis of diabetes came during a time when she was feeling bad and lethargic. Dad took her to the hospital, and they ran some tests and determined her blood sugar was extremely high, 500-600. She was hospitalized in Safford, and they began treating her by getting her blood sugar under control. She had to remain in the hospital for a few days. It should not have been any surprise to anyone, she was a classic Type II diabetes candidate. She was overweight, and her diet had too much sugar and enriched flour. She was also sedentary in her new life in Safford, with not much movement or exercise. I got too caught up in my own life during these years of mood stability and was just her son and didn't maintain my lifestyle management coaching for her. She had ballooned to nearly 190 pounds during this time. A significant weight when considering she was 5' 1" in height. At the hospital, she got some training on blood sugar management, diet, exercise and insulin treatment. I think most people don't take diabetes seriously enough because it is a slow, gradual killer. Eventually, it does kill everyone that gets it.

I remember visiting her in the Safford Hospital as she was recovering from her high blood sugar. I had just gotten a tattoo and was dreading the day of showing it to her in the hospital. I thought she would disapprove. Conversely, after looking at it, she smiled and liked it just fine. I really could do no wrong in her eyes.

Mom often complained of poor vision at this time. Some of it was due to side effects of her many medications and some of it was hereditary Glaucoma. Dad took her to see a specialist in Tucson and they thought her vision was dire. They told us that blindness was imminent. The specialist recommended that she learn how to read Braille. At this point, her trips to Tucson to see her psychiatrist would also include regular trips to see a Glaucoma Specialist. Her name was Dr. Alma Murphy. She was a tough, blunt lady and one of the top specialists in Tucson. I met her and attended a few appointments with mom. I never believed, like the growing consensus, that she was destined to be blind. I would scoff at the Braille and felt there had to be another path. I believed issues like these were as much mental and they were medical. Mom didn't particularly like her eye doctor. She generally liked male doctors better and often felt the female doctors were uppity.

During Christmas of 1998, I sat down with mom and dad and talked about places they wanted to go and things they wanted to do. I wanted to know their bucket list, mainly dad's bucket list as mom was content to go with the flow. Dad immediately said, *"I can't go anywhere with your mother."* I quickly interjected and said, I'll be going on all the trips, and it'll be fine. In the 5+ years since retirement, they hadn't traveled anywhere because of dad's apprehension with mom. I told him we would do it together, and I would organize everything.

With that settled, dad said he wanted to see the ocean again. So, we planned on a flight to San Diego. They both wanted to see the Grand Canyon, that would be trip number two. He wanted to take a passenger train all his life, that would be trip number three. We planned a trip, by train to see my sister Kristy. Finally, he said he wanted to see the new underground caverns just opening near Benson, Arizona. It was called Kartchner Caverns. So, the plans were made—a full schedule by planes, trains and automobiles. It was their bucket list and as the musical artist Prince said in his famous song, we were going to "Party like it's 1999".

In early winter 1999, the trip to San Diego was set. We were going to fly and then rent a car to drive to our motel on the beach. I did the driving, and I had the trip planned out. Dad wanted to eat at a nice seafood restaurant right on the beach. I remember mom getting nervous and choking on her food almost immediately, but I kept everyone calm and reminded her to eat slowly and everything would be okay. Social anxiety was the big reason why dad avoided public situations for mom.

As we were so close to the beach, we could walk down to enjoy the cool, balmy weather and feel the sand on our bare feet. The hotel had a jacuzzi, so we made sure to visit that amenity every night as we all brought bathing suits. We enjoyed room service, and the hotel had a nice restaurant as well.

We had a full agenda as we visited the San Diego Zoo, Sea World and the Wild Animal Park. All the attractions went just fine. They often required a lot of walking, and mom was overweight and out of shape. We took frequent breaks, so the experience wasn't overwhelming. We also took trams that gave our feet a break. All in all, it went well, and we were off to a good start. Dad was uplifted that we were able to get through the trip and also enjoy ourselves.

Our second trip was to the Grand Canyon in late spring. We drove to Sedona first and stayed a couple of nights. Then we drove to nearby Oak Creek Canyon and stayed in a woodsy environment for a couple of nights. Finally, we drove to Williams, where we boarded a train to the Grand Canyon. I took the lead in all the driving. Dad got to sit alongside and enjoy the drive and scenery. Something he had never done but enjoyed immensely.

Our first stop was Sedona. We arrived and checked into our hotel. We visited the Uptown area, a famous spot for turquoise jewelry and Native American  art. Dad had been making Kachina plaques for many years, and we wanted to look into ways to put his work out in the market for sale. We looked around at different shops and inquired and showed pictures. I remember we found a nice little ice cream shop, and we all sat down and had a nice treat, a favorite for mom was to get an ice cream cone. We took a couple of tours around Sedona in jeeps, and we all had a good time. Mom did fine getting around with a little help.

Our next stop was Oak Creek Canyon. We stayed in a cabin just a few feet from the creek. It was warm outside, so we got on our bathing suits and enjoyed some time in the water. I helped mom get in the creek, and she just decided to lie in the water. It might have started with a slip, but she settled in and enjoyed it.

77

Next on the agenda was the big trip to Williams where we would catch the Grand Canyon Railway up to the Grand  Canyon. We drove the car up to Willams and made our way to the train depot. It was an old-fashioned train with open windows and a flair for the old West. The view was scenic as we made our way to the Grand Canyon.

Dad was happy and content. It was a dream come true for him. About halfway through the trip, a few men by horseback rode along the train and held us up. They made the train stop and walked through the train making a big ruckus, shooting their fake guns. Of course, it was all part of the show—mom and dad were amused.

After arriving at the Grand Canyon, we walked around and enjoyed the incredible views. I remember it was hot, but still the trip of a lifetime. After seeing what we wanted to see, we made our way back to the train for our return trip to Williams and then back to our cabin. We stayed another night and went on our way back to Safford. Trip two in the books and again, it went very well.

Trip three was a highly anticipated trip because we were taking a train from Benson, Arizona to Alpine, Texas. It was an interesting experience. We arrived in Benson, at an empty parking lot along the railroad track. We waited in dad's truck for our train to arrive. All our bags were packed and ready to go. As our departure time arrived, we could hear a train approaching and we all got out of the truck and waited along the track. The train did not stop for long, so we needed to be ready.

The journey took about 10 hours to get to the Alpine, Texas, train depot. It was enjoyable for all, but particularly for dad. He soaked it all in and I could just feel how happy he was to sit by his window, watching the scenery and enjoying the experience. I noticed on this trip that dad was having bathroom issues. I inquired, but he didn't want to talk about it and didn't think it was a problem.

Once we arrived in Texas, my sister Kristy was there waiting for our arrival. It was a little bit surreal to take a train and end up at a small station just inside the border of Texas near New Mexico. It was a happy reunion for all of us to see Kristy. We went on to have a nice visit with her and her three daughters—Lisa, Lori and Krystle. Lisa had a new baby, Harley, and of course mom and dad really enjoyed their new great-grandson. After a few good days of visiting, we made our way back home and to our truck parked in Benson. It was another wonderful experience for all.

The final trip was back to Benson again. This time to the newly opened Kartchner Caverns. It had been talked about and under development for many years, something dad had been following in the news with interest. It was finally opened to the public. He jokingly called it Kerchner Caverns, it was an ongoing joke between us. We stayed in a hotel nearby and went down into the caverns. It was different from the more famous Carlsbad Caverns as it was a "living" cavern. It was wet and alive as they described it. The views inside were spectacular.

We made the trip a multi-stop adventure and visited nearby Tombstone. We did all the touristy things there, and we watched a show at the OK Corral, made famous by Wyatt Earp. After the fourth and final enjoyable trip, we concluded our goals for 1999. All bucket list items complete. It was a fun time for all and proved that mom could travel and interact with the public, and everything would be just fine.

With the new millennium under way, a life-altering moment was coming. I got the call in March of 2000; I was at my job in Morenci. I was not prepared for the news I received from my sister. She attended a doctor's appointment with dad in Safford. We had plenty of scares before regarding his health. In the past, he had melanoma skin cancer and a serious blood clot in his leg; they were both life-threatening. This call was different. She was upset and crying on the phone. She told me dad's results came back and his cancer was serious, and I should come to Safford now. I immediately walked to my boss' office and told him the news and that I needed to head to Safford. I got to town and assessed the situation. I realized immediately that it was indeed serious. I touched bases with mom to see what she knew and what she understood.

Dad had already resolved that this was the end, and there was nothing to do. However, we persuaded him to have colon surgery, and it was scheduled almost immediately. His cancer was stage IV, the most advanced. A difficult surgery like that was not ideal in a small town like Safford. The experience and expertise of surgeons in Tucson or Phoenix would have been the better idea, but in any case, the key to treatment with advanced colon cancer was the oncology afterword. Unfortunately, dad was not interested in traveling to a big city and was not interested in oncology.

He felt fairly good for a few weeks immediately after the surgery, but that was a small window of time to aggressively pursue radiation and/or chemotherapy. He hoped against all hope that the surgeon got it all, but that was highly improbable even for an expert surgeon from a top hospital.

Dad was sad in his last few weeks. He bought and listened to blues music all day and would not accept any visitors except family. I wish I had pushed him harder to try oncology. However, dad was a strong-willed person and he had made up his mind. I sat with him often in the living room and tried to comfort him. All his life, he was certain he would outlive my mother. He even signed up for his post-employment pension plan that would only pay out if he was alive, instead of a lesser amount that would continue with mom.

Now we talked about the reality that mom would outlive him. I assured him that I would take care of her. I think he had mixed feelings about it. He thought Kristy would be the better option, as he knew the huge responsibility and how it would alter the life of the one who assumed it. I was 31 years old and unmarried. I think dad didn't want caretaking responsibility on me at such a young age and yet to build a family. Yet, I knew, it could only be me.

I stayed in Safford regularly during these last few weeks to start transitioning life with mom and help and comfort dad as much as possible. He and I had been through a lot together during some of the worst moments of mom's mental illness. Our life together was as dire and difficult as any life experience could have been between a father and son. It is hard to even put into words the mutual understanding we had and the experiences we went through together. It was a deep bond to say the least.

Becoming mom's caretaker was a solemn decision, but it was the ONLY decision. The caretaking that mom required put me in a different role, much different than being a loving son. What most people don't understand—was that becoming a caretaker of someone with mom's health, required me to put my role as her son in the background and make the role as her caretaker my primary function. I got to be her son again from 1985 until 2000, now it would be different. Being a caretaker for a 64-year-old diabetic, schizophrenic woman who was going blind would be an extremely difficult job. I was 31 years old and had been on my own since I was 17. I never had any major responsibilities other than myself, not even a dog or cat. I knew full well that the responsibility of moving in with mom in Safford and taking care of her would be life-altering. The biggest responsibility of my life and the biggest responsibility I would ever have. As much as I loved mom and was up for the challenge, I knew I would be sacrificing some parts of my life. I had moments of bitterness from time to time. Ultimately, I just refused to put my life ahead of mom's life. She was mom.

Not only did we have her chronic issues of mental illness, diabetes and severe glaucoma, but she was obese, not often lucid, and had severe social anxiety from years of being a recluse. Dad was protective and thought he was doing the right thing. I think he was also embarrassed about her condition. Safford and Morenci were small towns where mental illness is something not well understood and often a butt of jokes. So, he just kept her home all the time.

Mom also had doctors she had been seeing. In Tucson, it was Dr. Fredman for psychiatry, and for her glaucoma, Dr. Murphy and a primary care in Safford named Dr. Standage.

As his cancer inevitably raged back after the surgery and no oncology, I recognized the situation as a potential double tragedy. Mom had been so fragile and so reliant on dad; it was easy to see his loss leading to serious if not terminal psychological effects on her. As dad's time slipped away, he started to get sick again, but this time much worse than before.

I wish we could have done something special during his window of good time after surgery. If not oncology, we should have gone up to Black River or a drive up the trail through Morenci. He was resigned to his fate. Sadness and bitterness were often his moods. He tried to quit smoking and drinking towards the end and that resulted in hastening his demise and his body had severe withdrawals from the cold turkey approach that was not healthy or helpful.

The night before he died, he started to feel terrible, and I decided he needed to go to the hospital. He could not walk, and we didn't have a wheelchair, so I had to lay him in a chaise lounge to transport him to the car. Mom was walking alongside the chaise lounge and when we got to the porch, she reached down to him. They hugged and kissed and exchanged, *"I love you."* It was a touching and poignant goodbye between mom and dad—46 ½ years after they met at the Christmas dance in 1954. I think they both knew it was their final goodbye. I told mom, *"I'm going to take him to emergency and get him cared for and then I'll be back as soon as possible."*

I remember how scared dad was in the emergency room. He was telling the doctor who checked on him that he stopped drinking and smoking. He was doing whatever it took. I remember one moment at the hospital that was a special final connection between us, something that only he and I would understand as a part of our long journey together. A patient was brought into the emergency room and placed by dad with a screen between them. Apparently, the patient had been hit by a car. Doctors and paramedics had mentioned they administered Haldol to him. Dad and I both turned and looked at each other and exchanged a look that only a father and son could have with the family significant word Haldol medication mentioned. It had been one of the first anti-psychotic drugs used on mom during her long history of mental health. It was used in extreme, violent episodes of mental illness.

After dad got assigned a room and was stable, I went home to check on mom and was planning to return the next morning. When I returned, dad had slipped unconscious. I don't know what happened or what they gave him, but he wasn't the same as when I left him a couple of hours previous. I was the last person to speak to him. He died later that day.

My sisters had all arrived and surrounded him throughout his last moments. I stayed separate from them and focused exclusively on mom. I knew dad was nearly gone and already unconscious. I had to focus on the future and mom during this delicate life transition.

PART 2
The Phoenix

"And when all that was left was ashes, she would again clothe herself in flame. Rising from the dust of her past to rekindle the spark of her future. She was a Phoenix, her own salvation; rebirthed, renewed, resurrected."

- *LaRhonda Toreson*

CHAPTER 5
Waking from the Slumber
(2000-2002)

*"You cannot defeat darkness by running from it,
nor can you conquer your inner demons by hiding
them from the world. In order to defeat the darkness,
you must bring it into the light."*

- *Seth Adam Smith,*
  "Rip Van Winkle and the Pumpkin Lantern"

Dad loved mom dearly, but he took the path of doing everything for her. For many years, I gave dad advice, but he had his own ideas on how to best manage mom's life. He would handle all the bills and all the groceries. He would personally oversee her medications throughout the day. They would never go and do anything outside of the house because he felt mom wouldn't be able to handle it or he was afraid she would have a public panic attack. No effort was put into diet and exercise for years, despite her diabetes diagnosis. She wouldn't even go to the mailbox on most days.

My strategy with mom was going to be different than dad's approach. First, I was more optimistic about her potential than dad. Secondly, I was ready and able to put in the work to get her to a better place. Dad didn't have the patience or perseverance to follow through day after day with vigilance. I knew she would follow my directions without question. I was going to be her beacon of hope, her drill sergeant and coach all rolled into one.

After dad died, I permanently moved to Safford. I maintained my house in Morenci for a few months and then finally moved out permanently. I believed what no one else believed, and I mean no one—mom could get better, a lot better, it was time to get to work. I moved into one of mom's guest rooms and set up an office in another room. Before this major change of life, I was actively trying to find new employment out of Morenci. I had several out-of-town interviews with other companies. I would continue the job hunt and knew mom would go right along with me if I ever moved.

Before any goals could be created and implemented, it's important to assess the starting point, and where we need to go, and then how we will get there. At the time of dad's death, she was 63 years old. Her height was 5'1", maybe a tad shorter and she was morbidly obese when we checked her weight, 188 pounds. She was on 10+ oral meds and had to inject herself with insulin multiple times a day.

Mom's mental health was stable, but quality of life had left much to be desired. We continued going to her appointments in Tucson every few months. I realized these appointments were not greatly productive because they weren't frequent enough. Mom continued to be diagnosed with schizophrenia and a mood disorder. Lithium was the key medicine prescribed.

Mom was diagnosed with imminent loss of vision through her advanced glaucoma. I knew there was something off with her vision and the diagnosis, I needed to dig in. People lacking experience with mental illness don't understand the power of the mind over just about everything else.

I knew the primary care relationship had to change. I got to know the doctor pretty well at the hospital through his treatment of dad, and I didn't like what I saw or heard.

I had three goals for mom that I had immediate control over: 1) exercise, 2) socialization, 3) firm routines to establish responsibility and a feeling of independence, accomplishment and self-worth. As we diligently worked on these goals, I would push for better health and better healthcare providers.

Exercise consisted of 1) walking on the treadmill, 2) taking walks in the neighborhood with the dogs, 3) Going to the local gym and taking water aerobics classes and lifting weights.

We would wake up each morning and check her weight. I would usually run on the treadmill first and then mom would take her turn and walk for 20 minutes before I left for work. She had strict rules to never walk on the treadmill without my supervision for safety purposes. Checking her weight was important in building a routine and building progress and momentum. It was a routine that dated back to the 80s when I came home during the summers, and we would walk up to the hospital to check her weight.

In the evenings when I would get home from work and on the weekends, we started going for walks in the neighborhood or we would go to the gym together.   Exercise and diet would be the centerpiece of everyday life. We would often take our little wiener dog Jennifer on walks around the neighborhood. She loved going for walks and we called her our little sled dog as she would pull and pull as we walked. Our house was about a 1/2 a mile from Safford High School, so we had a routine to walk down to the high school and along the grass fields and then circle back down Relation Street and back home, about a two-mile walk. On weekends, we would typically go for a longer walk up to 4-5 miles after she built up strength and endurance.

The third and most important part of her exercise regimen would also play a significant role in her reconnection with people. There was a health club in Safford that had an indoor swimming pool with a water aerobics instructor. It was mainly geared towards senior citizens. I joined the gym as well. Two long-time family friends were especially kind and helpful to mom's recovery. Bea Cervantes and Hortencia Figueroa both lived in Safford and had long ties with the family back in their Morenci days.

I arranged for Bea and Hortencia to alternate escorting mom to water aerobics classes at the nearby gym. The number one activity that epitomized mom's revival of her physical and mental health was her water aerobics. It helped her lose weight. It helped her regain social skills. It helped her regain self-esteem and purpose. Most of all, she really enjoyed it. They attended class three times a week on Monday, Wednesday and Friday.

Both ladies adored mom and would occasionally "bicker" over who would be taking her to water aerobics. They would pick her up and drop her off at her home. The classes took place when I was at work in Morenci. So, the ladies accepted a large responsibility to escort and guide mom through the classes. They would walk her to the front door and make sure she got into the locked house okay. They would occasionally go into the house to visit a little further, sometimes to have coffee.

The second major goal was for mom to return to the world and experience life and socialize with people. After being restricted to the house for a decade (The Lost Years), she had considerable social anxiety. She was shy, but with so much isolation, it had grown into a nervous anxiety. When people talked to her, she would freeze up and often not know what to say. In a restaurant, she would quite often choke on her food out of anxiety. She also had acid reflux and swallowing problems, but it was mainly social anxiety. Our efforts to exercise would often kill two birds with one stone. As she walked or visited the gym, she would engage in a lot of social situations. Bea and Hortencia would even take her to lunch at a restaurant after water aerobics now and then.

Usually, once a week, we would splurge on the diet and go to a restaurant in town. We had about five regulars we would rotate. There was La Casita in Thatcher, La Paloma in Solomon, Casa Mañana not far from the house and a couple of steak houses—the Manor House and the Branding Iron. Mom loved Mexican food, so she would be a little extra happy about going to one of the first three on the list. I would insist that mom order her own food and pay the bill herself, two things she hadn't done in a couple of decades. This would require her to interact and take responsibility. She would often be tongue-tied when someone would talk to her. At times, I would repeat the question to her or just ask her to answer the lady. Often people would turn to me for an answer, and I would diligently route them back to mom. I was not going to talk for her or take the easy route. We had to work on this.

Later, we started eating dinner out with Longo and Hortencia Figueroa. Longo and dad went back a long way and used to drink beer together on the porch. Hortencia would go on to help mom with rides to water aerobics.

For many years, we watched videos at my parents' home. It was safe and separated from the world. Now, there were a couple of new theaters opening in town, and we were going to go watch movies together in public and see all the new releases. We both loved to watch movies in the theater, so going to a weekly movie became a mainstay of our lives lasting for the next 18 years. It was a comfortable environment because it was public but still kind of private. We liked to sit up close to the screen and we would get popcorn, candy and drinks while watching the movies. I required her to walk unassisted without holding my arm. I would point her to a rail to hold onto, but that was it. She had to walk and talk on her own in the new world I was exposing her to. I would scan for obstacles and guide her through with whispers in her ear. We would usually attend one of the two theaters—either the one in the shopping center or the one behind the hotels heading towards Morenci. We also played miniature golf occasionally as a new business opened next to the theater.

Every Sunday, we would go to the grocery store and stock up for the week. In the past, she would only cook for me during my weekend visits, now it would be 7 days a week. Cooking for me was the highlight of her day; it made her happy. So, getting the proper groceries became important. She took it seriously and had a detailed list written out; she would work on it all week. Going to the store every Sunday became a weekly tradition that would continue uninterrupted for 18 years. I required her to do all the work at the grocery store. She made the list, pushed the cart and got all the groceries. We got her a debit card and I taught her how to use it instead of writing checks that she was accustomed to doing. When we checked out of the store, she would have to do all the interaction at the cashier. Occasionally, she would have a tough time following or interacting and lose her train of thought or get nervous. Often, people would look to me to takeover, but again, I would redirect the cashier back to mom and tell them she was the paying customer. Mom got to know where everything in the store was located and invariably wanted to take shortcuts around to get things. However, I would gently control the front of the shopping cart and make it go down every aisle, so we got everything, but also to lengthen the trip for social and exercise reasons. We were in no hurry, I would say.

About a month after dad died, we had a big public test with the high school graduation of her granddaughter Megan in Morenci. I loved these situations because I knew they were good for her socially and they built confidence. Mom and I drove to Morenci to watch her graduation. With hundreds of people in the stands at the football field and then all the family and friends meeting the graduates on the field, it was a wonderful experience, and very challenging. She had to maneuver up and down stairs and intermingle with all the people. I never held her hand or let her hold my arm, I insisted on independence.

I was determined for mom to travel. I wanted her to see her sisters, whom she hadn't seen in 20 years. I wanted her to see the ocean and visit new and interesting places. I wanted her to feel alive and excited through these new experiences.

The first trip we made was a flight to San Diego with my sister Donna and her two kids Danielle and David. We went to the beach and the zoo, and we took a boat ride. It was all a nice experience. This was a follow-up trip as we went on a trip with dad in 1999, about a year before. The trip was full of challenges and obstacles as we walked on ramps, stairs, and uneven flooring. We had lots of social interactions as we continued to build physical and mental confidence. Mom loved sitting out on the beach to get a tan and took a few walks out into the ocean.

Several months later, we flew to San Francisco to visit my Aunt Virginia, mom's youngest sister. They hadn't seen each other since the early 80s and only a handful of times during their adult lives. Mom was in bad mental shape when they last saw each other. This time around, she was stable mentally, but still in bad health with her weight.

Mom and I really hit it off with my Uncle Buck, Virginia's husband. Both were kind and supportive to mom, who was still drugged up and not completely lucid. I remember when they first saw each other at the airport, mom was a little wobbly, and Virginia helped stabilize her and helped her balance. I think mom couldn't believe she was back with her baby sister after all these years. Denise, my cousin, was also along for the trip we made. She was also kind and supportive of mom. Our trips to California were special for mom and me, it was so nice to see mom's side of the family after so many years.

In early 2001, my job required a week-long trip to Chile and Peru. It was a big test for mom to be away from me for that long. She did have some problems and anxiety, but for the most part, she did okay if I talked to her regularly on the phone. This was a time when she suffered a terrible fall in the parking lot at the local Safford Walmart. She didn't see a parking block and tripped over it. She hit her forehead flush into the asphalt and was bleeding badly. My sister was with her, and an ambulance was called, and she was treated at the hospital.

In the summer of 2001, we had a big family gathering at South Fork near Springerville, Arizona. After dad died, we buried his urn in the backyard of the house on Relation Street. Later, we decided to spread his ashes at one of his favorite places—a family gathering spot called Canyon Cove near the South Fork of the Little Colorado River. We all had an enjoyable time and spent a few days together as a family. Mom walked around and got along fairly well. She was still overweight and under the influence of heavy anti-psyche drugs.

In March of 2002, we traveled to visit her second sister, Beverly, who lived in Houston. We visited during Easter and were able to see most of Aunt Bev's family during an Easter dinner. Aunt Bev took us on a fun ferry ride from Galveston across the bay to the mainland. It was the first-time mom and I had met Aunt Bev's second husband Paul. He was nice and welcoming to us. We went out to dinner a couple of times and stayed at their house. I know mom liked him and enjoyed the visit. She had now seen both of her long, lost sisters in the first two years after dad passed away.

I was constantly coaching and assisting mom with discreet whispers in her ear or gentle touches of encouragement on the back. I was also scanning for hazards coming up or reminding her to eat her food slowly, so she didn't choke. I tried to do it as much as possible under the radar, so she had her space to retain her dignity and independence. If she wasn't talking well, I would remind her to speak up when someone talked to her, telling her "You can do it."

When I would leave the house in Safford and make the one-hour drive to work in Morenci, I would write down a few things she needed to accomplish while I was gone. I would be stern and ask her to get these things done and not to do anything outside the house that could lead to a fall or anything dangerous. The only thing she could do outside was get the mail each day.

Once she would get the mail, it was her responsibility to handle all the bills. She would also have to get stamps at the grocery store. It was her routine to have the bills ready for me to review and make sure the check and envelope were written correctly. She would leave them on the dining room table so I could take a quick peek. It was all part of the coaching and training, and I would point out occasional mistakes to learn from for next time.

Of course, every Monday, Wednesday and Friday, she would need to be ready for Bea or Hortencia to pick her up mid-morning. She would usually dress at the gym in the locker room and take a gym bag with her clothes along on the trip. The bag would also carry the key to the house and her wallet, so it was an important responsibility to pack and get ready for class. I would call her once or twice on my drive into Morenci and check how she was doing with her list and getting ready for class on those days. I would also call her after her class to see how she did and if she had any stories to tell about her adventures in water aerobics. Usually, her water aerobics escorts would also call her before they picked her up to make sure she was ready. When she would tell me about different situations, I would give her advice whenever I could, but occasionally, I would just say, well, that's life, that's how things go now and then.

Mom got comfortable with talking on the cell phone and memorized important phone numbers. I would ask her what she was eating and make sure she was documenting all her calories. As time went by, she started to fill notebooks full of her diet documentation. She even got into a routine of calling me a couple of times a day, occasionally just to ask how I was doing and sometimes to ask what I wanted for dinner. It would bring a smile to my face when I got a phone call from mom. Although, when she started asking me questions like— *"How's your day at work going?" "How was your drive into Morenci?"* Or *"What did you have for lunch?"* It brought a big smile to my face, and a little chuckle because she was really making progress! As I made my commute home each night, I would call her again to tell her when I would be home and to ask her what was on the agenda that night for dinner.

I would ask mom questions if she took her medications but not in a hovering sort of way, just as a part of our conversations. I gave her personal responsibility and treated her like an adult. I would then slip back and verify if she took the proper meds as they would all be in a pill planner. She would also check her blood sugar and inject insulin as needed. I would ask her what her blood sugar level was and how much insulin she took. I had no direct oversight of her diabetes until 20 years later. She took responsibility and managed herself. Before, dad had injected the insulin personally, but I required that she do it herself, and she got comfortable and at ease with the process.

Taking care of her cats, Fatty and Stinky, and her dog, Jennifer, was an important part of her day while I was at work. All three animals would compete over affection, and it wouldn't be unusual for them to fight about it and/or pile on top of each other. On occasion, mom had scratches and wounds to prove it.

One weekend, I was sitting in my back-office room at mom's house, and I saw a terrible incident with Fatty as he was drinking water in the adjacent laundry room. It was a large water bowl and somehow, he slipped and fell in the bowl. He was kicking around in a full panic as he seemed to be having some sort of neurological event or was just freaked out. I had to assist him out of the large bowl, and he started running around like he was completely out of his mind. He had no use of his front legs. He was running around with his face on the ground powered by his back legs. It was a terrible sight as he was running into walls and dashing every which way. When he finally came to a stop, he was tightly wound up in wires and cables under my computer and he couldn't get free on his own. I was going to have to get him out of this tricky situation even though he was still completely out of his mind. As I untied and unwound all the wires, he bit me over and over and scratched and attacked me without mercy. By the time I got him loose, I was bleeding severely on both arms.

It was so bad, I needed to go to the emergency room. First, mom and I took him to the emergency vet to see what was wrong with Fatty. I wrapped up both of my arms with towels as we visited the vet. Mom was carrying Fatty. I can't exactly remember what the diagnosis was, but Fatty could not walk any longer. The vet thought a regular dose of steroids over several weeks might help produce a miracle. He also strongly encouraged me to get to the hospital.

I drove mom and Fatty home and then made my way to the hospital ER. They spent quite a while cleaning up all my wounds. They told me I would almost certainly get a nasty infection, and they started me on antibiotics. After a couple of weeks of the antibiotic, the infection was still evident on my forearms and was traveling up my arms to my shoulders. I returned to the hospital to get another antibiotic started. It finally started to work, and my infection went away.

Fatty was having a terrible time with no use of his front legs. Mom gave him the antibiotic regularly and would hand feed him and help him drink water. It was not a fast miracle, but after several weeks of diligent, loving care by mom, Fatty began to regain the use of his legs. It was truly a miracle, but I believe any good miracle starts with love, and mom provided the love and care to make it happen.

Dad told me that Dr. Standage thought he was a hero for dealing with mom's mental illness instead of institutionalizing her. It was ironic that dealing with alcoholism was socially normal for a spouse to take care of, but not so socially normal to take care of a mentally ill person who was afflicted with a disease.

The doctor was fired on day 1 when I assumed responsibility for mom's health. We established a new primary care physician as one of our first goals involving healthcare. This was one of my earliest recognitions that not all healthcare providers really knew what they were talking about and that occasionally, they were simply wrong and gave bad advice. At the end of the day, I oversaw healthcare and would seek out smart, thoughtful providers who gave good advice for mom and me to consider.

We had eye surgery scheduled to help relieve the fluids that were causing pressure and damage to mom's optic nerve. It was damage to the optic nerve that caused the gradual and complete loss of vision with glaucoma. If the pressures could be relieved, the long-term vision would be salvageable. The surgery was successful, and we were hopeful the pressures would stay low and allow her to retain her limited peripheral vision. Her visual acuity was also considered legally blind, but we will address this later.

Ironically, about this time, I had eye surgery as well to correct my stigmatism. The procedure was called PRK surgery. I had the surgery in 2001 at a large, popular brand in the Phoenix area. The surgery went fine, my eyesight was corrected to about 20/25 in both eyes. However, post-surgery discomfort was high. I stayed in a dark hotel room as I was in considerable pain from exposure to any light. I was taking Vicodin for the pain, but it didn't seem to help. Mom and my sister Donna tried to give me relief, but nothing helped except time. A few days later, my corneas became increasingly cloudy, and it was becoming hard to see. I had several post-op appointments with an optometrist, and he kept giving me greater doses of steroids. The optometrist was aware the steroids were increasing the pressure on my optic nerve, but felt it was necessary to clear up the haze in my eyes. As it turned out, the steroids they were giving me caused permanent damage to my optic nerve and my peripheral vision. The optometrist finally allowed a Glaucoma specialist to see me, and he diagnosed the unthinkable, I had steroid-induced glaucoma.

That was my last appointment with that company, and I did two things. I saw a lawyer and moved mom and me to a new practice, Southwestern Eye. The glaucoma specialist was named Dr. Lewis, and it was an interesting scenario with both mother and son having dual appointments every few months together. Dr. Lewis was a kind man and was interested to hear about my case. I ended up settling out of court for the permanent damage done to my eyes. I had 50-60% of my peripheral vision permanently lost and I was in my early 30s.

My overriding goal was to improve mom's quality of life and to get her to a better place mentally. I knew a lot of changes needed to take place, and it was going to take time. I wanted to get mom back, the one I remember from childhood. The one that could be independent and manage her own life. This was a brand-new Shirley Biles that would be emerging. One that hadn't existed before. This version of mom was going to aspire to become independent and self-sufficient beyond any previous version of herself. No one thought it was possible, no one! Family, friends and medical professionals didn't know what I knew, she was tough. She would take and follow advice. Most of all, she had a fighting persistence that no one really knew she possessed, except me. She had an inner fire and drive that was indomitable.

In 2002, I applied for a job at the corporate headquarters of Phelps Dodge for the position of Global Casualty Manager in the Risk Management Department. My prayers of getting out of Morenci/Safford were finally answered. I was so happy and excited to get hired for this job. It had been my goal from the time I started working for Phelps Dodge in 1993 to get a job in Phoenix, where I would be happier and more comfortable. I did not have any background in risk management, as it was a specialized profession. However, I had experience working with contractors and a long history at the company flagship in Morenci. My new boss in Phoenix took a chance on me. Phelps Dodge had a generous moving package for its employees, so mom and I were on the move.

For the first time in 46 years, mom was returning to the big city of Phoenix. She was a country girl all her life except for a brief, but memorable glimpse of the big city after high school. Mom was on her way to becoming a city slicker.

CHAPTER 6
City Slicker
(2002-2005)

"You can take the girl out of the country,
but you can't take the country out of the girl."

-    *Unknown*

It was such an exciting time for mom and especially for me. I was finally moving on from Morenci and moving to Phoenix where I felt I belonged. It had been almost five decades since mom lived in Phoenix. She was just a young high school graduate of 18 when she lived with her Grandma Maddy in Phoenix while she attended Lamson Business College. Now all these years later, she was moving back to the big city. Country girl all her life, now she was going to be a city slicker. As for me, I was on cloud nine. Finally, after a decade in Morenci/Safford, I was living in Phoenix and working at the corporate office with a new opportunity.

The company moved us to Phoenix after we had a house selected. I already had a grand plan to someday buy a second house close to mom; allowing her to live independently and allowing me to live independently. Mom did a lot of research and decided on the home builder Pulte as our choice. She felt they were classy. My office was in downtown Phoenix, so I could have easily lived in any part of the valley. I decided on the west side of town, which was against the grain from where the family had normally lived. My aunt, uncle and sister all lived on the east side of town.

We searched around in the new developments of the southwest valley and found a perfect place at 67th Avenue and Lower Buckeye, a brand-new Pulte community. It was surrounded by farmlands on all four sides. It felt like the country; it felt like home. Mom bought the home in her name; she did all the mortgage paperwork, and she felt all the responsibility and independence of being a homeowner. We used an agent by the name of Kirsten Snyder. Mom thought she was classy, so she was hired. As we had future real estate transactions, we would keep going back to Kirsten. Mom's confidence was continuing to grow and grow.

Two miles away, a brand-new Fry's Food & Drug opened on 83rd Avenue and Lower Buckeye. Mom thought Fry's was the best as she remembered it was granddad's favorite grocery store. Inside the Fry's was a Wells Fargo Bank, which would be mom's new bank. There was a nail and hair salon in the shopping center, it was perfect. We loved our new big-city life in our new home and the new growing neighborhood in general. We felt like pioneers living in such an open, undeveloped part of Phoenix on the outskirts.

I remember mom was a little iffy about the painted concrete in the new Fry's, but then she decided it was okay. She was willing to overlook the lack of tile. We did our usual once-a-week grocery run—walking down every aisle as usual to her slight irritation. We would visit her bank if she had any business.

Of course, we had all our fur kids ready to start their new lives as well. We had our wiener dog, Jennifer, who was our special connection back to dad. I had grown extremely close to Jennifer as she snuggled with me every night. I took on the new role of dad in her life after my dad passed away. We had a new dog, Penny. She was a Rhodesian Ridgeback mix that had a heart of gold. Penny was found by friends of my sister Donna in a flowerbed. She was part of a wild litter of pups. We also had our two cats, Mr. Fatty and Stinky. Fatty was the alpha leader of all the animals. He demanded respect from all the dogs, the other cat and all humans that entered his house. He raised Jennifer from a young puppy and would require her to get a "cat bath" about once a week. As she grew into an adult dachshund, she dreaded the baths and began to rebel against them. They would get in terrible fights over those baths as Fatty would try and hold her down. If he couldn't lick her clean, he would start biting her and she started to bite back.

Mom used the proceeds from her Safford house as a down payment for her new house where we had a custom-built Jacuzzi installed in the backyard. Mom and I loved our Jacuzzi. It was not just any ordinary Jacuzzi; it was a big one. It could comfortably seat 6-8 people. We had our floating noodles and we enjoyed it almost every evening as we would get in our bathing suits and relax. By this time, mom was an expert on using a noodle floating device with her years of experience in water aerobics.

As for the yard landscaping, we first gave my cousin Doug the landscaping job. He had the best of intentions but was still struggling with drug addictions and was unable to stay focused or even awake long enough to get the work done. He was living with us during the renovation. He was addicted to methamphetamines at this time. I remember one day; it was the final straw for mom. She kindly but firmly told Doug he would need to leave and go back to his mom's house.

After our bad luck with Doug, we hired a professional yard contractor and had our yard built from scratch, and mom was involved in all the design. We had a beautiful plan laid out; it started with a lovely lawn. We've always lived in houses with a nice lawn and that was not going to change as we lived in Phoenix. Mom picked out the plants and trees she wanted and decided where they would be planted in the yard.

Regarding my new career, I was pleased with my job at the corporate office. I believed I was a good employee, but I know the reality of business. I got a lot of opportunities because of dad initially and then my brother-in-law Craig later in Morenci. Whereas this new career in Risk Management felt like it was all my own. I interviewed in Phoenix under the radar of my job in Morenci and got hired on my own merit. It was a tough job though. My new boss Rick had me under frequent performance pressure. I was hired into the position without a lot of experience and needed to learn and pick it up quickly. I was expected to learn the professions of insurance, safety, and legal relatively quickly, as they were all aspects of Risk Management. Along with this new career, I did a fair amount of travel around the state and around the country. My title was Global Casualty Manager. So, mom was on her own during many small trips I made around the country. This was a big reason why I would eventually move to the east side of town; I wanted her to be closer to family while I traveled.

We might have been most excited about the plethora of restaurant opportunities in the big city. In Safford, we had our favorite five places that were on regular rotation, but in Phoenix, opportunities were endless. We loved the experience of a nice sit-down restaurant with the ambiance of a nice dining room and the mystery of new eating experiences. We ate out at least once a week, and on rare occasions, twice a week. Some of our regular standards were Texas Roadhouse and Olive Garden. We experimented with dozens of Mexican food restaurants, that was mom's passion. We would get our chips and salsa and a coke for each of us. Mom would often get a beer in some places and a glass of wine in others. Time after time, I would hear mom proclaim after the meal... *"That was the best taco..."* or *"That was the best enchilada I ever tasted."* I would laugh because she often said that.

We also had to find our new go-to movie theater. Keeping up with new movie releases was one of our biggest activities. The

105

closest theater was at an old mall on 75th Avenue and Thomas which was called Desert Sky Mall. It was on its last leg twenty years ago, and today it is closed. Back then, it was our go-to movie destination. We loved the whole movie experience with candy, soda and of course popcorn, separate bags for each of us.

We looked around at several churches and tried out many of them in our westside community. They tended to be modern, progressive services that didn't really appeal to either one of us. We were looking for a more traditional church service, so we kept looking and trying new places.

A little update on me during this time. After returning from DC in 1992, I did not follow up on any of my political science college credit hours, which lead to incomplete grades and ultimately terrible grades when the classes were not completed. I think I was a little depressed and listless in my new life back in Morenci. I promised myself someday I would get everything fixed and finish the degree in political science if/when I moved back to the Phoenix area.

Now that I was back in the Phoenix area, I needed to properly honor that time in my life and not leave that degree unfinished. So now, I was back in Phoenix and could easily take courses to finish that degree, and I did. I got my second bachelor's degree from Arizona State, with an emphasis in political science. After a few semesters of coursework, I graduated in 2006.

Also, in June of 2004, I bought a townhouse in Tempe. After four years of living with mom, I felt it would be good for both of us to have a little more independence. I would often stay at my townhouse on weekends and stay at mom's house the rest of the week. It was a big step, but one we were both ready for.

Once in our new home and our new lifestyle in the big city, we had to continue all the great progress we made in Safford. That meant exercise, diet, and water aerobics. We had a regular weekly weigh-in as we kept working her excess weight off so she could live a healthier life and hopefully a longer life.

We visited several gyms around town but decided on a Naturally Women Fitness near Metrocenter in Phoenix. It was perfect because it was all women, and most of them were seniors like her. Mom was bashful and shy, so a group of all-women was perfect for her at this time in her life. They had a wide variety of class options for consideration with on our schedule.

So now, we had to figure out how she would get to her classes during the week. Since her great friends Bea Cervantes and Hortencia Figueroa were no longer around, we had no one who could assist in the big city. We did some research and decided on a service called Dial-A-Ride. This was a service specifically for seniors who lived on a fixed income and needed help to get around town. It was kind of like Uber for seniors before Uber came along. So, she was all set—she had her 3 times a week water aerobics and she had the rides set up. Each week, she would have to call the service and schedule her pick-up times from the house as well as schedule her pickup times back home. The process was to pay with cash after the ride was over. It was usually a nominal fee of $5-6 per trip. She would figure out how many dollar bills she would need for the week of trips and make sure she got the right amount of dollars during her Sunday grocery trip. It was usually $12 a day for 3 days, so she would need 36 single dollars each week for her rides. She would either get her dollars from Fry's or Wells Fargo Bank.

The drive to Metrocenter was about 15 miles from our home on 67th Avenue and Lower Buckeye. Her driver would take her up to the I10 Freeway then transition to the I17 Freeway North and then exit at Dunlap. I would try to teach mom the different freeways, so she had a clear understanding of how to get around town. It met with mixed results, but she would do pretty well, it was a big change from Safford. I had Bea and Hortencia who would look after mom like she was family. Now, I was at work an hour away in downtown Phoenix, and it was just mom taking charge of transportation with no backup.

Through the years, there were several problems with her transportation. Occasionally, they would be late and other times, they wouldn't show up at all. Occasionally, the no-shows were at her house and on other occasions, they wouldn't arrive to pick her up at the gym. She would have to call and arrange for new transportation. At times, she would get home a couple of hours later than expected. She dealt with her difficulties like we all do, with frustration but ultimately understanding she had to figure out a solution. There were only a few occasions in 15 years of water aerobics that I needed to personally intervene and help her. She would figure it out and then tell me about it later that night at dinner.

Naturally Women Fitness was such a wonderful experience. Her independence grew rapidly and best of all, she made lots of great friends. She would tell me all about the ladies in her class. She knew them all by name and all the ladies knew mom, and they all adored her. The ladies formed a tight bond and would also become friendly with some of the instructors. It was like a tightly knit ladies' club.

The club would discuss the different class options once the schedule came out and would decide which ones they would attend. This required mom to adjust her class times based on which class she wanted to attend and what classes the other ladies were taking. She would get a flyer each week to take home with the class schedule for the following week. Mom and her friends would not only attend all the same classes together, but once a week, they would get together and eat lunch somewhere near the gym in the circle of restaurants around Metrocenter. MiMi's Café was the group's favorite place.

Mom would attend the luncheons, and she would navigate how to schedule her dial-a-rides accordingly and where they needed to pick her up. I can't stress enough, she did this all on her own. As usual, we kept in close communication throughout the day. Mom had her cell phone and was quite proficient. She had all the important numbers memorized.

Mom had her own duffle bag to carry her bathing suit, wallet and phone. She was losing so much weight and attending so many water aerobics classes through the years, that she had to buy new bathing suits regularly. Mom was very modest and didn't like the modern locker rooms where everyone changed in front of each other. This gym had various areas of privacy where she could change into her suit. After the class was over, she would change back into her regular clothes. While away from the house, she kept it locked. So, she needed to keep her phone and keys in a safe place in her duffle bag. We would also keep an extra emergency key in a safe place in the yard just in case.

She would tell me all about her class and what areas of the body they focused on for each session. She would occasionally get into detail about which instructors she liked best and why. She liked to share some of the comments from the other ladies regarding the good and not-so-good instructors. Since it was an all-female club, I was only able to hear about the interesting banter that went on in the classes. I will say, there was a lot of lady banter going on. She especially disliked the instructors who would get in the water while they taught the class. She wasn't alone, several ladies would scoff at the instructors that would get in the water and they would look for alternative classes together. She liked it when the instructors stood on the side of the pool, and she could better follow the instructions. This seemed to be the consensus opinion of her circle of friends. She would tell me how good one instructor was every Wednesday or how another lady on Friday was new, but she had potential. With time, she might turn out okay, mom would say. She would at times get into detail on the locker room opinion of instructors. She would say, *"Some of the ladies liked her today, but me and my friends liked the one last Wednesday better. We hope our favorite will be on the schedule next week."*

When we moved to the east side of town, the ladies in water aerobics threw mom a going-away party at one of their favorite restaurants and some of them gave her gifts. It was a bittersweet moment as it marked the end of a beautiful camaraderie that she had with this group of ladies; unlike anything she had ever experienced in her life.

As we moved away from the Westside forever, I was sad that I took mom away from her close family at Naturally Women Fitness. If I had it to do over again, I would not have moved. It was beautiful, and I was so proud and so humbled at what she had accomplished with the travel logistics, courage and confidence at Naturally Women Fitness. It was perhaps her greatest personal growth. She did it all on her own. I just set her up for success and put her in the right environment to flourish. On a couple of

occasions, I met many of her friends, especially at her going away party. Mom introduced me to many of them.

In May 2003, mom and I went on a first-time cruise for both of us. We flew to Los Angeles where we embarked on the Carnival Ecstasy bound for Ensenada, Mexico. It was quite an experience. We tried to be active participants in all the fun they offered.

Both mom and I were introverted and shy, but we dressed up and went to dinner each night and sat at tables with fellow guests. Mom had wine and we chatted with them and shared experiences. We walked all over the huge cruise ship. It was warm in mid-May as we traveled down the coast to Mexico.

Once in Mexico, we spent the day on shore and walked around to see the sites. We bought a few trinkets and experienced the bombardment of local merchants trying to sell things to us. After a day on shore, we returned to our ship and cabin. We had a small, but sufficient cabin with double beds. Walking all around the ship was our exercise during the cruise. We had a blast.

In October of 2003, mom and I met her two sisters in Loomis, California, for a sisters' reunion. I worked with the other sisters and planned it all out. It was the first time they were all together since their dad died in 1981, over twenty years previous. Mom had been through a lot of tough times during those twenty years

that wasn't particularly common knowledge with her family. It was a bit of a triumphant return to the family as she had lost a lot of weight and regained a lot of her spice and vigor. The sisters commemorated the moment with a professional photo taken of the three of them. Aunt Bev told me that she and mom shared a bedroom in Loomis, and they stayed up most of the night talking about their childhood and their adult lives.

When mom wasn't busy with aerobics or the animals, she loved to listen to her Walkman, and then later her iPod. She  especially liked the Beach Boys and Elvis, but she liked a little bit of everything.

When we moved to Phoenix, part of the transition and rebirth was to start fresh with all new doctors locally. First and foremost, we wanted to find a local psychiatrist. We found a psychiatrist in the Phoenix area named Dr. Mirabe. She made a profound announcement to us. She said, *"Your mom is not a schizophrenic. She is just bipolar."* She went on to say that it was a common diagnosis in the 80s and 90s to call everyone with delusions, hallucinations and paranoia a schizophrenic. So, she made changes to her medications. Both of mom's medications were primarily used by schizophrenics, not as much for typical bipolar disorder. Lithium was completely discontinued. Moban and Cogentin were also discontinued. Finally, mom got a new 2nd generation antipsychotic medication called Zyprexa. It did the job of managing her moods and managed the delusions and hallucinations that accompanied her mental illness.

In retrospect, I feel Dr. Fredman got it right with his hybrid diagnosis of schizophrenia and mood disorder. I believe we were lucky that Zyprexa did such a good job with all her bipolar symptoms and her schizophrenic symptoms. In researching Bipolar Disorder, I believe mom had bipolar disorder 1.

Furthermore, the description and symptoms of a rare version called Bipolar Schizoaffective Disorder described what mom suffered from. Bipolar would be the reason for her mood instability--mania and depression extremes. It is common for delusions to accompany bipolar disorder. However, paranoia and hallucinations were most symptomatic of schizophrenia. So, mom most likely had schizoaffective disorder because she had suppressed hallucinations and paranoia to varying degrees during the last 40 years of her life.

After this initial meeting with Dr. Mirabe, we visited once or twice again, and the doctor told us she didn't need to see a psychiatrist anymore. She's stable with the new medication and regular consultation with her primary care doctor should suffice in the future. What a profound moment in our lives. Rarely people recover from mental illness, but it felt like a life-changing victory for mom to discontinue psychiatric care. She had been going to see the same psychiatrist in Tucson every few months for almost 20 years. What a life-altering change we made—not strictly for medical reasons, but mostly for personal psychological reasons for mom. It made her feel normal again; it made her feel like she persevered through an enormous life challenge and came out the other side.

I believed in this new direction with all my heart, but I studied mom closely and if a change or return to psychotherapy and/or new meds were needed, we would certainly have done it. Mental illness had been such a big part of her life for so long, there was anxiety and reticence in the family regarding this change. Nothing reminded a person more that they weren't quite right socially more than the need to see a psychiatrist every three months for the last 20 years. Now, that was the past, no more psych visits for the rest of her life.

The medical news continued to get better for mom. After a few regular eye appointments with Dr. Lewis—mother/son appointments—the doctor announced that her glaucoma was stable and not getting any worse. The fear of imminent blindness, which was virtually promised by her Tucson doctor, was not likely going to happen. The eye surgery was a complete success. Further, she took an eye test measuring acuity, and I was able to attend with her. She started saying the same things, she couldn't see anything, and I intervened with the test. I told her I didn't believe it and that she needed to read the top letter, she did. The doctor said the next line, she did. On and on, she read down the entire eye chart. As it turned out, she wasn't blind, she had near perfect vision—20/25. It was just a mental thing.

The final good news was that because of her nearly 50 pounds in lost weight, her diabetes was also stable, and she could move to oral meds and no longer had to give herself daily insulin injections. Because of her health and lifestyle, she was able to delay her insulin dependence for another 15 years.

Her great determination, discipline and endless perseverance translated into a physical and mental metamorphosis. The metamorphosis continued to build more confidence. The two most important drugs above all others that led to this rebirth were exercise and love! Exercise was the ultimate antipsychotic and antidepressant. Above all, the one drug that any psychiatrist will

tell you that's more important than any others is love (and support). Mom received considerable high doses of both exercise and love. She loved me dearly and trusted me implicitly. It took time and patience. With love, all things were possible, even miracles.

In 2004, the travel continued with a fun trip to Los Angeles with mom, and we invited her granddaughter Krystle for a trip to Disneyland. We also visited the Reagan Library and sat in on a taping of the show, Dr. Phil. Of course, Disneyland was the highlight of the trip. Mom was not shy about going on any of the rides. In fact, I would say the teenage Krystle was more nervous than mom with some of the rides. Just by looking at the expressions on all our faces, one could tell who had the most fun. There was lots of walking and mom did just fine. We were out there living our best life.

Mom and I made several trips to Minnesota to visit her daughter Kristy, who moved to a small town called Starbuck where she lived with her boyfriend, Dan. Mom and I made the first two trips by ourselves, and we also paid and facilitated trips for Kristy's daughters to see her up in Minnesota as well. A lot of the family was dubious about this move by Kristy, as none of us had met her boyfriend. He owned a cabin that was off the grid out in the middle of the woods a few miles away from the tiny town of Starbuck. Mom and I fearlessly made the flight and drove out to this remote cabin to visit, making sure everything was all right.

Our first trip was quite an experience and adventure. I remember the first night we stayed in a local motel. Right in the middle of the night, a stranger opened the door and walked right into our room. They had warned us the room didn't lock and unfortunately, a hunter walked into our room mistakenly. I remember our first drive was quite an adventure as we took several dirt roads to arrive at the cabin finally. Kristy was a gracious host and enjoyed showing us around the property where she lived, around town and the general vicinity of that part of Minnesota. On different trips, we also escorted a couple of Kristy's daughters up there and allowed them the opportunity to see for themselves that their mom was doing fine.

In March of 2023, it had been over 20 years since we moved into our Pulte neighborhood. It was nice to return to see the progress in the community and the overall neighborhood. It was my first time back since we moved in 2004. The old Fry's was still there, the Wells Fargo was still there, and the nail salon was still there. The two-mile drive that was all farmland between the commercial area and the Pulte community was completely built out. There was a clean, nicely developed commercial area along

Lower Buckeye and many new residential developments in every direction. All the major brands and stores were available along the way. I can still feel a hint of our excitement from 20 years ago as I drove and walked around the area. At that time, the excitement was great, we were both happy.

As I parked my Jeep in the community and let my dogs out, we began to walk around, and the memories started to flow back. Going back 20 years, when mom was walking our little wiener dog, Jennifer, and me walking Penny, our sweet mixed breed. The community had the most beautiful green belt picnic areas back then. As I approached them that day, they were every bit as beautiful, but even more so. The new trees of 20 years ago were now mature and majestic. They had winter rye grass planted. It was clean and as beautiful as I remember.

Also, as we were walking around on a quiet Sunday morning, we came upon a house with an older Hispanic gentleman playing his traditional Mexican music loud and proud. We exchanged waves. It was a reminder to me why mom and I loved the west side of town so much—it felt like home.

As we came upon the old house, I was reminded of the cute breakfast nook surrounded by glass on three sides with a pleasant view of the front courtyard. It was one of the big selling points as to why mom chose the house. I peeked over the fence to see that our beloved jacuzzi was filled in. There had been 20 long years, and things had changed, what wonderful memories though. I walked by the community mailbox that was conveniently right across the street from our house. Mom was able to check the mail each day with ease and convenience.

I took a drive from our house on Hess to Metrocenter and the location of her Naturally Women Fitness. It was about 15 miles and usually 20-30 minutes depending on traffic. Like most big malls, Metrocenter had been closed. Over time, it developed into a bad part of town with high crime and urban decay. The Naturally Women Fitness was gone and most of the restaurants lining the circle around Metrocenter were gone. Everything was gone. I began my drive back home. As fate would have it, I looked over to the right at a small minivan next to me, and it was a dial-a-ride. Not everything was gone, the wonderful memories live on.

CHAPTER 7
Independence
(2005-2009)

"Once adversity reveals your strength, and you know what you can endure, you become an irrepressible force of nature."

- *Abigail Damoah*

In September of 2005, mom and I got together with Kirsten Snyder, our realtor. We were ready to move to Gilbert and needed to sell mom's Pulte home on Hess Street. The timing of the market was ideal for mom, she sold her house for $250,000. In just 3 short years, she was able to double her money from her original purchase price of $125,000. This was an important nest egg for her to use for the rest of her life. She was pretty darn proud of herself. Going forward, mom would live in houses I bought for her, and she would save her money. I decided it would be good to remove mom's money from real estate and allow her to stay conservative, and I would take on the real estate risk. As it turned out, mom sold at the top of the market, and I bought at the top of the market. Good for her and not good for me.

We looked around quite a bit in 2005 and ended up finding a home at 330 East Hearne Way in Gilbert. Mom and I visited many houses for sale as we toured around with our agent Kirsten. We liked the lakes in the community and liked that it was just 5 miles away from her daughter, Donna, in Mesa. It was a three-bedroom house. Mom got the nice master bedroom, and I took a smaller bedroom. Penny and Jennifer liked the yard, and we all liked the neighborhood.

We got acquainted with the different walking paths around the nearby streets, as I would handle Penny and mom handle Jennifer, the little sled dog. One of our favorite places to walk was a park behind a nearby grade school. It was a ¼ of a mile from the house. We would take the dogs there and let them run wild in the big open green field. Fatty and Stinky made the transition from the west valley to the east valley as well. Stinky had a brief stint staying with me at the Tempe townhouse, but eventually needed to be back with her mama.

In the Summer of 2005, we decided to take a vacation to Los Angeles and spend a lot of time on or near the beach. This time, we didn't have any agenda, we were just going to walk around and get some Southern California sun on the beach. The weather was wonderful, and I remember mom had a particular pep in her step as the cool ocean breeze was invigorating. We found a couple of nice restaurants within walking distance that we enjoyed while staying in LA. We did have one bad incident...I had a fender bender while in a rental car, never a good thing. It was so minimal, that the other driver and I mutually decided not to report it. It was completely my fault as I was trying to navigate and drive at the same time. Mom saw it coming but didn't warn me fast enough. She said, *"I knew that was going to happen."* Other than that drama, it was a nice trip and we both enjoyed it. Mom was getting to be quite the traveler with probably a dozen flights under her belt by that time.

Just about 9 months after moving into the East Valley Hearne house, mom and I had a life-altering event. About 6 years after mom and I attended Megan's high school graduation, we were attending her wedding. It was held in Sedona in June of 2006. It was going to be a weekend ceremony, so mom and I got a place to stay over the weekend in Oak Creek Canyon. I made the decision that our dogs, Penny and Jennifer, could stay in the backyard for the short weekend visit as the backyard had plenty of shade, food and water, and a covered patio.

The ceremony went fine, but when we got back to our neighborhood in Gilbert, something seemed wrong as a neighbor was waiting for us as we got out of our car. She said, *"I'm terribly sorry, but I think your little dog is on the side of the road back near the school."* The lady had a look of heartbreak on her face. I immediately began to well up with tears and went into the house and got a towel and checked in the yard. Sure enough, just Penny was in the yard and a hole was dug underneath the front gate. By now, I was openly sobbing, heartbroken and feeling guilty. I took the solemn walk down the street to find my sweet Jennifer, dad's sweet Jennifer, had died on the side of the road, hit by a car. She appeared to be returning to one of her favorite places during walks, the big field near the school. I wrapped her up in the towel and walked her home with tears dropping down on her as I cried inconsolably. I set her in the back of the pickup truck and walked into the house and cried as I told mom. We both sat on the couch and cried together. I felt like I let mom and dad down for her to die so young and in a violent death. I believe one of the most important responsibilities for dog parents is to take care of their dog and allow it to die of natural causes, not violently.

Professionally, 2006 was a good year. After four years in risk management, I worked with the corporate maintenance leadership and developed a new department over contractor management in North America and South America. I absolutely loved my time in risk management, but it was highly structured and often highly stressful. I liked focusing on things I was comfortable and successful with—such as loss prevention and loss mitigation through claim management. My boss liked the policy underwriting nature of the business, so we had different areas of comfort.

Back in Morenci during the 1990s, I was given a chance to be an entrepreneur within the company and developed contractor management at one single location. Now, I was given a chance to build that infrastructure throughout two continents at our copper mine locations. I was allowed to be an entrepreneur on a grand scale. I continued to work out of the Phoenix corporate office as my base, but I was on the road at least 50% of the time— occasionally to South America, often driving around to the mines in Arizona and New Mexico. I completely controlled my own schedule and my own agenda. I reported to the leadership based in Safford, Arizona. It was truly my dream job, and I loved it.

When mom and I moved to Gilbert, we smoothly established a new fitness center for her to attend called 24-hour fitness off Val Vista, not far from home, only 2-3 miles away. It was a different dial-a-ride organization on the east side of town, but mom contacted them and was able to get rides set up just like she did

on the west side. I belonged to the same fitness club and would often attend the club at the same time as she. But I would not interfere or intervene with her rides. I wanted her to maintain that independence of taking care of things herself. She would go into the club just like any member and had to scan her membership card and get ready for class by going into the locker room and changing into her bathing suit. She must've worn out 50 bathing suits during her 17 years of water aerobics.

Mom got comfortable with her new club, maybe too comfortable. A few times, she would jaywalk across Val Vista from 24 Hour Fitness to a local Safeway grocery store to pick up a few items. She would tell Kristy about her secret of crossing the road, getting groceries and then heading back to the dial-a-ride pick-up spot. When hearing about it, I was horrified and would need to scold her for how dangerous and unsafe that was. It was a busy street that even I would never think of jaywalking across. In some ways, it was a notable example of her new independent mind, and she did it all secretly and within the parameters of her ride pick-up service.

Occasionally, I would see her walking into the club or exiting when I was already there. I would walk up to her and in a joking fashion, I'd shake her hand formally and ask her how she was doing. We would get a good laugh about it and then I would go on my way and tell her I would be by for dinner or visit shortly after lunch. I'd ask her how my laundry was coming along and what was for dinner; then we would go our separate ways.

One of my favorite parts of her water aerobics would be their last song. Throughout the class, the instructor played several fun songs for the students to follow along energetically. They would finish the class by playing the song YMCA, by the Village People. As soon as the song started playing, I could feel the excitement in the pool with all the students whooping and hollering. As the song would say the letters Y-M-C-A, all the ladies in the pool would mimic the letters with their arms! Mom had her favorite spot in the pool, and she would have friends who would often stand beside her during every class. It was kind of like being back in grade school, the ladies were by her friends. Some of the ladies really liked to chat during the class, and mom would occasionally complain to me, *"They talk too much, I'm not able to hear the instructor."* At least a couple of times a week, I would be in the steam room after a workout next to the swimming pool listening and watching her in class. I would smile from ear to ear during the YMCA song. Mom would see me walk into the stream room and she would be smiling and give me a wave. She was proud of her water aerobics classes and really liked that I was finally able to watch her in action. Moving to a new club was a real treat for me, as I never got to watch her at Naturally Women Fitness, so I enjoyed watching her every week with my relaxing view in the steam room.

In March 2006, we planned another get-together with Aunt Virginia and Uncle Buck. This time we decided to meet in Reno, Nevada, for a long weekend of gambling and socializing. It was nice getting to know Uncle Buck during all our visits. He and Aunt Virginia were always kind to mom. We had a fun time going to lunch and dinner with them and playing the slots. Uncle Buck had some history with the hotel where we were staying, so we got some of our stuff comped. In all, we had three visits with Aunt Virginia and Uncle Buck in about a five-year span.

A few months passed, and mom and I decided to look for a puppy. A popular book at the time was Marley and Me. A story about a mischievous yellow lab. The yellow lab was also the most popular breed in America and would go on to be for decades. We selected a breeder and visited. Mom fell in love with a vivacious, lovely little female. She decided to name her Brandy. She was a pure breed, so we needed to give her an official name for the records. We decided on Brandy Ellen Biles, the Duchess of Hearne. She was Brandy Ellen, just like mom was Shirley Ellen. Mom fell in love with Brandy. It was the beginning of a beautiful, long relationship that lasted for the next 12 years. Mom thought she was just about it.

As a puppy, she was a handful for sure. She tore up a lot of things around the house. Mom liked to tell how we would put puppy training pads on the ground and Brandy would shred the pad into a million pieces.

We decided she needed to go to obedience training at PetSmart. She was a rascal, but she passed the training and got a certificate. Mom and I were proud. We would both go to her training classes every week where she needed to learn new tricks and discipline. We proudly put her training certificate and birth certificate on the wall together with pride by mom's desk. I still remember her graduation ceremony, we were proud.

Penny didn't like Brandy too much in the beginning. However, they eventually grew to adore each other. Penny was like Brandy's surrogate mama. When Brandy was a little puppy, Penny was able to outrun her and keep her away, but as she got bigger, she had no way to avoid her constant love.

Mom and I would take Penny and Brandy for walks. When Brandy was a puppy, mom was able to handle the leash and I would hold the leash of Penny. We walked all over the neighborhood and got good exercise for the dogs and for us. As Brandy got bigger and stronger, I would need to hold both leashes.

We also started taking Penny and Brandy to the Cosmo Dog Park where they had a pier for dogs to jump off and land in the water. Brandy loved to retrieve, and she loved, loved, loved the water. She was a natural water dog and enjoyed running fast and then jumped off the pier on her way to a tennis ball in the lake. Mom and I enjoyed taking her because she had so much fun. Penny would usually wade around in the water and occasionally swim around the pier. As she was swimming, she looked for us to make sure we were watching. We would tell her she was a good penny girl.

Every few weeks, we would take them to the groomer. I'll never forget the time our groomer told mom that Brandy was getting too fat. Mom was a bit indignant, but it was true, and she knew it. The groomer told her to try green beans. Ever since that day, green beans became a staple in every dog meal, a special delicacy for the dogs. We both took the challenge to get some weight off Brandy like we took the weight off mom. It was exercise and diet, just like mom.

Our two dogs really loved to play with toys. Brandy had her tennis balls; that's all that mattered to her. Penny, on the other hand, had her special squeaky baby we called it Smoochie. She routinely had it in her mouth. Brandy respected Penny's toys and didn't take them or destroy them. Penny had her stuffed friends for all her life.

 After moving to the Hearne Way home in Gilbert in 2005, we noticed a nice simple church about a half a mile away on Guadalupe. It was called Gilbert Presbyterian Church, and the pastor was a kind man by the name of Dr. Terry Palmer. Mom and I tried it out and really liked the traditional services they had every Sunday morning. We decided we would be regulars and I mean regulars; we never missed a Sunday unless we were out of town. Sundays were a special day for mom and me. We would both dress up for church; mom would wear a dress and her best jewelry. Going to church gave her the perfect chance to get her heels on and shine.

We had our favorite row we would like to sit in, about 3 rows from the front and towards the middle so we could see and hear everything well. We would pick up the weekly announcement that led us through the service. We became known among the congregation of a couple of hundred regulars. Mom would hold my arm as we walked in and out, so she had stability while walking around a lot of people. All the congregation was kind and welcoming to us.

I remember our first service; they asked if there were any new visitors today. I stood up and introduced mom and me; we received a lot of nice welcomes. Mom loved to follow along with the schedule on the pamphlet. We would each have our own Bible but usually to keep up, I would take the lead and we would share one Bible or hymnal booklet.

We loved to sing! We both sang loud and proud even though I didn't have a particularly good voice. I think mom's voice was a little better than mine. She thought I should be in the choir.

We loved the way the services were organized. Lots of singing, praying and a good sermon by Pastor Terry. Once a week, they would have communion with the sharing of bread and wine (grape juice). At first, we didn't feel comfortable with the communion, but eventually enjoyed it. We would usually have communion while sitting at our pew, but from time to time, they would do the ceremony with each row going up to the front of the church and each person getting blessed by the pastor while taking the bread and wine.

Mom had the responsibility to write a check for the weekly donation and would put the check on the donation plate as it got passed around. The service would end in an uplifting fashion, usually some rousing song from the hymnal like "Hallelujah" and then we would leave on a high. The pastor would leave the building and wait just outside for everyone to part. We would greet him with handshakes and salutations. Occasionally, we would arrive late, and we hated it. We would have to sit in the back and not be able to follow as well. Plus, we both hated being a disruption to the service.

We loved the holidays at the church. They were especially festive and meaningful. It was a time when a lot of irregulars would visit, and the body of participants would swell. After the holiday, it would go back to the regulars, we were proud regulars.

There were a few of the regulars that we would speak to at the service each week. They mentioned a Bible study class each Wednesday. Mom and I discussed and thought that would be a great activity for her. A nice lady who lived near mom would pick her up and drop her off each week. All the ladies in the class would take turns reading scripture. Mom was no exception, she was shy about it, but she did her turns. The ladies would also take snacks to the class and mom would often make cookies for the ladies. It would be a bit shocking for me to stop by mom's house and see a plate of cookies naturally thinking they were for me, only to have mom say, hands off, that's for Bible study! Then she would reveal another plate that was for me.

We continued with this wonderful routine for several years. Participating in such an intimate, public gathering was the apex of mom's social renewal. She did so well, and we had a wonderful time in church each week.

In January 2007, I came home with a wonderful activity and challenge for mom. We would take a college course together at Mesa Community College. Mom and I enrolled in the class Introduction to Christianity, REL270. The class had lectures twice a week on campus. Each lecture was about three hours long, with a break in the middle. We traveled to the campus a month or so before our class and visited the bookstore. We bought two textbooks and all the related study material that went along with it.

The grade was made up of a mid-term essay, end-of-term essay, three in-class exams and weekly homework that had to be completed and turned in. Attendance was mandatory. Mom was nervous but excited about the challenge. She hadn't taken a college course since she was 18 years old. It was a night class, so most of the students were older adults. We would study together, and I would quiz her on reading assignments to make sure she understood the main concepts. The professor's name was Dr. Tom Shoemaker, and he was an interesting, gracious man. He taught a good class and was knowledgeable about historical Christian studies. Mom liked him a lot and he had a style where he would occasionally call on people in class. He was pretty kind to mom since she was so shy about things like that. Yet, there was one occasion he called on her and she answered his question pretty well. She handled herself quite well in all aspects of the class, even the exams in class. She finished with an A!

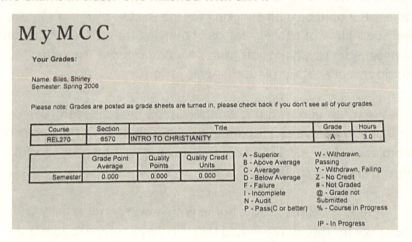

Taking a college-level class and doing so well—what an amazing experience and accomplishment for mom. The lectures were a bit of a grind—6 pm to 9 pm twice a week with lots of reading and study material that required attention.

In April of 2007 during our spring break at Mesa Community, mom and I flew to Washington, DC on one of our most epic journeys. It was an especially meaningful trip as I used to live there when I was an intern in the Senate. Mom was proud of my internship and was excited to see everything that I talked about in letters and phone calls home.

We stayed in a hotel a few miles from the Washington Mall. We used the DC Metro to get around town. Mom was at the peak of her fitness, and  she needed it. We walked around the mall and Arlington Cemetery, and I can say, at a minimum, it was 10 miles per day of walking. We saw all the usual sites in the mall—Lincoln Memorial, Washington Monument, Jefferson Memorial, the Capitol and the White House. We walked from the mall over the Potomac River and then walked around Arlington Cemetery, one of my favorite places. We saw the tomb of the unknown soldier and JFK's gravesite at the cemetery.

We also had a special request from Dan, Kristy's boyfriend, in Minnesota to stop by the grave site of his dad at Arlington where Dan had never traveled. We visited the special archive department at Arlington, and they helped us find the gravesite. It was no easy task, a lot of walking. We took pictures for Dan.

We had a rental car, so our next trip was to Gettysburg, Pennsylvania, to visit the famous battle site. Along the way, we crossed the Mason-Dixon Line, the separation between the north and the south. We also realized we were underdressed as it was quite cold in the early Spring. We found a clothing store in Gettysburg, and we each got a thick sweatshirt that helped a lot. We took a bus tour around Gettysburg and learned a lot and had a good time. For years afterward, we laughed about how important those sweatshirts were to us.

Next, we traveled down to Mount Vernon to see the home of George Washington. We toured the property and inside his house, with nice memories and beautiful scenery. We did a lot of driving in our rental car within several states—Virginia, Maryland, and Pennsylvania.

We were in DC during the annual cherry blossom season. It was quite an event. As we walked and drove around town, cherry blossoms were blooming everywhere. We were both exhausted from the trip. Mom was 71 at the time.

In May of 2007, it was another major transition for mom and me. Kristy had expressed interest in living with mom, so we reached out to our realtor Kirsten, and we started looking for a nice new house for mom to live in that would have plenty of room for Kristy. We found a lovely place at Val Vista Lakes on a street called Nantuckett. I moved into mom's old house on Hearne Way and rented out my Tempe townhouse. The Hearne house and the Nantuckett house were only about 3 miles apart. At this time, mom was completely independent and living on her own. I would just visit and get some nice home-cooked meals. Kristy tried living with mom in Gilbert but decided to return to New Mexico after living with mom for a couple of months.

The back and forth between the Hearne and Nantuckett houses would be our routine for the next 10 years. In all her adult years, it was her longest, most stable residence. She really was the lady of the house on Nantuckett.

As for the maintenance of the yards, that fell on me. I took pride in keeping the lawns, bushes and plants well maintained in honor of dad and just the lofty expectations mom deserved. Every so often, I would enlist her help with some of the work around the yards. She would gladly help in any way she could. We would visit nurseries and pick up several roses to plant. Mom had the job of pruning them. Roses were her favorite.

Another wonderful tradition that started when mom and I first moved to West Phoenix and continued for about 10 years thereafter was meeting my auntie and uncle for lunch and a movie. My auntie was dad's sister and Uncle Gene was the best man at mom and dad's wedding. We would take turns on where we would watch the movie.

As time went on, I made it easier on them and would go to their local theater for all our movies. We would start with lunch at a nearby restaurant. Chit-chat was fun, and we would update each other on both sides of the family. We all loved movies, so this was a fun event. Auntie would often have the responsibility of picking the movie. Auntie and mom would sit together with uncle and me on either side of them. It was nice to go out with auntie and uncle as I loved them dearly, especially because of the way they treated mom. They were not related by blood, but they adored her and respected her amazing resilience in life.

Auntie, uncle and I also had something else in common—we took care of our mothers to the end of their lives at home. They took care of my grandmother (Maymo). So, we had a special bond and connection because of our caretaking history.

When we weren't going to a movie with auntie and uncle, we continued our weekly movies together. We would usually go to an AMC theater near Alma School and the Superstition Freeway in Mesa, or a new recliner luxury theater that opened just a mile away from her Nantuckett home. We still insisted on separate popcorn containers, drinks and candy.

In December of 2007, mom's granddaughter Krystle got married. She had her ceremony in Colorado, so we booked travel and attended. We got our own cabin near the wedding party and stayed for three or four days. We had a wonderful time visiting with family and attending the wedding and reception. Mom was looking especially good at this time in her life.

Moving to the east side of town permanently opened new, exciting places to eat. As we drove around the nearby

134

neighborhoods, we had an eye on restaurants. Again, mom favored the Mexican food places Macayo's, Garcia's, Nando's, Rubio's and Serrano's to name just a few. She lit up like a Christmas tree when Mexican food was on the agenda.

In October of 2008, mom and I went on the trip of a lifetime. The trip started with a layover in Colorado, then we landed in New Orleans, Louisiana. We got a rental car and started to drive through Mississippi, Tennessee, Arkansas, Oklahoma, Kansas and Missouri. Mom was 72 years old at the time, as we visited 8 states in 8 days. She packed plenty of heels and boots as she walked around to see all the various sites.

I planned the trip meticulously, so we could spend time in New Orleans first. Then drive to Graceland in Memphis, Tennessee. On the way to our next stop in Oklahoma City, we stopped in Little Rock, Arkansas and visited the President Clinton Library. In Oklahoma City, we met mom's granddaughter, Lori. We watched a Neil Diamond concert and visited with an old friend. After leaving Oklahoma City, we drove north to Kansas and visited with my niece a little longer at her home and then headed off to Kansas City, Missouri, where we flew back home.

When I asked mom what she thought about all the travel and all the walking, she said, *"I'll make it. It won't be like when we went to Arlington Cemetery. I was barely able to get around. Although I walked everywhere the day before."* She was referring to our walking around the mall area of Washington, DC. She was looking forward to seeing Jack Langton who was an old, dear friend of the family from the early Morenci days. When mom interviewed me before the trip for a home movie, she started the interview by saying, *"How are you doing, Stephen? How did you like getting woke up so early?!"* The day of travel, we got off to an inauspicious start as she got confused with our start time in the morning and she ran in to wake me up two hours early.

135

Once we arrived at Sky Harbor Airport, we went through security as usual. On the other side, I asked her if she was glad to get through security, and she said, *"Yes, I always dread that."* By this time in 2008, she was quite a veteran traveler with over 10 flights under her belt. We had a brief stopover in Denver for about one and a half hours. The trip was smooth and easy.

We got to New Orleans late in the afternoon and just had plans to get to our hotel and rest. The next day, we woke up and walked down to the river to see the famous Mississippi River up close and personally. We couldn't find any nearby boat tours, so we just walked over to a large aquarium near the river and our hotel. The aquarium had numerous stairs and ramps all throughout the maze of flora and fauna. Mom navigated through this treacherous environment with not a single problem. Throughout the trip, she would get updates, or she would occasionally call Donna back in Arizona to check on her dogs. The great dog lover that she was, her dogs were regularly on her mind.

Later in the afternoon, we went on a swamp tour that took us back deep into the bayou looking for alligators and marveling over the strange, swamp environment. The tour bus picked us up at the hotel and drove us to the swamp. It was also amazing to see some of the houses deep in the swamp, often on stilts on the side of the river. Mom thought it was all amazing.

When we got home from the swamp tour, we got a ride over to the iconic Bourbon Street. It was busy and bustling with activity. There was a lot of random music and performances going on as we walked around. We went into a small bar and had a drink and listened to some live Jazz.

When we were ready to checkout from our hotel in New Orleans and get our rental car for the next 5 days, we discovered an unfortunate oversight, we got a car that was for a round trip instead of one way to Kansas City. At first, they could not locate another car for one-way travel on short notice. It looked like our trip was in big trouble. We had our big suitcases and mom was pulling hers around as I was pulling mine around trying to find a car so we could get on our way. We finally found a car at a rental facility that was half a mile away from the hotel. We did finally get everything squared away, and we were on our way to our next stop—Memphis.

On our way to Memphis, we drove through Baton Rouge and Jackson, Mississippi, on our way through the entire state of Mississippi from its southern border to its northern border on our way to Memphis where we had a hotel reservation for that night. It was a 400-mile drive, and it was pretty much driving all day except for food and bathroom breaks. Mom frequently commented on the beautiful landscape as we drove through the state of Mississippi. Once we arrived in Memphis, we just relaxed at our hotel that night. We thought about going out and watching a blues show—as Memphis was world-renowned for its blues. However, we decided to rest up and get ready for a big trip to

 Graceland the next day.

Mom had been a big Elvis fan and had been anticipating the visit with a lot of excitement. When we got to the parking lot for tourists outside Graceland, mom was on a mission I could barely keep up with her as she glided across the parking lot in her high-heeled boots at a fast pace. Once in the house, we walked around the mansion and saw a lot of interesting artifacts about his life. We concluded by walking to his grave site. It was interesting to drive through Memphis as they were certainly proud of their favorite son. Mom came away from Graceland with a lot of mementos including a sweatshirt and Elvis glasses to name a couple of items.

We stayed a second night in Memphis. The next morning, we had our customary breakfast at the hotel and went out to our rental car ready for the long journey to Oklahoma City. When we got to the car, we discovered our car's battery was dead. We were able to get help from the hotel, as they had jumper cables. We were finally on our way to Oklahoma City. It was about 500 miles, a good eight hours on the road. On the way, we traversed the entire state of Arkansas.

About halfway through our trip was the Arkansas capital city of Little Rock where the President Clinton Library was located. We decided it was a good place to take a break and walk around the presidential library. I teased her about how much she was looking forward to seeing the library because she was such a huge fan of Bill Clinton. She did like him as President because he was charming. After touring the library, I think she genuinely enjoyed herself. A little added fun outside the library was a big dog show. So, we stopped and watched some of the festivities as we were both missing our dogs back home.

Once we arrived in Oklahoma City, we checked into our hotel where Granddaughter Lori, her husband Jerry and her kids had already arrived. We visited with them a bit and then left to have dinner with Jack Langton at a local steakhouse. It was so nice to see Jack. Mom was especially excited to see him. It was a great connection to a happy part of her life as mom and dad would often socialize with Jack and his wife Bobbi. The two of them later divorced. Bobbi and their daughter, Brooke, had moved to California where Brooke made a name for herself as an actress. Brooke and I were the same age growing up in Morenci. She moved away when we were about five.

The next day in Oklahoma City, we toured the memorial site where the bomb was set by domestic terrorists killing hundreds of innocent people. Mom and I toured with Lori and her family.

Later we visited Jack Langton's house where he told a couple of stories about his days with my dad and all their mischief. He told the stories while sitting on  a couch with his arm around mom. He said, *"Come over here you succulent beauty!"* They were completely comfortable and really enjoyed each other's company. It was nice for Jack to see mom mentally healthy again as his last encounters were at times when mom was not mentally stable and was frequently hospitalized in Tucson. On those trips, dad would stop by and see Jack for sympathy and condolences. Back in OK City, Jack and I played a couple of games of pool as mom watched on. We finally said goodbye and Jack signed his book and wrote a dedication in it to mom and me.

When we got back to the hotel, Lori was ready to go to the big Neil Diamond concert. Mom liked Neil Diamond, and she had never been to a concert before. At 72 years old, she was standing up dancing singing and cheering just like everyone else including me and Lori.

The next day, we checked out of our hotel and followed Lori back to her house in Great Bend, Kansas, about a 300-mile drive. We stayed a couple of days with Lori and her family and had a nice visit. We received a tour of her church and, then we wrapped up our 8th state with a drive over to Kansas City, Missouri, about a 250-mile drive and flew back home.

Eight days of living and driving on the road. In all, it was nearly 1,500 miles of driving and over 30 hours from New Orleans to Memphis to Oklahoma City to Great Bend to Kansas City. The old saying that the journey was more fulfilling than the destination couldn't have been truer for us. We thoroughly relished the driving experience, the scenery, the many towns—both big and small. We enjoyed the lakes, the rivers, the people, the animals, but most of all—we enjoyed each other.

Just before our vacation in October 2008, the stock market was beginning to crash. Companies all over the country and the world began to see the collapse of their stock price and many were driven to bankruptcy. My employer for the last 18 years of my life was no different. Of course, the economy was driving the collapse of the stock market. It started with the housing market and spread to all facets of the economy. Then the layoffs began, and in many cases, companies started failing. My employer, Freeport-McMoRan, the successor company to Phelps Dodge, began its layoffs and closing some of its operations.

Panic was palpable, especially in my circles, as it was easy to cut the corporate overhead groups first. I was told my position was going away, but that I would get relocated to Morenci back in my old job and department with no reduction in pay. When getting this news, an inner calm and inner peace came over me. I decided I was going to resign from the company and walk away from my 18-year career and three generations of Biles men working for the company. I was going to make it on my own.

Although risky and against the prevailing wisdom of the time, I believed in myself.

I had some money built up in my 401(k). Over my many hours and hours of traveling and listening to satellite radio, I became knowledgeable about the stock market and trading stocks. My plan was to become a day trader and to a lesser degree, look for a company I could start.

Personally, and professionally, this was my moment of truth. It was where my responsibilities of caretaking mom and my personal desires to achieve something special came to a crossroads. Since I finished my political internships in 1992, I took the easy route and began working for the family company, Phelps Dodge/Freeport McMoRan. With the pressures of life, I settled on the course of least resistance. This time, I was going to make it work...I was never going to work for anyone again. I was going to figure out how to be successful, and I was going to continue to take loving care of mom.

In early 2009, I drove into the corporate office where my boss was having a meeting and I officially resigned. It was surreal, as I immediately felt different in the high-rise downtown building. I felt like an ex-employee, a visitor. I continued to feel that inner peace and inner calm that I was doing the right thing. My dad would have never approved or never understood my choice. He probably would have thought it was reckless and irresponsible. Mom supported me without a hint of doubt. I told her I would figure it out, and she was 100% behind me.

CHAPTER 8
The Culture of Dogs
(2009-2017)

"Once you have had a wonderful dog, a life without one is a life diminished."

-Dean Koontz

As early 2009 continued, I took a good assessment of my situation. I had money saved through my 401(k) over the last 15 years of my job with Freeport-McMoRan. Mom had a little money left in her savings. She was drawing Social Security as income. I had no income any longer. I had three mortgage payments and had the cost of living for mom and me. The real estate market had collapsed, so selling and consolidating was out of the question. I continued to rent out my Tempe condo as it was well located for continued usage by students going to ASU. I had been living in the Hearne Way house for the last three years. Mom had been living in the Nantuckett house exclusively by herself since May of 2007.

Our routine was regular and stable. Mom had been going to the same gym for 3 ½ years; it was the 24-hour Fitness on Val Vista and Elliott. She would attend the late morning water aerobics class on Monday, Wednesday and Friday. She had her dial a ride scheduled for pick up at the house and then pick up after class when it was over. I would generally work my schedule around her time at water aerobics. I couldn't resist going to the gym at the same time, so I could watch her YMCA water-aerobics conclusion. At times, I would be able to sneak into the steam room, but often she would catch me, smile and wave. I would smile and wave back knowing she caught me! I would generally take a quick visit to my house while mom was dressing and waiting for her ride home. I would see her at the Nantuckett house to hear about her class and usually get a nice lunch out of the deal.

The fur kid situation was stable. Penny and Brandy were the best of friends in mom's household. I would take them for a good run and walk while over at mom's house. I might do a little landscaping as needed while I was over as well. We had two cats—Fatty and Shadow. When Brandy was young, she was a little too much for the cats. They needed to stay up on tables and cabinets to avoid her puppy energy. By 2009, they were all getting along better. The cats would try to spend much of their time on mom's lap. Penny was sweet as ever; she was pretty much the perfect dog. Brandy was still high energy and needed her walks and her trips to Cosmo Dog Park to get her swimming in. Mom adored Brandy with every fiber in her body. She just thought Brandy was perfect.

I took Brandy and Penny's exercise seriously. I would take them for a run around the Val Vista Lakes community every day. We had several paths we would take on different days, usually about 3 miles total. Since we were running, mom would not attend. Although, we would still take our walks with her at several intervals during the week. Brandy loved the water so much. I couldn't help but let her jump in the many lakes along our running paths. I would keep her on a leash and just let her jump in and get wet. She loved it.

Mom and I would also take a few trips per week to Cosmo Dog Park where Brandy could get some serious swimming in. She was so singularly focused on retrieving the ball out in the lake; that she would completely block out the dozens of dogs all around her. On occasion, another dog would get her ball out in the middle of the lake. She would turn back to me expecting me to fix it. I would try and find another ball quick and throw it to her so she could come back with the ball I threw.

The year 2009 was the first year in a long time that I didn't have a job, I was unemployed. I hadn't been unemployed since my return from Washington, DC when I was stubbornly waiting for a professional position to open in Morenci back in 1992-1993. I had been gainfully employed for the last 17 years, but 2009 was going to be different. I was not getting a paycheck from another company, and the plan was to stay that way for the rest of my life.

My focus on earning income was day trading on the Stock Market. It was wild and woolly during this period of late 2008 and early 2009. It was very unstable, and trading was not for the faint of heart. The instability created an opportunity for quick rises in the market and quick profits. I was trading in my 401(k) account and a regular brokerage account. I would wake up early before the market opened and begin to assess the market on CNBC. I would make some trades and then monitor them throughout the day as I would work out, play with the dogs and visit mom. I would usually watch the end of the trading day shows on CNBC at mom's house to stay up to date on the daily trends and at times make some trades after the market closed in the post-market trading window.

Mom and I loved our Fry's right near Val Vista Lakes on the corner of Val Vista and Baseline. Shopping was one of the centerpieces of our lives. It was where she got her groceries, but also had social interactions, paid for her groceries, got her dial-a-ride money and got in some exercise. We visited that Fry's on Baseline and Val Vista every Sunday, I mean every Sunday for 13 straight years, from 2005 to 2018. She knew her way around; she knew all the cashiers. It was our grocery store home.

Our favorite Mexican food restaurants continued to be in regular rotation—Macayo's and Serrano's. We kept our eyes open for unfamiliar places opening all the time. Occasionally, we would plan out a lunch or dinner destination, but often I just liked to surprise her. Maybe it would be right after water aerobics midday or maybe in the evening, we would catch an impromptu movie and/or dinner together. Our life was structured and organized, but surprise was the spice of life. Now and then, I would bring food home with me; she loved Taco Bell. Every so often, we would order pizza from Domino's. We would buy three medium pizzas, two for me and one for her. She would get her pizza with mushrooms and pineapples. When I stopped by first thing in the morning, I would bring her a special hot drink, usually a Carmel latte.

As residents at Val Vista Lakes, we had membership to the clubhouse. On occasion, we would spend an afternoon on the clubhouse beach. It was such a beautiful facility; we didn't visit as often as we should have.

On Easter 2023, I spent the day at the Val Vista Lakes community reminiscing. What a beautiful community. It was built in the 1980s and had/has beautiful landscaping. I remember the paths mom and I would take Brandy and Penny around the neighborhood. Today, I have my two dogs Jonesey and Sakari. Sakari never knew this community, but Jonesey sure did. He lived at Nantuckett for three years. It's been five years since we lived there, but I could tell he remembered the area.

On a sad note, the Fry's grocery store was closed. I thought that it might have been shut down, but while taking the dogs for a walk around the clubhouse, I saw that it was closed. Also, the 24-Hour Fitness which had been such a centerpiece of our lives was closed. In both cases, the signage and branding were all gone, no sign that there had ever been a Fry's and a 24-Hour Fitness in that area. As a person who has worked with commercial real estate for almost 15 years, I understand how demographics change, and how traffic patterns change. Nonetheless, it was still sad to see something so important in our past gone.

It was during this period of around 2009 that we quit going to our church. In looking back, I think the best explanation I have was that I was just so singularly focused on making it as an entrepreneur that I didn't have the time to go to church. I certainly regret it because it was so good for us both, but I think at the time, I just needed to focus on making it on my own and I needed to focus.

As 2009 continued, my routine of day trading was successful. I began to gravitate around two business ideas to supplement day trading. One was to open a Bahama Bucks franchise and the other was to open a doggy daycare.

I loved the Bahama Buck's brand personally as a customer and thought it would be good to invest in a new franchise in the Phoenix area where they already had a few. I had discussions with the owners of Bahama Buck's based out of Texas, and I put together a loan request with my bank and was looking for a suitable location.

Simultaneously, I explored the doggy daycare idea. My cousin Doug was looking for work in which he could be with his blind/deaf dog, Roxy, not an easy task for him. He was living with his parents in Scottsdale, but his dog lived in a covered, vacant space at a Whitfill Nursery on a long chain in south Phoenix. Doug would take a bus ride to feed and visit her each day. He loved his dog dearly, but he had no other options. His parents would not allow her to live at their house. Whitfill would not allow Doug to live in the vacant space. He had struggled with various drug addictions for most of his adult life causing much instability with employment and living arrangements.

My cousin was at a point in his life where he had disappointed everybody who ever took a chance on him. I don't think anybody believed he could turn things around. Mom and I saw firsthand how unstable and unreliable he was when we hired him to landscape our yard a few years earlier in West Phoenix. We were disappointed, but we did not give up on him.

As I was formulating my business model, I saw excellent value in having a reliable night person who could stay in the dog boarding facility and help develop our brand of 24/7 service. Doug seemed like the perfect person. I began a 6-month interview/courtship with Doug. I met with him every couple of weeks. I wanted to see where his head was and if he was capable of being truly responsible. I would pick him up, and we would drive to see his dog, Roxy. Then we would visit other dog daycares and start to better understand the industry. I had an expectation that Doug needed to complete a multi-month dog behavior training course at the Arizona Animal Welfare League (AAWL). This would also show me if he could stick with something to its end. Again, he would have to take the bus to these courses. As I had meetings with Doug, I began to gain confidence that he desperately wanted this to happen so that his dog would have a better life. I saw in him the spark he needed to kick his addictions, and that spark was the love for his dog.

I got unwelcome news from the bank that my loan to start a Bahama Buck's franchise was rejected. I was unemployed and only earning investment income, not to mention we were right in the middle of the Great Recession. So, I decided to take the plunge

with doggy daycare because I didn't need a loan to start it. I just had to hope it made money before I ran out of money. It would be open 24/7 and it would be cage-free all the time. It was a radical, unique business model.

I co-signed for Doug to get an apartment and his utility bills so that he could get set up near the business. His new apartment was within walking distance of our business. I remember mom wanted Doug to get off to a good start in his new apartment. On our way to see him, she asked me to stop off at the grocery store and pick up a big load of groceries for him.

With the business, I had Doug working the nights and a few hired employees holding down the days. We called this new business Gilbert Dogs 24/7. I thought I could keep doing my day trading and the doggy daycare would develop into a company on autopilot. The dog daycare business would be a "hobby", but my

serious money maker would continue to be day trading.

Very quickly, that turned out to be fantasy. The company was bleeding cash every month. In the first year, I made just under $100,000 in sales, but spent well over $200,000. This big cash flow deficiency killed my ability to day trade because the cash I was using to trade stocks was disappearing into payroll and rent for the company. I saw the end of my business and the sad need to apply for a job if things didn't change fast.

In the first year after I quit my job, I spent every penny to my name. I still had 3 mortgages to pay and the costs of living for mom and me. Worst of all, the business was still bleeding money. Banks would not help with any loans or lines of credit.

I could either apply for a job or start withdrawing money from my 401(k)-retirement account I spent 18 years building up. If I took money from the retirement account that meant I had to pay income taxes on it and a 10% penalty. Yet, I was not ready to give up on the business, so I started withdrawing the $250,000 I had accumulated for all those years. Before I was done, I ended up spending all of it. Now, I was all in with the doggy business. It was my only hope. This meant both mom and I would be doing everything we could to make money for the business and make it work out.

I would try and take every job I could get with people calling us. I handled the phones and email traffic. If someone wanted a pet sitting in the middle of the night, I would take that job. If someone wanted a pet sitting in their house for 3 weeks of visits twice a day, on the other side of town, I would take that job. If they had an elderly dog or puppy that was not allowed in our daycare, we would take that client as well and they would stay with "Grandma Shirley" (my mom). She even had her own Facebook page that would show all the fun festivities at her house. She still had her two dogs, Penny and Brandy, and her two cats, Fatty and Shadow. The puppies and elderlies would just join her pack and she would take care of all of them. I think the most she ever had was three guest dogs at the same time, two puppies and an elderly dog. I had complete faith that she would do very well with the responsibility. I think she also liked it and I know she liked helping the business. We needed all the help we could get.

All in with the business also meant mom and I went all in with the culture of dogs. In the next five years, we would add five dogs to our family on top of the two we already had.

The first of five new dogs was a little wiener named Fritz. It was Barktoberfest 2009, and the business was just opening that month in October. Barktoberfest was a dog adoption event. I heard they had a wiener that needed a home. I felt a void in my life since Jennifer was killed while we were at the wedding in Sedona a few years previous. So, I asked if I could adopt Fritz. He lived with me at the Hearne house.

Fritz was the best little companion a guy could ever ask for. He slept with me deep under the blankets of my bed every night. He had a little stairway he could climb to get into my bed. As mom took the dogs too young or too old for daycare. Fritz and I took the dogs that didn't have the right temperament for a cage-free facility. One of our favorite guests was a big German Shepherd named Kaiser. Kaiser, when playing, would occasionally bite too hard. We call it a lack of bite inhibition. So, he would stay with Fritz and me. Fritz just loved Kaiser and all the big German Shepherds that would stay in our house. It must have been a German thing.

As 2009 quickly turned into 2010 and winter turned into spring, it dawned on me that it had been 10 years since dad passed away on May 1. Time had really flown by. Mom and I didn't have the money to do any travel like we did in the past, but it seemed perfect for the two of us to commemorate 10 years together and remember dad 10 years after his death with a camping trip at the South Fork campgrounds near the cabins of what used to be Canyon Cove. It was the place of so many great family memories near Springerville and where we spread the ashes of dad.

When I say camping, I mean we really camped! We stayed in a tent for a few days. We had a blow-up mattress and of course, the dogs came with us. Fritz stayed at my Gilbert Dogs facility. We packed up supplies and our dogs and headed up to the mountains. Mom took care of the old girl Penny, and I handled Brandy. We did a lot of exploring as we walked around the area. The old ruins of the Canyon Cove cabins still remained. It was late spring and still a little cold. We got good rain at times, and our trustworthy tent held up under the storms just fine. It had been a good 10 years; dad would have been pleased with how far mom had come.

To commemorate the return to South Fork, I created a home video to honor dad and our wonderful experience of camping. I used the song, "Somewhere My Love" performed by Ray Conniff and his singers for the music to the video. This beautiful song and memorable video would be a future source of nostalgia for mom and me. The video shows the story of our trip to honor dad at the place where his ashes were spread and a walk through his life through pictures.

Not too long after we returned to the valley, I was taking Fritz for his usual walk down the canal behind my house on Hearne Street. We saw something up ahead and saw it moving, but we weren't sure what it was. As we got closer, I could see it was a puppy. He was tied to a tree with a rope and had some ant-infested dog food by him in a plastic bag. Fritz and I got to him and couldn't believe it. I looked around in every direction up and down the canal, but there were no people for a half a mile in either direction. He was left there abandoned. He was a happy little guy and was especially happy to see us. I told Fritz, meet your new brother. He responded by pulling on the leash and wanted to keep moving along with his walk. I told Fritz, this guy was going with us! I untied him from the tree, and we finished our walk together and then took him to the vet to get checked out. He was probably about 3 or 4 months old, a mix between a golden retriever and a border collie.

Although I only had Fritz at my house and mom had Brandy and Penny, two big dogs, once I took the new dog over to meet mom and her dogs, I knew his new home would be with them. We called him Bubba. Now mom had three big dogs. They all got along famously. It was a beautiful cycle of life with the elderly Penny, the adult dog Brandy and the puppy Bubba who had enthusiastic respect for his elder Penny. He loved playing and competing with Brandy for balls during fetch. They both loved the water. Most of all, mom loved Bubba and Bubba

loved mom. It would begin a lifetime of love and protection between Bubba and mom. He could be found by her on the couch or by her feet on the floor, protecting her. At night, he was lurking just under the bed where mom slept.

As 2011 began to move on, we had a new problem, but a good problem. Gilbert Dogs was starting to take off. Our space was small, only about 1,500 square feet. It was formerly a pizza place. We were starting to fill up and our sales doubled during the 2nd year, still relatively small around $200,000, but enough to pay the bills of the business and our personal bills. Then, an opportunity came in the nearby city of Chandler.

A couple had opened a dog daycare in Chandler and largely modeled it after my cage-free business. As 2011 carried on, they decided the business was not for them and asked if I wanted to buy it. I was just starting to get some success at Gilbert Dogs, but I was a born entrepreneur and risk taker, so I negotiated an acquisition and changed the name from Happy Tails Pet Resort to Chandler Dogs 24/7. We opened in November of 2011, almost two years exactly after I had opened Gilbert Dogs 24/7. Chandler Dogs was three times the size of Gilbert, with over 4,000 square feet. I felt the dog volume that was overflowing at Gilbert would be an attractive fit for some of them to move to Chandler, and that was what happened.

Back at Nantuckett, Mom continued to take in the puppies and elderlies, but now for two shops. I would often take incoming calls, so I would hear all the opportunities that would have normally been declined. I wanted to take in the elderly because mom was such a kind and loving host for them. The puppies were often rascals, but mom loved them as well. The puppies would often "graduate" from Grandma Shirley's Bed and Breakfast and then join the big dogs in the shops of either Gilbert or Chandler.

Mom was getting used to caring for her three big dogs. It was a piece of cake for her. I would stop by every day to take them for

154

walks and runs. It was quite a sight to see the four of us running around the neighborhood.

Our favorite game at bedtime was what we called "Bed drop". It was a rather complicated game that involved all three dogs at mom's house. Mom was in bed watching and Brandy was up on the bed with her. Bubba, Penny and I would be positioned on the floor. I would throw a tennis ball to Brandy on the bed, and she would catch it perfectly and then Bubba would rush to the end of the bed where Brandy would be standing. I would say, "Bed drop Brandy, Bed drop!" She would drop the ball into Bubba's mouth, and then he would rush over to me as I lay on the floor in the corner of the bedroom, and he would give me the ball. Then we would start the cycle again by throwing it to Brandy. Penny's role in the game was to kiss my face and especially my eyes so I couldn't see well enough to play the game with the other two. We loved to play bed drop almost every night until it was time to turn out the lights and go to sleep. I would exit out of the garage and back to my house where Fritz would be waiting.

The Val Vista Lakes community was close and family oriented. They did Christmas wagon rides around the holiday season. Also, Halloween was a big event in the neighborhood. No one waited for the kids to knock on the door, everyone set up chairs out in front of their houses, and traffic was stopped in the evening. Mom and I enjoyed our Halloweens at Nantuckett. We would buy so much candy but ran out early because it was so busy. We would have to retire into the house and turn off our lights notifying trick-or-treaters we were closed for the night.

As 2011 was winding towards an end, it would be my first year of navigating the busy Christmas season at two shops. A family came in and wanted to board this big white dog. I talked to them quite a bit and learned that they had had him for two years but unfortunately, their newborn was allergic to him. I really connected with this big guy called Saint. He was about 120

pounds, and his breed was kind of rare in the US, known as an Akbash. They told me that he was going to a shelter after their two-week board at Gilbert Dogs. We tested him out, and he did okay but was a dominant personality in an open, cage-free environment. I decided he would stay with me during Christmas 2011. I was secretly and privately testing him out at home to see if he would get along with Fritz. My wiener had a dominant personality as well, but he was outweighed by over 100 pounds by Saint. Fritz spent most of his time hiding under the bed for the first few days. I took them for frequent walks together and they eventually became friends. After the two-week board was up, I made sure to handle personally Saint's checkout with his parents. I asked them, *"Can I have Saint?"* It was so touching that the mom broke into immediate tears. We hugged, and she told me, YES!

Saint was our third new dog in two years. Mom had her three big dogs—Penny, Brandy and Bubba at Nantuckett. I had my two boys—Fritz and Saint. I brought mom over to meet Saint and she loved him to pieces. He was so loving to mom and gentle. When he was happy, he would smile showing all his teeth. He smiled big when he was with mom.

Mom's move to Nantuckett was not only the place where her family of dogs swelled, but also cats. She had Fatty and Shadow when she arrived at the new house at Val Vista Lakes. Additionally, there were some strays in the neighborhood. One big white cat was particularly friendly. Mom and I suspected he was left behind by the previous owner as he seemed to gravitate to our house. He was a dirty white cat, so we named him Dirty Snow. We eventually allowed him in the house. He got along with our two cats just fine. He seemed comfortable and at home inside the house. Unfortunately, our house cats were not vaccinated, and we believe Fatty probably caught something from the outside cats and sadly died a couple of years after moving to the Nantuckett house.

Along with Dirty Snow, there was a young female kitten that seemed to be close to Dirty Snow. She was feral, and not friendly with humans. We called her Little Mama. Unfortunately, we couldn't capture her and get her spayed. So, she proceeded to have a litter of kittens. We allowed her in the house for the event. She had five kittens, mom named them Sam, Misty Ann, Darth and two unnamed kittens which were adopted out. They lived indoors all the time but were never friendly as Little Mama taught them the ways of being feral. Darth got out and was never found again. Little Mama got out as well. I was able to get Misty Ann and Sam spayed and neutered. Unfortunately, little Mama got pregnant again and had another litter. She again had them indoors. When they were old enough, I was able to get the entire litter adopted out by the Humane Society. Little Mama had one more litter after she got out once more. We tried preventing her from going outside, but some mistakes were made. We got the entire litter adopted out by a local shelter, Friends For Life.

Dirty Snow died a couple of years after we moved to the new house. We suspected he was old. We were happy he had some peaceful time indoors at the end of his life. Only a couple of years old, Little Mama died as well. She was a Little Mama all her life. Her true love and the one she spent every waking moment with was our neutered male cat, Shadow. Little Mama's first two kittens, Sam and Misty Ann, survived her and Shadow.

With the cats living in the main part of the house, the dogs were relegated to mom's bedroom and a doggy door outside. With the design of mom's house, it was the best we could do with the animal situation. It wasn't the fairest arrangement as the feral cats and Shadow got most of the house and the more beloved dogs had relatively limited access to the house and to us humans.

In 2013, the two locations of Gilbert Dogs and Chandler Dogs continued to thrive. I was looking at opportunities to move Gilbert out of its tiny original suite. About a mile down Gilbert Road to the corner with Guadalupe, I found its new home. It was about 4,000 square feet of space for the dogs. That equaled the size of Chandler Dogs. I had two facilities of about 4,000 square feet now and my business continued to grow.

Mom and I had a big loss in 2013. Our dear sweet Penny died that year. She died at home with mom in her bedroom. I was unfortunately unavailable when it happened. It was sad to hear a voicemail from mom telling me that Penny had died. As soon as I got the news, I rushed home and took our sweet girl off to the vet. It was a good way to die for Penny, she was surrounded by her dog siblings Brandy and Bubba and comfortable at home with her Mama.

In 2014, it was a busy year for me personally. I went back to school full-time at Arizona State University. This time, I was pursuing three objectives: a third bachelor's in history, a certificate in sales/marketing and a certificate in religious conflict, all concurrently. My goal was to take all my needed classes over two semesters and one summer session to receive the degree and certificates in one year. It was about 40 credit hours. I was fortunate to achieve my goal and make the dean's list both semesters and maintain straight As. All the classes were on campus with lectures, which I loved. I enjoyed the classroom interaction with professors who were experts in their fields.

In the summer of 2014, I adopted my darling, Sasha. Cha-Cha Fancy was my special nickname for her. She was originally a client's dog that was attending daycare at Chandler Dogs. Her mom was moving out of town and wanted to re-home her in town. Sasha didn't feel like a good fit at first. She was a bit distant and aloof. Everyone knew I loved huskies so I kind of got pressured into taking

the plunge to adopt her. When I took her home for the first time with Saint in the Jeep, she was terrified of him. I didn't think she was a good fit for my household. I first tried her with mom as she had lost Penny and had her two dogs. I didn't feel she got along particularly well in that household either. Her play style was a lot rougher than the less-physical, straightforward fetch and retrieve that Bubba and Brandy were used to. Bubba was afraid of her; he would hide from her. So, my groomer Melissa tried to adopt her, but again, she didn't fit in with her household of older smaller dogs and Sasha tended to pick on the little ones.

One day, Melissa's grooming employees were watching Sasha and she got out of their home and escaped into the city. I felt terrible and guilty. It had only been a few weeks since my favorite husky, Kira, a client at Gilbert Dogs, had escaped his house and was killed by a car. I searched day and night for Sasha. I was in contact with rescue groups and police who had received leads on

159

her whereabouts. About 36 hours later, and several miles from her escape location, I got a good lead from social media. I arrived at the apartment complex and found her. She did not run away from me; she ran to me! That was the moment I finally made a connection to the future sweetheart of my life. I was determined to make it work with the boys' club of Fritz, Saint and me. We were going to have a princess—that was Sasha, Cha-Cha Fancy. We made it work and the rest was history.

Mom and I had our fourth new dog during this era I called the culture of dogs. I had my three dogs Fritz, Saint and Cha-Cha, and mom had her Brandy and Bubba Boy. Our family was almost complete.

Our regular routine usually meant a drive to Cosmo Dog Park so the dogs could swim and chase balls or a good run around Val Vista Lakes. One of our favorite easy activities each day was for mom and me to sit on the swing in the backyard and throw the ball for the dogs. Bubba loved everything Brandy loved. She loved to retrieve; he loved to retrieve. She loved to swim; he loved to swim. Bubba was a little bit devilish though. He liked to get the ball and keep it from Brandy and tease her. He would lay in a bush in the backyard thinking he was hiding, but we could all see him clearly. We called it the "Bubba Bush." Brandy would run up to him and bark, demanding he give up the ball or take it to us on the swing. He would do neither; he would just hide in the "Bubba Bush" and smile.

Another big year for the company, for mom and for me personally was 2015. One day, my groomer, employee and good friend Melissa told me she had an adorable rescue dog she was giving a complementary groom, to help him get adopted. He lived in a shelter and needed a home. She suggested I stop by the shop and meet him. His name was Jonesey, and he was an Australian Shepherd. He was smart and loving, characteristics I noticed immediately after meeting him. I told Melissa, *"You know what, you got me!"* Let me take him home to meet mom, Bubba and Brandy. It was instant chemistry, mom adored him as he was so loving to her. Brandy liked him but she liked all dogs. Bubba was the true test as they were both young males. It was love at first sight for the two boys. They immediately began wrestling like they had known each other all their lives.

Jumping up on the bed and down to the floor wrestling and taking time to go say hi to mom in between rounds. Our family was now complete. Mom had three big dogs —Brandy, Bubba and Jonesey. I had my three dogs—Saint, Cha-Cha and little Fritz. We were all dogs all the time—24/7 in the culture of dogs.

As for the company, 2015 was the year we opened our third location, Tempe Dogs 24/7. We had considerable pushback from the community, but we eventually got approved by the Tempe City Council and the mayor and opened in the late fall of 2015, almost the same time as the two previous locations opened in 2009 and 2011. Tempe was about 15 miles away from each of the other two places and was a natural location for many of our clients at both locations as it was new, near the freeway and run by the same, trusted company many had followed for years. We needed more capacity as the two original places were starting to fill up with those 8,000 square feet that we had for dog guests. Tempe added a new 6,000 square feet of capacity to our company in the east valley.

I was so proud that mom was able to attend my grand opening and open house with me. She was proud of me, but she was supportive and proud of everything I did or tried to do, whether it succeeded or failed. She was my biggest cheerleader. I walked her around the shop and showed her everything. We sat down at our conference table and enjoyed dinner together as I had a food truck serving all the customers who visited the grand opening.

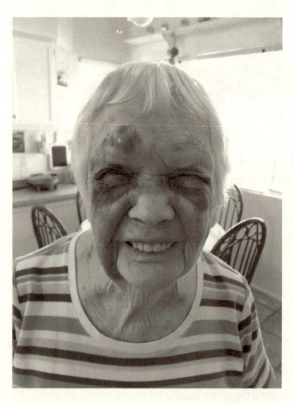

As 2015 progressed, mom had three emergency room visits. They probably all played a role in her future health. On May 17, 2015, mom took a terrible fall while walking out to get the mail at her house. I was with her at the time doing some yard work. She fell and hit her forehead. She got up on her own and tried to say she was okay, but her forehead was swelling. Unfortunately, she did not break the fall with her hands at all, it was solid contact with the cement. It looked terrible, I told her, *"I have got to take you to emergency to get you checked out."* Her face was bruised very badly after the fall. They did not think she had any permanent injuries from the fall, but a hard hit to the forehead at 79 years old couldn't be good for her delicate brain.

In late November and early December, she had two more emergency room trips caused by extreme back and neck pain. It was during this time that she began getting regular epidural steroid injections to help her manage the pain. Unknown to us at this time, she was experiencing advanced heart disease. Regular steroid shots not only spike the conditions of patients with diabetes, but they are bad for people with heart disease. These regular injections were leading to catastrophic health problems in the future.

Since our camping trip to South Fork back in 2010, it woke up an old, but great love we had for South Fork and Springerville. We no longer traveled around the country on trips, but we regularly traveled up to the White Mountains of Eastern Arizona.

In the Summer of 2016, we had a trip planned, a once-in-a-lifetime goodbye to our former places of residence. We packed up all three of her dogs into the back of the Jeep. My three dogs stayed at the new Tempe Dogs facility. We started with a drive to Safford to see our old house on Relation Street. It was mom's first trip back in about 13 years. We got out and walked on the sidewalk around the house. Mom was quiet. I could tell the memories were rushing back. The house had changed a lot; it wasn't kept up like my dad had maintained it, but that was understandable, as it was a large lot with a lot of work.

Our next stop was a drive to Morenci. We drove to the house on Ironwood Street first. We didn't get out or look around that much, just a couple of drives by. Next was the big one for both of us, our beloved home on Mariposa.

Probably the house we both lived in the longest during our lives. I was able to pull over near the house at 140 Mariposa. I let the dogs out and off the leash; I immediately realized that was a mistake. I had forgotten how things work out in the country. Often neighbor dogs roamed around or hopped the fence whenever they wanted to approach a new dog. Plus, it lit up the neighborhood like firecrackers on the 4th of July with all the dogs in their front chain link yards adding their two cents to our arrival. So, I put them back in the Jeep and walked around without them. Mom got out as well and looked around. She was genuinely sad from the experience and even a little shaken. I could only imagine the memories that were flowing back to her—good and bad. It had been almost 50 years since she moved into that house. It showed its wear and tear. It certainly wasn't kept up to my dad's standard. Much of the buildout that so clearly defined our house was gone. The treehouse was gone. The pool table room was gone. The extra bedroom where my sisters lived was gone. Even the cement sidewalk where all the kids had footprints and handprints was gone. We stayed around for a while and decided it was time to leave. We talked about all the good times and tried to remember how it was then, not how it was on the day of our visit.

Our next journey was to drive all the way up the Coronado Trail and stay in the South Fork area. No small trip to say the least. As we drove through what used to be known as Stargo, we stopped at the mine lookout. Let the dogs have a good potty break and got out to look at the mine one last time. Mom got right up to the tall chain link fence and reached out to hold on. She looked around at its majestic size as I finished up the potty break. We all got back into the Jeep and continued our journey up the beautiful, but windy road. For the longest time, the road up the Coronado Trail was known as US Highway 666. It was later changed as the numbers 666 (a sign of the Devil) was not a good name for a highway. It was later changed to Highway 191. We had several more stops along the way, notably at Hannagan's Meadow. By now, it was getting late in the afternoon. We were just winging it; we didn't have a place to stay that night. I figured I better reach out and get something set up. I was able to get a cabin for us at the X Diamond Ranch. A big spacious cabin for all of us. We stayed there for a few more days and reflected on our goodbye trip. Mom told me, *"I am not interested in visiting Safford and Morenci again, that was enough, that was goodbye."*

A favorite part of mom's day was making me a great home-cooked meal. She knew I didn't eat very well and liked to make something home-cooked as often as possible. She loved making me happy and eating her special meals made me happy. Yet if the truth were known, mom's feeding of her dogs also ranked as a high priority with her.

Mom and I had this age-old disagreement on how many times the dogs should be fed. I wanted twice a day, but she wanted three times a day. So, "we compromised", and the dogs ate three times a day. One of the meals would be primarily green beans, but she would sprinkle in a nice helping of dog kibble. She kind of ranked how many green beans each dog would get based on seniority. Brandy got the most, but Bubba was starting to warrant a bigger helping. Jonesey got the smallest helping because, well, he hadn't earned it yet.

How did she feed three big dogs as she turned 80? It used to be just taking their bowls out on the back porch and setting them down. However, Brandy and particularly the younger feisty Bubba would like to get done with their bowl and start shopping around in the other dog bowls. As a seasoned dog boarding facility owner, I knew this was not good practice and not safe. So, we instituted a new program back in her bedroom. I nailed special hangers on the wall spreading out each of the three dogs and attaching their leashes. When it was time to eat, mom would get the three dogs hooked up in their eating stations where movement was restricted. Then she would carry in the bowls of food and set them beside each of the rambunctious dogs so eager to eat. It was quite a sight to see, but I was happy because it was safer.

During the year 2016, Mom had two more emergency room visits. She had another bad head injury from a fall and a bad high blood pressure episode. These visits were back-to-back on May 20th and May 21st.

The head injury was like her fall almost a year prior. She did not break her fall and hit cement flush in the head. Her swelling and a large hematoma were present almost immediately after the fall. Again, they did not think any permanent damage was done from the fall, but I'm sure it was detrimental to her long-term health.

After returning home from the head injury, she felt terrible the next day and asked to return to the hospital. Her blood pressure was running high; it was checked out at 220/100. So, I rushed her back to the emergency room for treatment. Again, a prelude of things to come for her health in mid-2016.

As the Summer of 2016 ended, we had one more big trip up into the mountains. We had a Biles family reunion scheduled with the kids, grandkids, great-grandchildren, great-great grandchildren and spouses of Maymo and granddad's Family. These were decedents of my paternal grandparents. It was quite a nice event, Doug traveled with mom and me. We rented out most of the cabins at the South Fork Ranch. I rented the biggest one so several family members could stay with mom and me. Mom and auntie are pictured hugging at this event. My aunt and uncle were in good health, and mom was in good health. It was nice to get them together with all their kids aka "The Cousins." We had some big family meals. We did some fishing. We did a scavenger hunt. All told, we had a nice get-together. We took several family pictures on the final day to commemorate the event.

We didn't know it at the time, but there was also a life-changing event that happened at the reunion. Mom complained of chest pains. We discussed with her the seriousness of them, but ultimately, they went away, and no follow-up was made at that time. It was later determined that she likely had a minor heart attack at the Family Reunion.

PART 3
The Indomitable

"Some people when they have taken too much and have been driven beyond the point of endurance, simply crumble and give up. There are others, though they are not many, who will for some reason always be unconquerable. You meet them in time of war and also in time of peace. They have an indomitable spirit and nothing, neither pain nor torture nor threat of death, will cause them to give up."

-Roald Dahl

CHAPTER 9
Heart Surgery
(2017)

"You have to accept whatever comes and the only important thing is that you meet it with courage and with the best that you have to give."

- Eleanor Roosevelt

The beginning of 2017 was uneventful. Life continued along its normal trajectory. My auntie had been in and out of the hospital a lot. Doctors were having a challenging time locating the source of internal bleeding in her GI tract. She seemed to be in good spirits but frustrated.

Then suddenly and unexpectedly my dear auntie passed away on March 23. On social media, I posted this poem in her honor.

Remembering my Auntie

I was just nine or ten when I went on a wonderful vacation.
My Auntie took me to San Diego, I was full of elation.

Auntie took me to the Wild Animal Park, Sea World and the Zoo.
Some of the greatest memories a little guy ever knew.

In the 80s and 90s, Auntie's house was the place to be.
We would set up the Scrabble table—Auntie, Doug, Cindy, Maymo and me.

I so enjoyed all the movies, when I moved back.
Mom, Uncle, You and I, we were quite a pack.

From the time I was a little boy all the way to the end,
Your great love and grace will always transcend.

I will miss you so much and the family will be sad.
But it gives me solace to know you are once again with dad.

During 2017, we lost the centerpiece of the greater Biles/Underwood family, the matriarch, my aunt. Auntie was one of those people who was full of life; so full of energy, it was hard to imagine life without her. Auntie was the glue of the family.

I would spend a lot of time at my auntie's house in the 90s when I was going to college. We would watch the TV show Dallas together every week and usually play a game of Scrabble in my paternal grandmother's bedroom (we all called her Maymo). My cousins Doug and Cindy would often join in. We would have a lot of laughs. Then after everyone went to bed, Doug and I would continue playing games, usually many hours into the night. Inevitably, Doug and I would start laughing so loud that my auntie would scold us from her bedroom. They were good times.

I was so happy that my auntie passed away knowing her beloved son Doug had a great, stable career in my dog daycare company. She worried about him frequently through the years as he struggled with drug addictions and stable employment. At times, no one in the family knew his whereabouts. It was so hard on my auntie. Although at the time of her death, Doug was an enormous success—on his own and stable. He was loved and admired by so many inside and outside the company. He had made a big mark on the world with his signature kindness. His mom and dad were so proud.

The family had invited me to do the eulogy at my auntie's memorial service on April 22. It was the biggest speech of my life and one of my greatest honors. I was not crazy about public speaking, but I had to deliver a good speech in honor of my auntie, her family, mom and my family. I took the responsibility very seriously. I made trips to visit my auntie and dad's cousins, Bobby and Shirley. Growing up, the four of them were close. It gave me perspective on my auntie's childhood, growing up during the Great Depression. I also spent a lot of time with my uncle and learned all about how he and my auntie met in Morenci. I practiced for a couple of weeks with mom as my audience. The eulogy had to be perfect.

During the day of the memorial service, I was not nervous, as I was well-practiced. My dad's cousins Bobby and Shirley were at the service. It was not easy for them to attend because of their age and health, but they were a major part of my speech, and I was glad they made it. It was a big venue, I wished they could have sat up closer to get a better experience of my narration and their contributions. Of course, mom was close to the stage, and I mentioned her a few times during the speech. It was about a 20-minute eulogy. The church was packed, I would say 200-300 people in attendance, maybe more, as my auntie was loved by a lot of people.   I think it went well and it was a proper tribute to my dear auntie.

A month later, on May 19, I took mom to our nearby hospital, Banner Gateway. She was complaining of chest pains. She was given several thorough tests. Next, they wanted to transfer her to Banner Baywood, a few miles away. Baywood is the premier heart hospital for Banner in the Phoenix-Metro area.

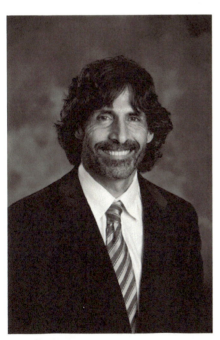

Mom's cardiologist, Dr. James DelGiorno was going to remove the blockage in her arteries with an angioplasty procedure in the cardiac cath lab (catheterization lab). Mom went off to get the procedure done and probably 15-20 minutes later, Dr. DelGiorno emerged with his usual big smile, but he couldn't have done the work so quickly...he told us three out of the four arteries were completely blocked, and the fourth artery was 95% blocked. He said that she would be returned to her room, and he and a heart surgeon would return a little later.

A few hours later they returned. A decision needed to be made on whether to go into surgery the next day, with lengthy, difficult open-heart surgery. Mom was 80 years old. Because of her age, they decided the procedure would need to be a "beating heart" surgery. The surgeon would operate while the heart was active and beating. This makes it even more challenging to work on a beating heart, in other words, a moving target.

Due to her advanced age and the long, difficult procedure, it was a hard decision on whether to attempt the surgery. The good news was that mom was in excellent shape for an 80-year-old and up for the challenge. She had been walking several times a week and going to water aerobics several times a week for 17 years. All her hard work had led to this moment of decision. If anyone could endure the surgery and the difficult recovery, it would be mom. A decision had to be made that day.

Dad was presented with the same life or death decision after his colon cancer surgery. He had the choice of oncology or just living out his life over the next several weeks. He chose the latter. It was a personal choice and obviously a difficult choice for all of us when presented with an end-of-life decision.

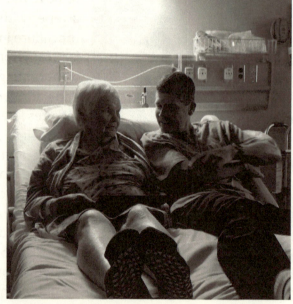

I sat down with mom in the hospital bed and had that solemn discussion with her. She did not hesitate. She was up for the challenge. She wanted to live. Whatever challenge came her way with the surgery and recovery, she was up for it. Surgery was scheduled for the next day, May 21, 2017. It was important for all of us to get a good night's sleep if that were possible. Surgery day was going to be long and hard.

It was one of those moments in life that was thrust upon me unexpectedly. One day life was normal and then the next day, the world, my world, was on hold. Everything was going to change; everything was going to be different. Life as I knew it, my future, mom's future was unknown.

Surgery day had arrived for mom. She was going to be in surgery for 5 to 6 hours. It was unthinkable for her to be under anesthesia and under the knife for so long...not to mention the incredible endurance and concentration of the surgeon and her staff. It was the first of many moments ahead where I was beside myself with anxiety, nerves and fear of losing mom. The surgery had a window of time to get as much done as possible, but I was continually cognizant of the extreme strain put on mom's body to go through such a lengthy surgery. I was able to go back with my sister as mom was getting prepared for anesthesia. The doctors and nurses throughout the process were kind and supportive of mom and the family.

We were in the waiting room knowing it was about time to hear something regarding the surgery; it had been several hours. Finally, the surgeon, Dr.

Iva Smolens, emerged and walked over to us. She said the surgery went well, and mom was stable. My goodness, it was such a relief to hear those words from the doctor. She went on to tell us how she performed a "beating heart" surgery. We all just listened in awe of her skill and ability. It was going to be challenging times ahead as she was getting transferred to the intensive care unit (ICU) during recovery. She was coming out of the anesthesia soon.

Mom and I had many challenges to date, but I was anxious to see her conscience and lucid so I could see how she came out the other side. Was she still going to have all her famous spirit and spunk? Soon enough, we got our answer. Yes, she was recovering very well, thank God, and she was up for making progress so she could get out of ICU and into a normal hospital bed. I think it was about 24 hours after her anesthesia wore off and the pain medicine wore off. She was in a lot of pain from the surgery, understandably. Regardless, she was up and walking in just two days and taken out of ICU where she recovered for a few more days. As usual, I was with her every day, every hour of the process.

On May 29, I said, *"Day 10 in the hospital. Mom made it out of ICU after open heart surgery. At 80 years young, she is such a strong, inspiring woman. Lots of pain, but no narcotics for last 5 days, just Tylenol."*

Two days later, on May 31, I said, *"Mom was discharged from the hospital last night transferred to an acute rehab center. It has been almost two weeks since her open-heart surgery. She had three hours of intense physical therapy, occupational therapy and speech therapy. She is doing very well."*

On June 10 after mom made it home, I said, *"A message from mom—after 22 days in the hospital, triple bypass surgery, ICU and rehab, she is home."* Mom said in a video message – *"Thank you for all the well wishes and prayers that everyone has given me. Thank you."*

About a month after surgery on June 18, mom was home and getting her nails done and returning to normal life. A week after that on June 24, *"We went out to a local park, Freestone, and fed*

the ducks and got a good 20-minute walk in." We took rehab seriously. We were building up her strength and stamina.

On June 25, we went out to do our normal grocery shopping and she did all the work as usual. We walked up and down every aisle and she picked up all her groceries meticulously.

On July 8, I celebrated 50 days since her heart surgery. It has truly been an inspirational journey of love, faith and tenacity. More than anything, she wanted to get home to be with her dogs.

The next few months were quiet months of healing and getting back to normal. No significant issues, good or bad, had come up. We continued to go to cardiac workouts and her usual walking and water aerobics regularly. We continued going on our weekly trips to the grocery store and our occasional visits to larger stores. We would visit malls and large department stores to get good exercise in a cooler environment. One of our favorite places to go was Superstition Springs Mall where we had lots of good challenges with walking. Mom had a lot of mixed feelings about using a walker; she wasn't crazy about it. However, it was doctor's orders for a while as she was still recovering after discharge.

In July, we made a trip up in the mountains with my sister Kristy. It was therapeutic for all of us. The dogs loved the time up in the rivers, lakes and mountains near Springerville. We played games, sat out on the porch and enjoyed the cool mountain air away from the heat of Phoenix.

In early November, I visited the dog industry expo in Hershey, Pennsylvania. It was my second annual visit. Getting together with others from the industry and hearing many of the experts give advice was one of the best ways for me to get advanced education and one of the real secrets to growing the business.

Thanksgiving 2017, we had our biggest emergency to date with mom. I had left mom's house on Nantuckett Street that night with everything seemingly okay. I knew she wasn't feeling great, but there was no sign of her being deathly ill. Somehow after the big meal, her underlying illness must have rapidly developed. As I was driving home to my house, I got a call from mom. She said in a gasping voice, *"Help, I can't breathe!"* She was becoming faint and drifting in and out as she talked. I could tell it was something bad, she was struggling to talk and even breathe. I told her, *"I'll be right back to the house, I'm calling an ambulance."* As mom was talking, she would randomly fade to silence, and I would raise my voice, *"Mom, mom stay with me, talk to me!"* I put her on hold and called 911 as I turned around my car. I told them of the emergency at mom's house on Nantuckett and told them I was returning to the house as well. I also called my sister Donna and told her I just got off the phone with 911, and they were on the way to get mom. I said, *"She is in really bad shape. You should get to the house right away."*

I got to the house a couple of minutes before the ambulance. Mom was almost unconscious, on the floor, and gasping for breath. I quickly tried to comfort her and encourage her. I told her the ambulance would be here soon. By the time the ambulance came in, they checked her oxygen level and discovered she was at an incredibly low 60% oxygen saturation. The paramedics gave her oxygen right away, got her on a gurney, and made their way to the ambulance outside. She was in critical condition. Donna just arrived as mom was departing. I can't remember if mom was conscience enough to see her.

When they arrived at the emergency room, she got a thorough evaluation. She was moved to a ventilator to assist her with breathing. As it turned out, mom had been suffering from upper respiratory infections, bronchitis. She was positive for RSV—Respiratory Syncytial Virus, a virus like COVID. It can be serious and life-threatening with older adults. [RSV is the most common cause of bronchiolitis (inflammation of the small airways in the lung) and pneumonia (infection of the lungs.)] This combined with her already existing congestive heart failure was a bad mixture. She was filling up with fluids and the more she filled up, the harder it was to breathe. She was admitted to the Intensive Care Unit (ICU) for critical, lifesaving care.

On November 24, *"UPDATE on our mother. She tested positive for the RSV virus. Thank you all so much for your sweet thoughts and prayers. For those that don't know, she was hospitalized last night with a breathing emergency. She is doing better than last night but still hospitalized. Please continue to pray."*

After three days in the ICU and a nine-day overall hospitalization, they were able to get the respiratory infection under control and pull the excess water out of her system through diuretics.

For a couple of days afterwards, she was a little gun-shy with her breathing, and we had a return trip to an urgent care and another trip to the emergency room. We finally got the problem under control medically and psychologically.

Looking back, this was such a close call. Of all her near-fatal CHF (congestive heart failure)/edema (swelling caused by too much fluid trapped in the body's tissues) close calls, this was the most serious, because it required her to take the initiative and call me on the phone while she was already in critical condition. It was one of the biggest signs of her great will to live. So many people would not have the ability or the will to make a phone call when their oxygen saturation level was at 60%.

If not for her ability and special awareness to call me just before falling unconscious, I could have easily arrived on the morning of November 24 to find my mom deceased. Gasping for air and falling in and out of consciousness, she was already far beyond critical condition, but she had the wherewithal to call me to save her life.

It is important to note, that these episodes of edema were hard on her body. Pulling the water off rapidly through IV diuretics was exhausting, painful and hard on the body. Ultimately, we could see the breathing improve hour by hour, day by day as the excess water was removed. The quality of her kidney function was eroded because of everything her body went through—the water gain/water removal process.

In general, mom was still living a relatively independent lifestyle in 2017. We had done considerable work to get back to her pre-open heart surgery baseline. She was walking without a walker or cane. She was active and had great stamina. She was living alone in her home at Nantuckett, but my visits were more frequent during the day and longer in duration.

There was not much to report on my business during 2017. I had the three locations of Gilbert, Chandler and Tempe, and they were all doing well. Substantial changes were coming in the new year.

On December 18, *"This year marks the 18th Christmas with mom since dad passed away in 2000. We have a tradition of going out, picking our tree, and decorating it together, well she does most of the work."*

On December 19, *"Mom and I are excited as we were going to watch the new Star Wars movie <u>The Last Jedi</u> at Fat Cats in Gilbert."* Mom and I loved our movies, and we loved the Star Wars movies. She walked into the theater under her own power, and we got our usual snacks and popcorn.

A decline in health leading to end-of-life happens to all of us. Mom's end-of-life decline started in 2017. She spent 43 days in the hospital that year. We all handle and deal with the end-of-life differently. Mom dealt with the end-of-life in the same manner she lived her life, with endless amounts of grit and grace.

CHAPTER 10
Stroke
(2018)

"Success is not measured by what a person accomplishes, but by the opposition they have encountered and the courage with which they maintained the struggle against overwhelming odds."

- Charles Lindbergh

We started 2018 full of hope, but we were wary after the serious scare during the previous Thanksgiving. It started to feel too risky for mom to be alone. I instituted a life alert service for her to carry around her neck in case of emergency. The service would be instructed to call me if mom pressed the button and mom would be able to talk to one of the operators directly on the device after she pressed the button.

On January 4, *"The lease has been signed; location number 4 has been born. More announcements to come."* Glendale Dogs

 was the newest location added to my family of shops. I took over a commercial suite that was previously a dog daycare but closed for months. So, when I finally got it open, it was like starting from scratch. It was a big challenge to start a location from scratch that was over 30 miles away and often a one-hour drive.

Also in early January, we got the sad news that mom's dear companion, Brandy, had severe congestive heart failure after getting an echocardiogram. Her ejection fraction which measured her heart function was low, and she was not expected to live much longer. She was so important to mom. She was the centerpiece of mom's motivation to get home after heart surgery. They had a close bond ever since we brought her home at 4 months old.

Towards the end of January, I made a trip out of the country for the first time in 12 years. Mom was stable after her heart surgery, and more importantly, she was stable mentally so I could go away for the short 4-day trip, and she would be okay. My sisters stayed with her, and everything went fine as I visited the Panama Canal.

On January 29, I captured a picture of mom and her best girl, Brandy out on a walk in the neighborhood. The two were both suffering from advanced congestive heart failure, and they were out on their first walk together since they both returned home from the hospital. They were both slowed considerably by their CHF. Of the two, Brandy's condition was more serious.

At the end of February, mom's health took another turn for the worse, she had a serious stroke. I took her to Banner Gateway, just a couple of miles from her house. She was disoriented and feeling ill. Unfortunately, she was not diagnosed soon enough, so corrective measures were not taken in a timely fashion. She was severely anemic, which was likely the precursor to the stroke. Anemia is a condition when the body does not have enough healthy red blood cells or hemoglobin to carry oxygen to the body's tissues. The anemia was likely brought on by a bleeding ulcer that had yet to be diagnosed.

It was a vicious cycle of bleeding internally from an ulcer that was brought on by stress and diet. The internal bleeding would lead to anemia that would lead to more severe conditions such as stroke or heart attack. The bleeding internally was sporadic and could never be resolved, just managed the best we could. Through the years, she went through extensive testing with gastroenterologists. They never could find where she was bleeding specifically. And again, even if they could, the bleeding ulcer would come and go.

We did not fully understand the severity of her condition until they came back with the stroke diagnosis. It was not a major stroke, but not a minor one either. Her ability to speak and walk were both impaired from this episode. She was transferred to the nearby Banner Baywood Hospital which was the regional base for heart and stroke issues. In all, she was in the hospital for four days. She was given a couple of blood transfusions to help with her low hemoglobin.

On March 1, she applied and was accepted to attend the acute rehab facility, Rhodes Rehab. It was a blessing that she got

accepted to Rhodes again, it was considered one of the best rehab facilities in Phoenix, and it would mean her therapy would be conducted by many of the therapists we got to know so well after heart surgery. Acute rehab is intensive rehabilitation, often 3-5 hours per day which helps expedite recovery after significant issues such as stroke and heart surgery. Not everyone qualifies, only people who are deemed with the character and ability to do the demanding work during acute rehab. This time, speech therapy would be the primary focus and concern.

On March 3, *"Working the bike after a 300-foot walk."* Her sense of balance was permanently impaired this time around. She would need a walker going forward. She was also having difficulty speaking and had some comprehension problems. It was such a blessing to see Brian at physical therapy once again. He was mom's physical therapy after her heart surgery in 2017. Mom and I were both fond of him. He was tough and firm, which is exactly what mom and I both respected. I had so much admiration for him and all his colleagues in rehab. I could have seen myself doing something like that in my life. It would have been a rewarding career.

Also, on March 3, mom's sweet dog Brandy came to visit her at the rehab center where she was living temporarily. Brandy was extremely ill with advanced congestive heart failure, but I think she liked coming over to see her mom as the dogs were wondering about her absence. Mom felt she needed to get home to take care of her.

A week later, on March 10, she was now about 8 days into her acute rehab. We tried to get her outside as much as possible for fresh air. She was so happy to see Jonesey and all her dogs when we ventured outside. We would frequently make a video call from home to the hospital so mom could see I was feeding them correctly. It gave her great satisfaction to see the live video, but she still wanted to get home as soon as possible to do it herself.

During the time between therapy sessions, I would frequently show mom videos of memorable moments together to bring her some happiness and motivation to return home. One of my favorite videos to show her was the trip we made to South Fork in 2010 to commemorate our first 10-years together after dad's death and to remember dad. The song used in the video, "Somewhere My Love" by Ray Conniff and his singers had become our favorite song through the years. I would play the video and song, and I would encourage mom to sing the words as it was good practice to help her with cognition and speech after the stroke.

On March 12, it was 14 total days in the hospital when combining hospital plus rehabilitation. The rehab center tried to do meals in a community environment, and it was nice. We were sitting at the community breakfast table, ready for our work/rehab schedule for the day. I would preach three major points to mom – *"Eat well, sleep well, and work hard--God will do the rest."*

After 19 days in the hospital, mom came home on March 19; it was a long, hard time. She had a lot of challenges and the work in rehab was difficult and tiring. Speaking was a little more challenging now and her balance was impacted. She was on anti-stroke blood thinners, but this is where another major problem emerged. Blood thinners are not prescribed for people who bleed. She had that bleeding ulcer problem causing anemia and all the other problems previously mentioned like more strokes and heart attacks if her hemoglobin gets too low. Conversely, without blood thinners, the likelihood of a severe stroke was greater. This would be an ongoing challenge to manage this complex health predicament.

On April 1, I had a ribbon-cutting ceremony to open the newly built Chandler Dogs. I was able to renovate a suite in the same shopping center and have twice as much space for the dogs. This was my first major renovation with a bank loan after 9 years of running the company.

I was nervous about spending a half million dollars on a renovation, but I had faith it was going to work out for the best. To keep growing, at some point, it's important to involve bank loans to help the growth continue.

I wish mom could have attended the ribbon cutting, but I decided it was best for her to stay home so soon after her stroke. It was a nice event, there were a lot of people that attended the ceremony. This was my second major venture in a month. First, I opened the brand-new Glendale Dogs in March and now the new Chandler Dogs in early April. It was an exciting time, but a financially stressful time to have 4 locations and a big bank loan.

In mid-April, we visited a local urgent care to have them look at mom's arm. Mom had very thin skin and would roughhouse with the dogs. At times, it would lead to skin flaps getting torn. This occasion was bad enough to require a visit and medical attention with a proper wrap.

In late April, I captured a great picture of mom and Brandy out in the yard enjoying each other's company.

I was also realizing mom needed to live in the same house with me again. She was still independent, but it was clear that her health was declining over the last 1 ½ years— with her triple bypass, open-heart surgery and now a significant stroke. I was spending increased time with her at the Nantuckett house. The problem with moving was my business loan. The loan had a lien on my house, and it wasn't so easy to move the lien. I began working on it knowing it had to be done. For over 10 years, we had lived in two separate houses, about 3 miles away. I needed to sell both houses and move us into one new home.

In late May, Doug and I took our regular trip up into the mountains for some rest and relaxation and always competitive games. I won Scrabble and Dominos; Doug did best with Trivia. My dogs Saint and Sasha were also joining us on this trip. It was a nice break after the stressful time in the hospital with the stroke and difficult rehab. Going out into nature has long been my mental health therapy.

190

In early June, mom and I watched the Food Channel a lot. We liked duplicating some of the deserts we would see on television if they didn't appear too difficult. On this occasion, we made a pistachio cake. I bought a green flower arrangement to go with it. Mom and I did a lot of cooking projects together as a team. We would get the shopping list together, drive over to our favorite Fry's and then methodically go through the recipe step by step.

On June 9, it had been 12 years since a beautiful love affair for the ages began, and I had a great partner in the care of mom. Her name was Brandy. She was the yellow lab mom fell in love with and was the light of her life. Through the years, they were constant companions. They were perfect for each other because they were both sweet and kind-natured souls. Brandy's heart finally failed on June 9. Oh, what a special heart it was. On Friday, June 8 she was not able to stand any longer. I tried throughout the day to help her. I asked a trusted employee to come over and look at her. We thought it best to schedule a vet appointment for the next morning. I decided to sleep with her on the floor to comfort her through the night. She started to have seizures and gasped for air, both complications from her heart failure. It was terribly distressing to experience. I was crying as I tried to comfort her. At 1 a.m. Saturday morning, I woke my frail mother and told her we needed to take Brandy to the hospital and stop her suffering. We can't let our girl suffer any longer, and we need to be with her. Mom agreed.

When Brandy suffered her initial heart failure in January, it wasn't her time. She had important work to do for 6 more months. She had one closing chapter of purpose, to give and receive love from mom. She had to help mom get through her stroke and rehabilitation. From the terrific book, <u>A Dog's Purpose</u>, the

conclusion was that a dog's purpose is to love us. Brandy loved us so much and loved mom so much. She was mom's special guardian angel for 12 years. Thank you, my dear Brandy. You were the daily motivation through heart surgery, stroke and several weeks in rehab along the way. For mom, it was all about getting home from the hospital to see Brandy. What a beautiful journey.

About a week after Brandy passed away, mom was experiencing chest pains. We visited the local hospital, Banner Gateway, and had her checked out. She stayed overnight and was released the next day.

On June 19, I posted on social media how much I loved Sasha, a.k.a. Cha-Cha Fancy. With mom's health and my business, I needed stress relief. In the caregiver world, it is called respite.

192

The dictionary definition of respite is *"A Short period of rest or relief from something difficult or unpleasant."* I did not get a whole lot of respite over the years, but I managed my own stress and mental health by spending time with Cha-Cha. It was short walks when I was able or a car ride around the neighborhood. I just thought the world of her.

We returned to the emergency room on June 22. Mom's arm was swollen, and it was hurting. The swelling made her arm twice the size of normal. She had an infection and remained in the hospital for a couple of days for care and treatment.

At the end of June, I had one of my scariest moments. I was waking up one morning and my sleeping companion and wingman for the last 10 years, Fritz, was also waking up. He did his normal routine of walking down his stairway off the bed and walked outside to go potty. I heard him jump through the doggy door twice (once out and once in) knowing he was heading back into bed. He climbed up the stairs, and then just suddenly fell over.

I looked up and saw that he was lifeless. I started to panic. I picked him up and ran around not knowing what to do, then finally ran out into the garage, only to realize I was still in my underwear. I ran back into the house, by now sobbing. I gently laid Fritz on my bed while I put on clothes as fast as I could. I thought to myself, if only I could rush him to the hospital, maybe they could shock his heart. After finally getting dressed, I picked him up again, got into my car and started racing to the nearby pet emergency room. I held him in one arm as I drove with the other. I called him hoping he would wake up, but he wasn't moving, he was lifeless. It had now been about 15 minutes before I arrived at the emergency room parking lot. I ran into the emergency room lobby asking for help. I said, *"I don't know if he's alive, please help him!"*

They took him back and set up an emergency, critical care triage for Fritz. It was about 15 minutes later, they came out and told me, *"He's still alive, but in critical condition."* They treated him for about 3 days in the emergency hospital. He was having congestive heart failure, and his lungs were filling with fluid, as his heart and kidneys were no longer efficiently removing the fluids in his body causing a tear in his heart. They started him on a couple of different diuretics.

I got to take him home finally, but he was extremely weak. My other dogs, especially Sasha helped me nurse Fritz back into reasonable health, but his health was deteriorating. Within a span of a week, I almost lost two of my dear fur children from the same health problem—congestive heart failure. I was so thankful that I was given a little more time with Fritz. I enjoyed every minute with him after that scary early morning moment.

 At the end of August, Doug and I went on a trip of a lifetime, it was a bucket list trip. We took a passenger train from Flagstaff, Arizona, to Denver, Colorado, and then through the Rocky Mountains all the way to the California coast and San Francisco. From there, it was down to Los Angeles and back over to our stop in Phoenix. The trip took about a week as we slept and stayed in our private cabin on the train. It was quite an experience for both of us.

The rest of the summer and early fall were quiet and stable for mom and for Fritz. On October 16, I took Fritz to his 3-month echo

194

follow-up with his cardiologist, and everything looked good. He was starting to get back to normal, slowly but surely.

On October 17, I took my big fur kid Saint who was a 115 pound, 10-year-old elite athlete, for a run. He had been running with his sister Cha-Cha Fancy and me for years. When he started to run, he was a force of nature, a runaway freight train going down the track. Cha-Cha and I held on for dear life. By the Fall of 2018, Saint and I had been running every morning for over six years. When Sasha joined the family in 2014, the three of us would run every morning. It was an exciting time and an amazing sight to see this big guy running at full gallop.

On October 30, Cha-Cha and I visited the Halloween party at Chandler Dogs. The Chandler team blew me away with their decorations. I think they got a hundred visitors that night. Sasha and I were dressed as his and her Sun Devils.

All year, I had been working on a project to sell both my house and mom's house. As previously mentioned, it was hard to do as I had a business lien on my personal residence. With mom's health deteriorating, I needed to live in the same house with her again. I did a lot of research and found these homes called NextGen. They were two homes under the same roof. A  normal main house and a smaller house with one bedroom, one bathroom, its own kitchen, its own backyard, its own garage and its own front door. Mom and I were roommates again, but still maintaining some independence at "Shirley's Place."

I was relieved to have her under the same roof again, but mom was downright giddy to be living with me once more. Of course, she was in on the secret move, but I did not tell anyone else until the walkthrough day which just happened to be on mom's birthday. I got all my sisters in the car with mom and told them we were going on a surprise trip. They could not imagine where we were going. They had no idea; mom kept the secret perfectly. We drove up to the new house, and I announced, "Welcome to our new house—Mom and I." They were so happy and shocked. They also were nervous about mom living alone a lot of the time when I wasn't there. I got everything worked out with the selling of both houses, buying one new house and getting the business lien transferred. It was a great ending to a big year.

On December 10, mom had a bad hyperglycemia event with her diabetes. Her blood sugar level exploded to over 600. She remained in the hospital for 3 days to get her sugars under control.

The year saw mom's stroke and rehab, selling both of our houses and moving into a new one. With the business—moving my Chandler location to a new place and opening a new facility in Glendale. With our dogs, it was the passing of our sweet Brandy girl and the near passing of my wingman Fritz.

The year 2018 was finally ending after 33 days in the hospital. We were optimistic and in a better place with all those emotional ups and downs. We finished the year with Christmas number 19 together, in the new house.

CHAPTER 11
Shingles
(2019)

"Courage is not having the strength to go on; it is going on when you don't have the strength."

-Theodore Roosevelt

We were hopeful that 2019 was going to be a good year. We even dared to think it would be a return to normal. Yet, it was destined to be the year of the shingles. As in 2017 with open-heart surgery and 2018 with the stroke, mom was in another battle in 2019. This time it was the shingles virus and its related complications.

As 2018 ended and 2019 began, I was continually looking for ways to take preventive measures for mom's health. The doctor recommended she get vaccinated for shingles. It was a two-shot regimen during a 60-day window. She got her first shot. Then, as either luck would have it, or the vaccine caused it—she developed the shingles rash.

Shingles (herpes zoster) is an infection that causes a painful rash. It is caused by the varicella-zoster virus (VZV). This is the same virus that causes chickenpox. After a person had chickenpox, the virus stays in the body. It may not cause problems for many years.

In early 2019, we made the momentous change, from mom's house with two dogs and two cats and my house with three dogs, to a new blended home with all of us together. Mom's connecting house and my house each had private backyards separated by a fence, so the dogs were kept separate. Most of them would have gotten along, but I didn't want to risk any issues with the two alpha males—Saint in my house and Bubba in mom's house. Plus, Bubba and Jonesey were mom's dogs primarily and her therapy dogs. Fritz, Saint and Sasha (Cha-Cha) had been my dear furkids for many years. We had been inseparable for the five years since Cha-Cha joined our pack in 2014. Saint and Fritz go back even longer—eight years since they started living together. We were all happy to be in the new blended home.

On a personal note, I was getting back to my avid reading habits in the winter of that year. I love to listen to audiobooks, and I set the goal of about 50-70 books a year. By the end of March, I had completed over 30 books. I generally read history and biographies. I consider life a continuous classroom of learning. I know I am in a good place when I am reading. It is one of my good habits that usually suffers when things are not right in life.

I was also active in attending Arizona State basketball games. They had a good team that year, and I attended several games with various family members. I would often splurge on the tickets and get seats close to the floor for everyone to enjoy. I treated my brother-in-law and nephew to tickets and accommodations at the big year-end tournament in Las Vegas in March. We stopped by Hoover Dam and enjoyed the sights on the way to Las Vegas.

Since my best friend Fritz had his near-death experience in July of 2018, I was enjoying every precious day with him. I wrote an article on April 4 of 2019 to commemorate our wonderful life together and the difficult experience we had the previous year. I said in the article regarding time since his ailment...

"Nine months and two days later, Fritz is doing very well. He is running around living his life and barking his head off like a good wiener was supposed to do. At times, he is even more spirited than before. He continues to have heart problems, but every day is a

blessing. A great lesson for us is to sometimes be a dog, live in the moment and enjoy each day."

The shingles journey began in earnest in early February. I wasn't sure what was going on. I was seeing a relapse of mom's bipolar disorder behavior. She was complaining of terrible pain and acting peculiar. It was hard to know what to believe when bipolar was involved.

For mom, it was an utterly miserable and an excruciatingly painful illness. We tried narcotics first to help her with the pain, but it was not working. In a rare occurrence of recklessness, mom took a heavy dose of unsupervised narcotics, resulting in an overdose. She was not herself and certainly in an altered mental state. I checked the narcotics pill bottle and noticed she had taken several pills to help with pain. She was having a tough time staying conscious and lucid after the overdose.

On February 10, I rushed her to the hospital and checked her into the emergency room. They kept her in the hospital for 3 days. Not only were the narcotics ineffective for her shingles pain, but she was having a bad reaction to them. She was prescribed a drug called gabapentin to help with the pain. Gabapentin was a medication for neuropathic-related pain. It was her savior and her demon at the same time. It did give her some relief from the pain, but one of the side effects produced uncontrollable muscle spasms causing her to lose her balance and occasionally fall. It also had a strange interaction with her mentally. She was beginning to have more mental illness issues such as delusions and hallucinations that had been dormant for 25 years. It was a daily struggle to battle the physical pain and the mental delusions caused by the illness. Her shingles raged on for several months.

On February 22, mom was hospitalized for more complications related to shingles. When mom was in pain, she would bleed internally from an ulcer. The bleeding would make her anemic and great stress on her already failing heart and kidneys. She would experience heart attack-like pain and experience fluid overload due to the heart not working efficiently. With fluid overload came congestive heart failure/kidney failure and difficulty breathing. On this hospital visit, she required a blood transfusion and intravenous diuretics. Mentally, it was the neuropathic nature of shingles that I thought was tapping into her dormant bipolar disorder. She was hospitalized for about a week this time. The pain from the shingles and how to treat it properly was difficult especially with how it was interacting neurologically with mom. She came home on February 27.

Mom fell in the kitchen due to her gabapentin related leg spasms on March 1. She hurt her shoulder, and I took her to urgent care first and then they recommended we go to the emergency room. This time, I traveled up to our old Banner Hospital, Gateway. I wasn't completely satisfied with the Mercy Gilbert Hospital experience; so, I changed hospitals. They took X-rays and luckily did not find any fractures or injuries. She was discharged the same day.

On April 9, I called 911 at 4:42 PM, mom was having an acute breathing emergency. Paramedics arrived at the house and administered oxygen and tried a breathing treatment. They proceeded to rush her to the emergency room at Banner Gateway Hospital. They required 10 days to get her symptoms under control. She had a UTI (urinary tract infection) which contributed to the fluid overload, a symptom of her congestive heart failure. She also had highly elevated blood pressure (hypertension). She was probably 10-15 pounds heavier with fluid which greatly limited her ability to breathe. She was still in an altered mental state from the gabapentin medication she was taking for shingles. Also, her electrolytes were out of sync. All of it was intermingling and making a proper path for care and recovery difficult.

During this hospitalization, I was taking a break from the hospital on an April day in 2019. Then I got a phone call from my sister Donna at the hospital. She said, "Mom is unresponsive". They called a rapid-response team to her hospital room to begin emergency procedures to gain a response. I was driving at the time and immediately redirected myself back to the hospital. My sister was in a panic, and the hospital response team was not having any success.

I was concerned, but not overly worried. I knew mom's current condition was heavily influenced by an illness and medication causing an altered mental state—shingles & gabapentin respectively. I returned to the hospital and then to mom's hospital room. The room was full of medical professionals. I maneuvered myself to her bedside, and I started talking to her and told her to respond, with emphasis! She began talking and a sly grin emerged. Everyone, including the medical professionals, thought she had taken a terrible turn for the worse. I suspected mom just didn't feel like talking and was being cantankerous.

The medical staff eventually got her excess water pulled from her body and her kidney function continued its downward spiral as it would get damaged with each subsequent episode of edema— swelling caused by too much fluid trapped in the body's tissues. Edema can affect any part of the body, but it's more likely to show up in the legs and feet. Her kidneys were not failing yet, but they continued to progress towards inevitable failure. After 10 difficult days, she was discharged.

On April 23, by a vote of 7-0, the City of Tempe approved our permit to build an outside area at my Tempe Dogs location. It was nice to get final approval from the Tempe City Council to build an outside area. In the dog business, having an outside area was a big deal. Tempe Dogs 24/7 had gone four years without an outside area after its initial permit was approved in 2015.

By May, mom was starting to recover from the shingles. We had lived in our new house for a few months and were enjoying it. Since I gave all the dogs a daily walk, it was a lot easier having everyone in the same house. By now, we had a good daily routine. We celebrated by baking a double-decker lemon cake that we ate slowly over about a week and a half.

Later in the summer, mom, Kristy and I met in Greer to enjoy some cool weather and watch the annual parade in that small town. We took mom's dogs Bubba and Jonesey with us as we all enjoyed the cool weather.

Also in June, I was out for my normal walk with Saint and Sasha. I had retired Saint from running about a year earlier because his breathing was labored. This morning, we had gotten about a mile away from the house and Saint started to struggle with his breathing. I stopped and tried to calm him down, but nothing was working. I was a mile away from the house, and my gigantic dog could not breathe and was unable to walk. I knew he needed to get to the dog emergency room right away, so I wrapped his leash around a road sign and tried to secure it. Then, I ran home with Sasha; I was in a panic. I was completely exhausted when I got home and quickly got Sasha in my Jeep and drove back to where I left Saint along the road 10 minutes earlier. I was able to get Saint in the Jeep, and we drove as quickly as possible to the veterinary emergency room. Saint received emergency treatment, and they got his breathing under control. He was diagnosed with a collapsed trachea which wasn't allowing him to breathe normally. I was so thankful he made it. From that day forward, he had to retire from, not only running but also from, walking as well.

It was Saint who started the tradition of car rides after his June 2019 breathing incident. Since he couldn't go for walks any longer, I would take him and his sister Sasha for a car ride each day. He loved to get out to see, smell and feel the world around him. We would drive to the local convenience store and get a snack as part of our morning ritual. I would open the windows and let him enjoy the experience to its fullest.

We would get home, and I would take Saint into the house and then pack up Sasha for a one-on-one walk at one of the nearby nature preserves. I tried to make it as painless as possible for Saint as he hated to miss out on the walk with Sasha, and he didn't understand why he was missing out. I would walk them both into the garage and into the house, but only to let Saint in. He would usually lay in the hallway connecting the garage until our return. When Sasha and I returned, he was still waiting for us, and she would run down the hallway and jump over him each morning. I think it was her way of rubbing it in that she got a walk, and he didn't. He would quickly go and smell her and try and figure out where she had just come from. He knew he missed out on something.

In the middle of July, mom and I went out to one of our

favorite places, Dairy Queen. We loved DQ because we could get a delicious meal, and then have our favorite dip cone afterwards. We were regularly getting out and enjoying life whenever we could. Life is not about getting to a destination; it is about the journey. It is all about the little things in life that bring enjoyment, even for just a few minutes.

On July 23, we had a big announcement, it was

the opening of our 5th location, Phoenix Dogs 24/7. The doggy daycare, boarding facility and grooming salon near 32nd Street and Shea was rebranded to the name of Phoenix Dogs 24/7 on July 23, 2019.

After opening four locations from scratch, I tried the acquisition route for the first time in July of 2019, making it my fifth location overall. It was a successful acquisition, and it was one I hoped to duplicate many times in the future. I rebranded the facility and inherited its fine staff and loyal clientele. Madison Van Houten was the manager of Phoenix Dogs and would go on to a position of senior leadership and a close confidant.

One week later on July 26, my wingman and best friend, Fritz, died suddenly from complications related to pancreatitis. The death of a person's dog can be every bit as hard as the loss of a family member, sometimes even greater. We raise our dogs from when they are puppies, and they are our children. It feels very unnatural for a "child" to die before the parents, but that is what happens with our canine loved ones.

In the case of Fritz, we were inseparable for 10 years, day and night. He laid under my blankets down by my legs every night for 10 years. That sort of relationship is irreplaceable. I wrote this note at the time of his death in remembrance of him.

Thank you, Fritz. Thank you for making me laugh. Thank you for being my co-pilot in business and in life. Thank you for unapologetically barking your head off anytime you wanted. Thank you for your continuous devotion and love. Thank you for the wonderful memories that I will forever cherish. Our 10 years were the best 10 years of my life. I will miss you terribly.

When I took Fritz into the emergency room for a second time, I felt deep down that this might be it. He was not himself, and something was horribly wrong. I remember quietly sitting in the waiting room sobbing to myself. I also remember a young family in the waiting room at the same time and a few of them were crying as well for their loved one. Animal emergency rooms are sad places. This time sticks out to me as I felt despair and loneliness at the possibility of losing my Fritz. I didn't have anyone in my life other than my mother who was able to comfort me, and with all her medical issues, she wasn't in her right mind to be my comforter. I came to realize that great losses like this are often turning points in life as I sat there in the emergency room alone.

On July 27, the kind people at the rescue where I adopted Fritz put out this post.

"The Friends for Life Nation is sad to learn that little Fritz, adopted years ago at BARKtoberfest, has crossed the Rainbow Bridge. His dad, Stephen, owns Gilbert Dogs (and Tempe, Chandler, Mesa etc.) and has been a supporter since the first day they opened their doors. We were so happy when Fritz and Stephen found each other that day, and our collective hearts hurt for him now. Thank you, Stephen, for giving Fritz the home we dream of for all our furry friends. Hugs to you and your family as you mourn your boy."

The next day on July 28, mom and I traveled to San Manuel to the memorial service of my dad's close first cousin Robert Mayes.

Bobby was more than a first cousin to my dad; they were best friends growing up. I got to know Bobby pretty well when I traveled to his house before my auntie's memorial in 2017. I wanted to visit with him to learn more about their childhood together in research for the eulogy. I found Bobby to be a kind man. Mom, even with all her medical issues, traveled to San Manuel with me for the memorial. I got up and spoke at the event and talked about Bobby's childhood with dad. Mom and I got in town early enough to enjoy some local Mexican food for lunch before the memorial.

On August 7, I wrote a final article about losing Fritz. I went through all the emotions associated with grief and loss.

"A Wonderful Life"

During the sickness and death of our loved ones, we go through a rollercoaster of emotions.

Resentment – I was resentful of the emergency room vet for not diagnosing him properly given his symptom of excessive vomiting.

Guilt – I felt guilt for not taking him to the emergency room sooner. I felt guilty that I didn't recognize his proper diagnosis myself through better personal research.

Hope – I gathered hope when I took him to my personal vet the next day where he got the proper diagnosis with a positive test of acute pancreatitis. They began immediate, aggressive intensive care.

Guilt & Anger – After researching acute pancreatitis, which was on the list of 20 possible reasons for excessive vomiting, I felt the guilt again for not figuring out the diagnosis and the anger again at the emergency room.

Sorrow – When driving to meet with my vet to plan out his next step in recovery, I got the call that he had taken a turn for the worse and was in critical condition. I was asked to please hurry. I immediately started sobbing behind the wheel, impairing my ability to drive safely. It hit me like a sledgehammer.

Grief – I arrived in time to stop his pain and put my boy to rest. He was being kept alive but could no longer make it on his own. My profound sadness was overwhelming.

Loneliness – Fritz was the center of my world for 10 years. My other dogs – particularly Sasha felt the sadness and loneliness as well. We were lost and lonely.

Gratitude – Friends For Life Animal Rescue ran a post in honor of my boy Fritz that touched me deeply. Barktoberfest was a special time for Fritz and me. For nine years, we proudly walked in the alumni parade. It meant so much to both of us.

AND THEN a couple of days after the post, a lady I had never met, named Tara O. responded. She said she knew Fritz. She was at Barktoberfest on that October day in 2009, the day I adopted him. She and her family had decided to adopt him after lunch. As fate would have it, I arrived just a few minutes before she returned to adopt him. She was disappointed, but decided to adopt another dog, and she had renamed him Fritz in honor of the original Fritz, my boy.

Appreciation - This post response had a profound effect on me and made me think that I had arrived just minutes away from not having the best 10 years of my life. I am so grateful I got there first; my life had been so positively impacted by my little wiener boy. Tara O.'s Fritz was still alive, and they had a wonderful life together too.

Love – *Some things are out of our power and control. Life happens, and sometimes it is hard to rationalize. Bitterness, anger and guilt are emotions that can overwhelm us. I missed Fritz and cried often from losing him. But I'm so thankful for that post from Tara O. It put everything into perspective for me. What a wonderful life we had. Until we meet again, on the other side of the rainbow bridge, I expect to see his spirit in other dogs that I meet along the way. And God, please be patient with his barking, that is just who he is.*

In mid-August, I took a trip to Rome. I played it safe with a short trip, only four days counting travel. With mom's health, I didn't want to be gone long. One of my sisters stayed with mom. I visited Vatican City and went on several tours in Ancient Rome. It was tedious with my non-stop schedule. I had a tour that started within an hour after the long flight across the ocean. I saw a lot of sights that I had wanted to see for a long time, but it was not as enjoyable as I would have hoped because it was so rushed.

On August 31, mom and I attended a special 90th birthday party for my Uncle Gene. Both mom and I loved him dearly. It was a big party with a lot of people, held at his assisted living facility where he was living. It was hard for mom to attend the party, but she arrived under her own power and loved spending a few minutes with my uncle. We bought him several fun gifts with a Coors Beer theme. It was ironic that most people at the birthday party would have believed that mom was in worse health than my uncle. It was not an easy

210

path for mom to live at home instead of assisted living, but it was what she wanted. She wanted to be home with her dogs and me.

On September 8, mom complained of feeling weak and not right. I took her to the emergency room at Mercy Gilbert Hospital. After two days of treatment, she was discharged. Her hemoglobin was down to 5.8 which was far below normal. They gave her a blood transfusion of one unit of blood to raise it up to 8.3 which was still below normal. So, more problems with hemoglobin were destined soon.

On September 20, I had lunch with mom on my birthday. We ate at one of our favorite restaurants for lunch, Texas Roadhouse. She got her usual--a big country fried steak with a baked potato and green beans. I have never been a fan of parties or any fanfare. It had usually been just mom and me.

On October 5, mom complained of chest pains, so we took her to the hospital. She was kept for observation for three days. Her hemoglobin was stable, so she wasn't actively bleeding. Blood pressure was elevated. She was stabilized and later discharged.

On November 2, mom turned 83 years young. Six weeks after my birthday, we were out celebrating mom's birthday at one of her favorite restaurants, Olive Garden. It was about two miles away from our new home in south Gilbert. She loved ordering soup as a starter, then her favorite, lasagna, and a glass of red wine. We stopped by the jewelry store, and she picked out a bracelet as a present. She would collaborate with the store attendant to find the most expensive jewelry available. I smiled mischievously at her and the attendant for their bracelet selection.

On November 8, I called 911 at 5:49 AM for mom. We normally woke up at about 5 AM each day. We tried a breathing treatment, and it wasn't helping. Her oxygen level was low, and she was struggling more than usual.   We needed emergency help at the house. Paramedics would arrive fast, usually five minutes or so. Mom was taken to the emergency room where they gave her diuretics intravenously while simultaneously supporting her breathing with a ventilator. She was discharged from the hospital two days later on November 10, and she attended Uncle Gene's memorial on the very same day where she sat 2 rows away from the front where I gave the eulogy.

On November 10, I had the great honor of giving the eulogy at my Uncle Gene's memorial. I loved my uncle and shared a kindred spirit with him as he and I had a similar experience of taking care of our moms for many years. I shared a note he  sent to me and a poem I wrote in his honor during the eulogy.

Before my uncle died, he sent me a private message on Facebook that I cherish.

"Have been meaning to tell you something for a long time. I so respect you for the way you take care of your mom. You are an exceptional person. Decided to get this said before I go out yonder. -Uncle"

My eulogy poem in honor of my uncle was entitled "Out Yonder".

Out Yonder

You had a big personality from Texas, the lone star state.
Moving to Arizona to impact our lives was your fate.

A lifetime of people, they all knew you were smart.
Yes, a big brain, but an even bigger heart.

Your kindness was beyond compare.
Your storytelling always told with a flair.

You were a good mentor, a good provider, a good dad.
It was Papa with the next generation, ah to know him, everyone was glad.

Oh, your laugh, so infectious.
You made everyone happy, it was so precious.

Your heaven on Earth was Black River, fishing for bass.
Later in the night—it was poker, steaks, Coors, and a little bourbon in a glass.

All your adulthood, you were with your wife.
Gene & Jean—what a couple—what a beautiful life.

I imagine you now with my dad and granddad back at Canyon Cove.
Planning your next trip to the reservation, hiking down to Black River at Stove.

Life after death was tough for you and for all of us to ponder.
My dear Uncle, you were one in a million and we all hope to see you again out yonder.

On November 19, I needed to take mom to the emergency room at Banner Gateway Hospital. Mom was short of breath and didn't feel good. This stay was relatively brief for her, just 24 hours. They gave her various breathing treatments and extra diuretics. They thought it was something allergic.

December 11 was a full family car ride in the morning. By this time, we were having a daily ritual of a long car ride every morning with mom, Saint and Sasha. I would set up a ramp for Saint to climb into the jeep. He could no longer jump in.

On December 14, I called 911 at 1:08 AM. Mom called for help in the night with her panic button. As I got into the room, her oxygen was low. We tried a breathing treatment and calming exercises, but it didn't work, and I called 911. Paramedics arrived quickly as usual. They performed further treatments but couldn't get her stable. They rushed her to the emergency room at Mercy Gilbert Hospital for further treatment. At the hospital, they treated her with intravenous diuretics and antibiotics. She showed steady improvement and was discharged after three days.

On December 22, we celebrated our 20th Christmas together,  just mom and me. We finished up our first year in the new house together. It wasn't what we hoped it would be, but life rarely is what we expect. We navigated the tough times and enjoyed all the little moments of life, even if they were for just a few minutes.

On December 24, we opened presents as usual and drove around the neighborhood to look at the lights and listen to Christmas music. We even stopped by McDonalds and got a milkshake to add to our night of tradition. She went to bed around 8:00 PM.

A couple of hours later, she had a breathing emergency. She pressed her panic button asking for me to rush into her bedroom. After evaluating her condition and oxygen level, I called 911 at 10:10 PM that night. Paramedics arrived quickly and checked her vitals and found her blood pressure was 240/93 and an oxygen level of 68. They rushed her to the hospital and started her on a nitroglycerin drip, antibiotics, and a diuretics drip as well. She was

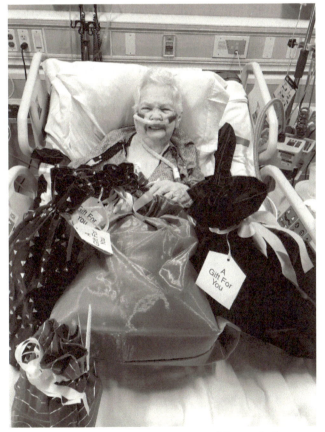

then transferred to the ICU. This was not going to be a quick fix. She had infection in her lungs, edema, and out-of-control hypertension.

After she was stabilized, I brought the rest of her presents into the hospital since it was going to be Christmas in the ICU this year. After much work, the medical professionals got her stable and she was discharged after seven days in the hospital. As usual in these situations, her condition was often critical, and survival was far from a sure thing.

With the year now at an end and mom going home just before New Year's Day, it turned out to be another difficult year, progressively harder each year. It was a year of profound loss with the death of my uncle and the death of my Fritz. When totaling mom's days in the hospital during 2019–it was 39. There were four 911 calls, seven trips to the emergency rooms and three transfers to the ICU.

I think in 2019, I wanted to believe life would get back to normal. The worst was behind us, I thought. I wanted to believe we learned from past issues, and we were now better prepared, and it was going to get back to normal. That was our attitude— whether it be my hip disease as a child or her bipolar disorder in her midlife—we would face the challenge and conquer it.

However, dealing with end-of-life decline and more importantly, accepting the decline was a foreign concept for me. For better or for worse, it was not in my DNA, and I never handled it well all the way to the end. We conquered and defeated things and then moved on. I think after 2019, I continued with this internal yin/yang dichotomy...between slowly accepting decline and fighting it tooth and nail.

CHAPTER 12
Congestive Heart Failure
(2020)

"We don't always succeed in what we try, certainly not by the world's standards, but I think you'll find it's the willingness to keep trying that matters most."

-Fred Rodgers

As mom came home from the hospital on New Year's Eve 2019, my brother-in-law, nephew and I flew to El Paso to watch Arizona State in the Sun Bowl. Mom was stable at home and Donna was staying with her. We flew back the next day on January 1, 2020, to Phoenix after an ASU win.

Unfortunately, mom's health deteriorated again quickly. Late in the night on January 4, mom called me on her panic device. When I arrived in her room, I could see she was not doing well; she was speaking and was okay with us driving over to the emergency room at Mercy Gilbert Hospital.

At check-in, her respiratory rate was elevated, her blood pressure slightly high, but her weight was extra high, over 140 pounds. Her body was experiencing severe edema—water retention and swelling. Her hemoglobin was low, 8.3, and her blood sugar was high, over 350. These were indications her body was fighting hard and under extreme stress. They moved her from the Emergency Room to the Intensive Care Unit (ICU). As her stay in the hospital progressed to day 2, her white blood cell counts skyrocketed indicating infection. Her electrolytes were all out of kilter because her kidneys were not cleaning her blood properly.

This stay exhibited the classic challenges of treating her complex health profile. She needed a blood transfusion, but not until her fluid overload was removed. After fluid removal and a blood transfusion, the hope was that her kidneys would perk up and start treating and cleaning her blood properly to clear up the many electrolyte irregularities in her blood. Also, she was simultaneously treated for an infection with intravenous antibiotics.

After ten, grueling days (half in the ICU), she was discharged on January 14. She went home with a stable 16 respiratory rate, 125/67 blood pressure, stable electrolytes, and stable kidney function back to normal, but with her advanced kidney disease. Her breathing was stable on room air.

The year 2020 was off to a tough start, but she did get thorough treatment and was stabilized very well. We just had to maintain the delicate balancing act of avoiding infection, avoiding blood loss through stressful ulcers and keeping the fluids off.

In early March, the fears of Covid were starting to peak around the country. Sporting events were canceled, and people were asked to isolate themselves. We had two good months of stability with mom at home. The worst thing in the world right now would be another stay in the hospital. They were not allowing family members in with the patients and in general, hospitals were a good place to avoid, since the Covid virus was so prevalent in the hospitals. We were extra careful with any exposure to mom.

I still left the house occasionally but tried to keep my distance from people and tried to stay outdoors mainly when leaving the house. In my isolation, I followed my usual stress management strategy, I went on walks with my dogs—especially Cha-Cha. I would come home from my walks rejuvenated from her happy-go-lucky take on life. She had such a presence that everyone would notice her and come away with a smile when seeing her. She would almost float on air with her walk. She held her head high with a big smile as she trotted along like she was a runway model. I would literally get 10-20 comments per day about her.

We had another month of relative stability at home after the Covid scare began, but in mid-April, she was having complications from the usual suspects. It had been 3 months since she was last hospitalized. I was extremely anxious about any possible hospitalization because I knew how easily proper treatments and care could skew without my oversight and input into her medical history and her psychological issues. Hospitals were extremely busy during this time, and it would be easy for the least "squeaky wheel" to not get as much attention.

On the morning of April 23, she contacted me with her panic device. I came and assessed her condition and immediately called 911 at 4:52 AM. It was a 4-minute 911 call, as her condition was dire. Only one minute after I hung up with 911, the paramedics arrived by fire engine as usual. They would not allow me to accompany her and would not allow me to see her in the emergency room. They wanted to intubate her by sticking a breathing tube down her throat and putting her on a ventilator. I strongly resisted this treatment as it is a serious step and people who get intubated have an 80% mortality rate. In the past, she was able to hang on with the usage of a BiPap ventilation system. The emergency room doctor argued with me by phone as I could only talk from the parking lot. I told him to just give her a chance. *"She does not have Covid. She has congestive heart failure and is experiencing fluid overload while sleeping and has a tough time breathing at night."* Using a BiPap was against protocol in the Covid era with a patient suspected of having Covid as it would recirculate Covid germs in the air within the emergency room. She was in critical condition, and I would not give permission to intubate her. Slowly and gradually, she improved enough to convince the doctor to keep the ongoing treatment of BiPap for breathing while giving her diuretics intravenously.

Her vitals in emergency showed evidence of another infection as her white blood cell count was high. Her electrolytes and kidney function were relatively stable. Her hemoglobin was slightly below average, but not bad. They did some testing that showed her blood was clotting too much and that she had advanced congestive heart failure, which of course we knew already. Excessive clotting is an early indication of future stroke as well. I think basically she needed the excess water removed. It had been three months since her last hospitalization and over that time, her heart and kidneys slowly and gradually couldn't keep up.

After the emergency room, she went into Covid isolation for 48 hours. She continued getting treatment in the hospital for the next six days. I was not able to visit and only talked to her a couple of times as she was usually asleep or under the influence of sedatives or narcotics. The hospital called me saying she was ready to go home on April 29, I arrived to pick her up. She was a terrible mess! She was now on oxygen going home, something totally new for her. She had never needed oxygen before as a regular supplement for breathing. They ordered her a BiPap machine for home as well. Her white blood count was extremely high on discharge day; she had a slight fever and an obvious infection that needed treating. Almost all her electrolytes were abnormal. Her oxygen level was only 91%.

I was upset to see her in such bad condition and getting discharged. This was clearly an unwise decision, there was no thought of Dairy Queen. I wasn't even sure I could get her into the house safely. I got to her home and the effort it took to get inside was too much for her. I called 911 immediately after getting her home from the hospital discharge at 3:10 PM. I asked the paramedics if they could take her to a different hospital, and they said they had to take her to the closest hospital because of her dangerous vitals. I was angry because I couldn't even confront the doctors who discharged her in such bad medical condition. However, I could not allow her care to continue at that hospital, so I ordered a hospital transfer. The next day, on April 30, she was transported to Banner Baywood Hospital.

Unfortunately, Banner had equally strict Covid protocols with visitors. I demanded access to her and her medical care. I called the administrators and left messages. I let everyone know I had power of attorney, and she needed representation in her current state. It was still to no avail. I wanted every decision to be run by me for approval. I was on the phone for hours a day, so I was not popular with the staff, and I didn't hesitate to go up the chain if I wasn't getting heard. At first, her condition completely regressed worse than ever. Her labs after getting admitted were poor. Her hemoglobin was 7.6, and she needed two units of blood. They were not checking her weight every day and didn't have her on a diuretic drip at first. It was difficult to talk to the specialists and hospitalists in charge. They changed shifts so frequently and had so many patients that I would get new specialists and hospitalists that did not understand her history, and I would have to talk through her medical history with all of them. They frequently had her on narcotics and strong sedatives without permission. She was unable to speak on the phone because she was so drugged. She didn't eat for many days because she was either sedated, or they couldn't trust her to chew and swallow properly with her dysphagia (the medical term for difficulty swallowing and chewing) which would occasionally lead to aspiration (when food or fluids enter the airway and into the lungs). I had a few doctors hang up on me when I challenged their approach or their hopeless diagnosis. They would say, "Your mother is extremely sick. You need to accept she might be drifting away." I would not accept it. It was the same set of complications we worked through a dozen times before. She spent the next 14 days at the Banner Hospital, now almost an entire month between the two combined hospitals. I would receive her daily labs and then talk to the hospitalists in charge. The numbers were getting better, and it was harder for them to continue the pessimistic narrative. The labs were not ideal, but it was all relative to the progress that the patient was showing.

With Mercy Gilbert, she was obviously discharged too soon. In contrast, now at Banner Baywood, her stay was dragging out far too long. Eventually, the idleness, lack of therapy, lack of contact with family and lack of hope would lead to her demise. I got to know a specific hospitalist and was able to convince him that she needed to go home now. She hadn't received any therapy for a month. She had been in bed, often sedated, and most of the time not eating anything. So, no food, no exercise, little human interaction from staff and zero visitors.

On May 10, I commemorated 20 years of caregiving to mom. We had never been apart for more than 4 or 5 days. She had now been in the hospital by herself due to pandemic rules for 17 straight days and well over 20 days between the two hospitals. I said, *"My mother is a warrior and continues to find new levels of courage and determination! I'm hoping and expecting she will come home very soon."*

I knew that her only hope was to go home and for me to take care of her, feed her and get her moving again. Because of the Covid outbreak, she got little attention from staff, and she looked like a patient at the end of life. When I would visit her at previous hospitalizations, I would insist on eating and therapy. I lost my ability to influence the staff with only phone contact. Also, mom could sometimes block everyone out and not communicate very well without me as her mouthpiece and advocate with staff. The hospital staff thought she was basically a vegetable unable to speak, eat or even move. I knew better.

The doctors did not think she would make it very long at home but finally agreed to allow the discharge as basically a hospice arrangement; they thought it was not fair to her or the family for her to die in the hospital with no family support. I refused to commit to palliative or hospice care. So, they allowed the discharge and I arranged for a medical transport company to deliver mom to the house.

She was coming home with less-than-ideal vitals. Her oxygen level was still low. We had an oxygen machine and a BiPap and it would now be totally my responsibility to bring her back to health. She could not walk on her own and she was not lucid when she got home. She did show a couple of smiles. I found that it was essential for her to move around to fight the effects of edema overload and ultimately shed some water weight and breathe better. So, we got to work.

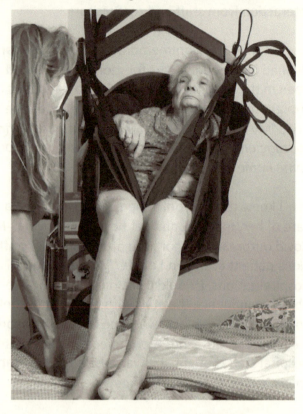

I had a medical sitter hired 24/7 for the first couple of weeks and my sister Kathy stayed in the house to help. The first couple of days were dire. It was important that her fear of breathing didn't turn into a greater problem that would lead to hyperventilating and an actual breathing emergency. One time in the first 24 hours, she was doing quite badly, and she was panicking to breathe. As she would often do in these times of fear, she would want to hold my hand. I would look her in the eyes and give her encouragement to stay calm and trust the ventilator. I would ask her to take slow, deep breaths and I would talk to her calmly and confidently. I worked with her for hours to calm down. If she had been hospitalized again this time, I don't think she would have made it. It was imperative for her to stay home and work her way back to better health.

At home, we had the BiPap machine that gave her a lot of comfort and we also kept her on oxygen all the time for the first

couple of weeks. I believed home and her dogs were the best medicine. She trusted me implicitly, and I think immediately started to feel more comfortable and slowly started to feel better. I could literally see her recover right in front of my eyes living at her home and with her dogs.

The dogs knew something was wrong and were compassionate. She received constant doses of love from Sasha and Saint as she lived on my side of the house and on her return home, I moved her bed into my bedroom. Occasionally, I wheeled her over to her apartment where she could see Bubba and Jonesey, her dogs.

I was anxious 24/7 for the first couple of weeks—agitated, scared and on high alert. It was exceedingly difficult, but it was an amazing process to see life return to her. The hospital thought it would take her 6-8 weeks of physical therapy for her to regain her mobility if she survived her first few days at home. We took that as a challenge.

Two days after her return, she was getting a lot of movement in her wheelchair, eating and drinking normally and getting some fresh air outside.

On May 18, Day 4 of rehab, they thought it would be an 8-week plan to walk again. Amazingly, she was walking in only 4 days after coming home. We were over the worst parts of her early recovery, her O2 was getting better daily. She was eating, gaining strength and gaining confidence.

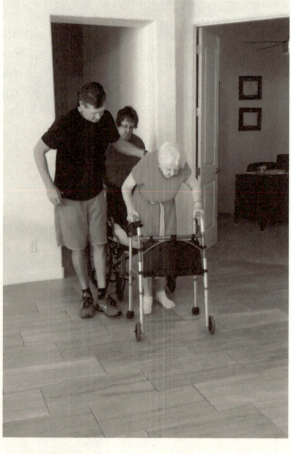

Simultaneous to this tough time with mom, my company was under extreme pressure from Covid. At one point, there was a fear that dogs could catch Covid. Then we had the hard isolation shutdown in the Phoenix area. I closed three of my night programs and kept two open. I laid off about 50 part-time employees. The business was losing money hand over fist, and I was just trying to keep the business afloat. I will give a better summary of the business survival later in the chapter.

Mom's recovery continued very strongly. On day 10 after her return home, she was playing with her Elvis cards and feeling feisty as she wore her Elvis glasses she got at Graceland.

On social media, I repeated a funny interaction mom had as she overheard a doctor's comment. *"A doctor told mom hospice. She responded with thank you! She thought he said hot stuff."*

On July 16, I left town for a much needed 3-day excursion up in the mountains with my Cha-Cha Fancy. We did a lot of hiking along the upper Black River near Springerville and Big Lake. Taking Cha-Cha out of town, just the two of us, was wonderful. I had my brief respites each day when we would go on a walk together, but getting out of town into nature was medicine for my soul. She had so much fun too. It also felt good and therapeutic to go to a place my dad and uncle loved so much—Black River in the White Mountains of Arizona. We also loved wandering in the woods where we could feel the vibe of the Mexican Grey Wolf who was reintroduced to the wild.

After returning to the valley, Cha-Cha, Saint and I added a new regular member to our car ride club; it was mom. Saint needed his ramp and mom needed her step stool. Cha-Cha was still able to jump in the jeep. Our morning car rides were a special time for us. We would get out, roll the windows down, and let our hair down as we'd play the radio and sing along loud and unashamed.

We would start our ride with a stop at the local convenience store where everyone would get a treat. Saint and Cha-Cha would get a piece of cheese. Mom and I would get a drink and a snack. Occasionally, a lot of wild howling would go on. Saint was looking for a dog he could bark at to show he was still the alpha dog in the neighborhood.

I had satellite radio in my jeep, so we were able to play hits from the 1950s and 1960s. We would invariably find a song we knew some of the words to and we would sing along. Some of our favorites were "Personality", "Que Sera Sera", "Calendar Girl", "Get a Job" and "Open Pit Mine". When the George Jones song, "Open Pit Mine" would play on my playlist, we loved singing the first verse extra loud...

From Morenci, Arizona, where the copper mines glow,
I could see Clifton in the canyon below.
In Clifton lived Rosey, we danced, and we dined
on the money I made in the open pit mine.

We were proud of where we came from, Morenci, Arizona. The Doris Day song, "Que Sera Sera" was our unofficial theme song. We loved singing the verses...

When I was just a little girl
I asked *my mother, what will I be*
Will I be pretty? Will I be rich?
Here's what she said to me.

Qué será, será
Whatever will be, will be
the future's not ours to see
Qué será, será
What will be, will be.

I would chime in after those verses and repeat whatever will be, will be, the future's not ours to see. During all our many days of illness and unknown future, the words would ring true for us... that the future is not ours to see, what will be will be. Let's enjoy the moment on this car ride, and sing.

After we picked up our snacks, we would take a ride around the neighborhood that would usually last about 30 minutes. Our drive would go to the outskirts of south Gilbert where the city would border with a local Indian reservation. There was a lot of open space and mountains. We drove by a church that was being constructed from scratch. As we drove by it, we would say, there's our church once it's built. Mom took a keen interest in its progress. As we were heading east ready to turn back north to our house, we would see a big mountain. I would say there is Shirley's Mountain. We would end the car ride with a stop by the mailbox where I would hand mom any mail she received. Mom was able to identify with Saint who was unable to go for walks and exercise any longer due to health issues. Our car-ride club had a real sense of shared experience and connection.

When we got home, I would help mom back to her apartment and get her situated with some television and a Diet Pepsi. I would take Saint back into my house. Then Cha-Cha and I would go on our personal one-on-one walk to the park for about an hour. After dropping her off at the house, I would check in on mom and then take Bubba and Jonesey for a run in the neighborhood and sometimes a car ride too. It was a full morning routine of exercise, socialization and therapy. It was hard to achieve any big victories at this stage, but every morning during our car ride, we chalked up a small victory. We got out in the world, rolled down the windows, felt the wind, saw some pretty scenery and we sang.

On July 26 at 5:50 PM, I called 911 for mom. She didn't feel well. After getting evaluated in the emergency room, her white blood count was irregular, her hemoglobin was a little low. They kept her for observation until July 28th when she was discharged. Thank goodness, the hospitalization was not a major ordeal for her this time. It was the anomaly from her otherwise smooth sailing after her miracle return home in June and the implementation of her nightly BiPap ventilator.

After mom's miracle return home in June, we settled in for a long run of no hospitalizations. It would be a wonderful nine months before her health faltered again. Excluding the short observation visit in late July of 2020, mom was hospital-free for almost a year! When her health faltered, I would look for a path forward. Having a BiPap at home was her current path forward and we relished her good health.

In August of 2020, I took another solo excursion to the mountains with Cha-Cha. On this trip, we decided to walk entirely around Big Lake near Springerville, Arizona. It was 7 miles around.

The challenges of the pandemic continued with my business. It was a bitter pill for me to swallow. I had all my locations open 24/7 since their openings. It was odd for our locations not to be open 24/7, but that was the nature of our economy. It was a hard, cold recession and we were trying our best to keep our heads afloat. Our quality kept shining through with awards in the community. We worked hard to help the healthcare community that needed night services while they worked in the hospitals. I think the hard work we put in during the pandemic helped us afterward in 2021 when things started to turn around.

In September 2020, Cha-Cha and I drove to San Diego

together. The highlight of the trip was visiting Dog Beach (an unfenced dog park) where I allowed off leash for the first time in her life. She was never trusted off leash, since her famous escape in 2014. She was a flight risk with her wry smile and her dubious history. Her first instinct was to run, and she did for about 15 minutes. Luckily it wasn't too fast, and I was in good shape. After she got her 15 minutes of running out of the way, I was able to trust her. She walked around, got in the water, and interacted with the other dogs. It was a beautiful time for us.

Sasha and I had been close, the love of my life I would say, but this trip, I feel we bonded even more. We stayed in a beachfront motel and enjoyed our time in San Diego. No matter if we were in Arizona or California, the compliments people made about her were non-stop. I would beam with pride every time someone would make one. I feel like she knew everyone loved her. She had a way of improving her cuteness when people came around and she would prance. She loved the attention too.

On October 5, we celebrated Doug's 11-year anniversary with the company. We made a point to celebrate every year. He was loved by the staff, the clients and the dogs. Many of the senior staff had been with the company since the beginning. It was a family affair.

On October 22, it was the 6-month anniversary of mom's miracle discharge after nearly a month in the hospital by herself during the early times of Covid. Small victories, and small successes were our mantra. Six months out of the hospital was an enormous success!

On October 27, we got out and voted early before the 2020 general elections in November. Throughout all our 20+ years together, we never missed an election. We did our civic duty; it was just the way I was raised. Mom was a lifetime Democrat. It was unthinkable for her to be anything but the party of my granddad, Sonny Biles. Similarly, like my granddad, she skewed conservative. She liked Bush Jr.; she liked McCain but also liked Obama. She also liked Trump. I think she admired how an older man could still run and win the presidency. She didn't like Hillary Clinton at all, but she liked Biden okay.

Mom's birthday celebration in 2020 was especially precious after her Herculean survival earlier in the year and the wonderful stability we got with the BiPap ventilator at night.

It was her 84th birthday and a rare gathering of all four of her kids to celebrate.

I made a double-decker homemade yellow cake for the occasion. I liked making her birthday special with a homemade cake instead of something store-bought. She really got in the spirit of it during the celebration.

Later in the month, we celebrated Thanksgiving at Donna's house. We would invariably overindulge at the dinner table, prompting extra insulin that night to combat all the sugar and carbs she ingested. Sometimes it would be a ridiculous amount of insulin I would need to give her. It would have to be slow over time with constant rechecks of blood sugar. The fear would be to give too much insulin ultimately resulting in a low-sugar emergency which is far more dangerous than a high-sugar reading. I must say, it was worth it. She loved to eat, and on this one day, she could indulge.

Right after Thanksgiving on November 27, I headed up into the mountains again to spend quality time with Cha-Cha Fancy. This time it was fun in the snow. I laughed and laughed as she frolicked in the snow.

In early December, another award came in for my business, this time Glendale Dogs won a Best in Industry award. By this time of the year, things had started to improve quite a bit with the Covid economy and people started returning to work and to travel. I was able to open all five places to become 24/7 once again. It felt good and we had a sense of real accomplishment that we seemed to have survived and kept all our full-time employees with no layoffs.

The hardest year in my business life was almost over. It was scary to think I could have lost it all after devoting so much of my blood, sweat and tears to the business. Few people were traveling and so many people were working from home during the year. However, there was a group of loyal, diehard customers that came in to support the business during the difficult Covid days of survival.

Also, 2020 was the year of the "dog boom". Millions of new dogs were adopted during Covid to help people with their stress and depression. Of course, leave it to "Man's Best Friend" to help us get through one of our toughest times. The dog boom resulted in a whole new generation of dogs and dog owners looking for services such as mine.

On December 7, I celebrated the birth of my girl, Cha-Cha Fancy. What a wonderful year we had together. She started to slow down considerably in the near future, but 2020, was a beautiful year for us. And to think I originally regretted adopting her. It goes to show sometimes things need a little time to develop, but when the relationship developed, it was the best I've ever known.

On Christmas Day, mom woke up to what she liked waking up to, loving dogs. However, this time was especially poignant as she woke up in her own bed this Christmas instead of a hospital bed like in 2019. Kristy joined up for Christmas in 2020.

Bubba had the time of his life with the wrapping paper. It was a good Christmas and a year of thanks for mom's ability to overcome insurmountable odds.

In 2020, mom needed four 911 emergency calls for paramedics to save her life and rush her to the emergency room. After starting the year off with 10 days in the hospital in early January, she went on to spend another 25 days in May and June in two different hospitals. Finally, the 3 days of observation in July. A total of 40 days in the hospital. Over 10 of those days were in the intensive care unit. A true year of miracles.

CHAPTER 13
Kidney Failure
(2021)

"When you get into a tight place and everything goes against you, till it seems as though you could not hold on a minute longer, never give up then, for that is just the place and time that the tide will turn."

- *Harriet Beecher Stowe*

The early months of 2021 started with continued stability for mom and no hospitalizations. It seemed like we had it figured out, mom had sleep apnea, a condition where she would stop breathing at night while lying in a horizontal position. During sleep apnea, the airway is narrowed or closed, and breathing stops. We think it started with her stroke and it was related to her dysphagia—trouble swallowing properly. The BiPap would force proper breathing patterns and help prevent sudden sleep apnea events.

On January 15, mom and I traveled to a big public vaccination site for the new Covid vaccine. It was held in a parking lot near the Arizona Cardinals stadium. Since mom was severely at risk, she was able to get her vaccine sooner than most, and I was able to get mine sooner as well because I was her caretaker. It was quite an experience to go through the lines that day. Covid was life or death with mom, and I loved any help I could get to lessen the chances or the severity of mom contracting the illness. I am proud to say, she and I never got Covid during her life.

On February 5, mom got her Covid booster. It really took a lot of pressure off. Mom's quarantine from the public unfortunately happened during her most stable, healthy time. There was not a lot to do except car rides.

In early March, we took an excursion to the Phoenix Zoo. We spent a good 4 hours walking around and seeing all the animals. It was an arduous task for me as mom was in a wheelchair and there was a lot of walking and a lot of steep slopes. I tried my best to just make it a pleasant experience for her. I think she had a good time. She loved animals, and it was a way to get out into the open air and not worry about Covid so much. I tried to give mom some new and interesting experiences, but we were limited. I wish we could have done more.

For the rest of March and most of April, our life was pretty smooth. We did our group car ride each day. I took Cha-Cha on her park walk every day. Mom watched her TV. I was always working on my business in the background by email as it continued to slowly come out of its doldrums. The economy was bouncing back. Most important of all, I was keeping mom out of the hospital. That all ended abruptly as we approached the end of April.

On the morning of April 30, mom was resting in her bed and doing relatively okay. Nonetheless, by evening, I called 911 at 5:59 PM for help. Mom had been experiencing discomfort when it came to breathing for a couple of days, and I let her stay in bed a lot. It had been over 11 months since she had a serious hospitalization. When the paramedics arrived and the ambulance, I instructed them to take mom to the closest Banner hospital, which was Banner Ocotillo Medical Center.

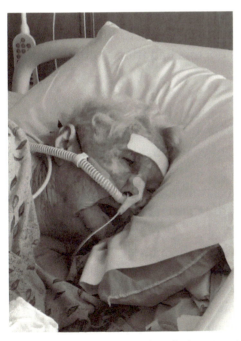

After arriving at the emergency room, her vitals and labs were poor. Her breathing was assisted by a BiPap. White blood cell count was running abnormally high, indicating an infection. Her kidney function was running as low as I had ever seen it, the GFR (glomerular filtration rate) was at 15, indicating near complete failure. The GFR is considered the optimal way to measure kidney function. Some of her electrolytes were abnormal, further indicating inefficient blood cleaning by the kidneys.

Mom was transferred to the intensive care unit, and thank goodness, Covid protocols were eased substantially. I was able to stay with her in the ICU. She was fighting for her life now and the situation was dire. She was not responsive to me or outside stimuli while she was fighting to breathe with help from the ventilator. The treatment course was familiar—she needed the excess water removed from her body by intravenous diuretics. She needed intravenous antibiotics to fight her growing infections. Most importantly, she needed the BiPap to help her breathe during these difficult times. Eating would be out of the question indefinitely. Something as simple as phlegm could be dire to her ability to breathe. I'll never forget the utter pessimism in the ICU. None of the doctors or nurses thought she had a chance. They were chagrined by my hopeful disposition as they saw it as unrealistic.

The major new complication during this hospitalization was sepsis. Sepsis is when the entire body is under attack by infection and antibiotics don't seem responsive. Over 50% of all diagnosed with sepsis do not survive. The doctors had tried multiple antibiotics with no success.

The second new development was that her kidney function was not kicking back into gear and cleaning her blood. What we had dreaded for the last couple of years was starting to become a reality. We could not count on her kidneys any longer. Ineffective kidneys also make the diuretic treatment ineffective as the waste and toxins normally excreted through urination was not working.

After several days in the ICU, her EWS (early warning sign) scores were poor. The EWS was used as a way of indicating a person nearing death. One of the most troubling vitals was her respiration rate (RR), it was abnormally high, routinely over 30 breaths per minute, and often near 40. A healthy respiration rate is 15 breaths per minute.

It had now been a few days on the BiPap, with the extremely high respiration rate and a high pulse. Her breathing was rapid and desperate. No signs of real communication, she was hunkered down fighting for life.

The head doctor at the ICU asked for all the children to travel to town and convene in her conference room where she could speak to all of us at once. For days leading up to this meeting, her intentions were clear to me. She had argued and disagreed with my seemingly misguided hope. She made several statements leading up to the meeting that the family needed to do right for mom and know when to let her go. As difficult as it was in 2020, during her Covid isolation, this was by far her most serious condition. Kathy was the final child to arrive in town from Tucson.

It was May 3, with all four children in the conference room, the doctor began by saying, *"All voices in the family need to be heard and respected. The family needs to come together and make the right decision for mom."* The doctor continued by stating mom's serious diagnosis. She stated that the time had come to let her go. The doctor went around the room one by one, asking each of us to speak. Some of my siblings said they didn't want to see mom suffer any longer, then teared up and cried. Others made similar comments, and then said they would stand behind my decision. The doctor was building an environment to an inevitable outcome—her recommendation. Nobody believed she could make it, not one single member of the medical staff or family— except me.

I finally spoke and was steadfast in my belief, I saw a path forward, she needed kidney dialysis. In the past, diuretics helped shed the excess water and jumpstart the kidneys, but now, mom needed help from dialysis. A dialysis machine is in essence, artificial kidneys.

If there was no hope, no path forward, I'd be the first to agree it was time. Yet, this was not the time. I reminded everyone, including the doctor, that I had power of attorney, and my decision would be final. The doctor responded by saying she did not think mom was a candidate for kidney dialysis. She felt mom was too old and weak to handle the rigors of kidney dialysis multiple times per week. Further, she said mom was not a candidate for the surgery to add a dialysis port to her chest. She was not very cooperative with nurses and showed a lot of fighting and resistance.

I advocated giving her a break from the BiPap which had been dominating her face for several days. Let her calm down and continue the antibiotics to get the sepsis under control. The meeting adjourned without a decision; it was a bit of a stalemate. I kept a respectful tone in all my discussions with the ICU Chief and tried to advocate for mom, calmly but passionately.

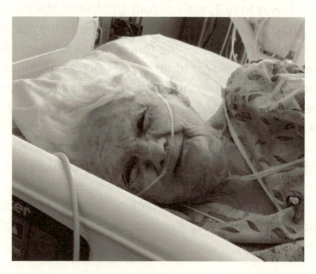

I told her, *"Do not be deceived by this tiny, elderly woman. She is a lioness and just needs a couple more days to fight through it. Let a fighter fight."*

They finally took the BiPap off and put a nasal cannula on her so she could communicate without the loud, dominant BiPap ventilator on her nose and mouth.

I was able to talk to her and explain what was going on and what her path forward was—kidney dialysis. The doctor observed my conversations with her and finally saw that she wasn't a lost cause. The head of ICU saw her smile and agreed she was now a candidate for surgery to install a dialysis port linking her jugular vein in her chest. The surgery was scheduled for May 9.

In the meantime, they were continuing to give her new antibiotics to finish off the sepsis infection. They finally found an antibiotic that was working. She needed a blood transfusion as well because her hemoglobin was low. She had not eaten or gotten out of bed in several days, so that was also high on the agenda. She was hungry and anxious to eat some food. However, her ongoing dysphagia was an impediment and the fear of aspiration.

On May 9, she had her dialysis port surgery. The surgery installed a catheter with two ports directly into the jugular vein. There's an arterial port where the blood comes out of the catheter into the dialysis machine to clean the blood. Once the blood is clean, it's then returned to the body through the venous port. After surgery, she was ready for her first dialysis treatment, it would usually take 2 to 3 hours. During that time, all the blood in the body circulates through the dialysis machine to get cleaned– the task usually handled by healthy kidneys.

Mom would often feel better and sharper after a dialysis treatment. She received 3 treatments in the hospital before they were ready to discharge her with an outpatient regimen at a local dialysis center.

Kidney dialysis was a challenging process for people, especially the elderly. Doctors did not believe she was strong enough mentally or physically for the rigors of kidney dialysis. When kidneys fail, the blood fills with toxins, and the body's electrolytes become out of balance. The person feels terrible, lethargic and then deathly ill. The second important function of the kidneys was the removal of excess water from the body through urination. To allow a patient with advanced congestive heart failure the ability to breath properly, timely water removal was vital.

When the patient gets dialysis treatment, she feels good for about 24 hours, but dialysis takes its toll on the body. The constant removal of the body's blood into a filtration machine, and then reintroducing it back into the body is a traumatic process. Further, each dialysis treatment required the removal of 5-8 pounds of water that was previously handled by urination. By the end of treatment, blood pressure is typically low, sometimes dangerously low. When it trended low during treatment, dialysis would have to be stopped. Of course, the problem with stopping treatment was the obvious fact of water not getting removed and blood not getting filtered.

It was counterintuitive to want high blood pressure with a patient like mom, but that was exactly what we needed prior to dialysis treatments. We knew the treatment would drive her blood pressure so low that they would at times be unable to complete the treatment. Therefore, we needed high blood pressure before it would go dangerously low from treatment.

During her first few dialysis treatments in the hospital, I talked non-stop with the technicians as I learned the process and learned about their experience with elderly dialysis patients. The key ingredient they would tell me was family-patient support. The patients that got the support were able to tolerate the process. The ones that didn't get the support eventually gave up on life.

On May 15, she was discharged and made it back home to her dogs. Every year seemed to yield a greater miracle in the story of mom. The struggle at Ocotillo Banner Medical Center from April 30 to May 15 of 2021 was the toughest battle she would ever win. She had spent 15 days in the hospital with 7 of them in the ICU.

She had a double infection—a lung infection with pneumonia and a urinary tract infection. She survived sepsis shock. Her kidneys completely failed, and she had acute congestive heart failure.

We tried to take the most positive spin on her new medical condition. We wanted to believe her kidneys could make another comeback. Some of her doctors were also optimistic. I think it was good to pursue every possibility to find a better quality of life. However, our optimism would lead to risk that would make things more difficult in the future.

Living the kidney dialysis life had many challenges ahead, and it would push my mother's indomitable spirit to its highest levels of tolerance. Yet, our routine was to celebrate the victories, no matter how small. Going home, sleeping in her own bed, loving her dogs, drinking coffee in her own kitchen, and yes going on car rides.

In June, another one of my locations won an award, this time it was Gilbert Dogs. By summer, the bounce back was strong. People were starting to travel again, and the huge dog boom of 2020 was starting to show itself with more dogs needing daycare and boarding. We were well positioned with our cage-free business model. Most people inherently dislike cages. Many felt more comfortable in a cage-free environment.

On June 12, I went up into the mountains with my cousin Doug. He had been suffering heart-related illnesses for quite some time since he had a pacemaker put in around 2013. He was severely obese in 2020 when we took our usual summer trip up to the Springerville area.

Once we arrived at our cabin in the town of Alpine in 2020, Doug started complaining of breathing problems and was in a panic. We had to cut our trip short and drive home.

I stopped off at a Walmart and bought Doug a scale. I told him he needed to start exercising and dieting every day, or he wouldn't be living much longer. I asked him to weigh and send me the results daily for accountability.

One of our goals was to get weight off so we could go up in the mountains again. Over the next year, Doug pumped iron and dieted. He lost an amazing 80 pounds. I had no doubt he added time to his life.

Returning to June of 2021, Doug had lost those 80 pounds, and I longed for our trips together. Doug was a special person to me. He was my link to a time and a place that didn't exist any longer—a connection to his parents, our grandparents, my dad, and my childhood past with family. He worshipped my dad, and I loved his parents dearly. We had so many good times together.

We chose a location that didn't have the high elevation of Springerville, a town called Strawberry, Arizona. We had a couple of good days, but again, Doug was short of breath and began to panic, so we came home early. Sadly, that was our last trip together in the mountains. We were not able to renew our trips together, but the most important thing was Doug's improved health and lifestyle. He was terribly fearful of Covid. He wanted to stay in his apartment all the time. His job with me allowed him to work from home. Socially this was not healthy for him.

On June 16, we celebrated mom's kidneys. They had bounced back enough for her renal doctors to discontinue her dialysis. I even got her a cake and made it a big party. Her kidneys were producing plenty of urine and the tests were encouraging.

In my years of working with specialists, I appreciated the optimists. It was not fully reasonable to think her kidneys would hold out much longer. Yet, her renal specialist helped us go through the process of testing her kidneys and then when the lab results indicated that her kidneys were functioning, we had her catheter removed from the jugular vein on her chest. What we would learn in the coming months was that her kidneys functioned; however, they were very depleted, and it was impossible for her body to maintain the delicate balance. After all, her kidney disease was quite advanced. It all was based on the twin diseases of CHF (congestive heart failure) and CKD (chronic kidney disease). Further, it was her diabetes over the last 30 years that was the precursor to those twin diseases. They were all part of metabolic syndrome.

On June 21, we returned to the car ride circuit. After the dogs were loaded in the back, mom was able to walk by

them in her walker and give Saint a big kiss on her way to the front seat. Saint enjoyed those kisses and so did mom.

I'm not too embarrassed to say that occasionally we would sing along with the radio, but often we all howled together, including mom and me. Saint usually laid down in the back of the jeep, but he was able to see above the back gate. Every now and then, he would spot a dog or what he thought was a dog, and then everybody would join in and support Saint's condemnation of that dog through group howls.

On June 24, I achieved a major milestone of surpassing 100 employees in my company. It was especially gratifying to surpass this goal with all the recent struggles in the Covid economy. I was proud we kept a stable, consistent workforce during the troubled times, and it started to take off in the better times.

On June 29, I mentioned a book I read about diabetes. During mom's long recent hospitalization, she went on a forced fast of probably about a week. About this time, I was reading the book, "The Diabetes Code" by Dr. Jason Fung. He stresses over and over how diabetes can be reversed with diet, exercise and intermittent fasting. Well, mom went on a long intermittent fast and I could see that clearly her A1C improved and continued in a downward cycle through fasting and low-carb intake.

I read a lot of books about fats, sugars, salt and diets. It is a fascinating business of making food, especially in the modern world we live in. The clever formulas that chemists come up with to addict the public. It is also the main reason diseases such as diabetes, heart disease, high blood pressure, kidney disease and Alzheimer's have erupted in the 20th and 21st century. The human body has not evolved the ability to handle the high intake of sugar and processed flour in our diets today. The result is an epidemic of diet-related diseases—the metabolic syndrome.

On July 8-10, I skipped out of town with just Jonesey. Hiking was getting more difficult for Cha-Cha, and it was out of the question for Saint. Bubba wasn't crazy about walks or hikes. So, it was just me and Jonesey on this one, and we planned to do some epic hikes.

Jonesey and I had the goal of 30 miles of hiking over three days. We would do one in the morning and one in the late afternoon over 3 days. Our biggest accomplishment was the hike to the top of Mount Baldy, with its 2000-foot climb and 16-miles round trip. We were both tired and sore but felt accomplished on that day.

When I got home, I was completely focused on Cha-Cha. She was going into surgery for a mass removal that was malignant. I was anxious when she went into surgery on July 23. I just didn't know how I would be able to deal with losing my darling.

Also, in July and after consulting with mom, I decided to bring home a new puppy husky. I named him Sakari. He was really a load, like all puppy huskies. Sakari means sweet one in Eskimo. It was fitting but also didn't describe what a hot mess he was.

We decided Sakari would live with mom and her two dogs. Cha-Cha was healing from her surgery and Saint just wanted to eat him. Bubba loved him to pieces and Jonesey tolerated him. August 12 was his first day of school, he dressed up in a tie for the occasion. He loved lying underneath mom's walker or by her side on the couch. At night, he slept on the bed with mom while the two adult dogs laid in their usual places under the bed.

After almost three months out of the hospital in mid-August, mom had an 11-day hospitalization for congestive heart failure and kidney failure again.

In retrospect, we were hopelessly optimistic about her kidney rebound. Her kidneys were so impaired that it took a perfect lifestyle to maintain a safe status quo. The poor kidney function would directly impact her congestive heart failure as her body was taking on too much water and resulting in labored breathing. It was a complicated set of health challenges mom suffered from. No one doctor would really piece it all together. We were on our own.

Mom was originally hospitalized on August 15 after a frantic 911 call. Paramedics arrived and stabilized her health as usual prior to the ambulance's arrival. The rest of her stay in the hospital was an effort to get her congestive heart failure stabilized. It was the usual challenges of infection, low hemoglobin, out-of-balance electrolytes, and excess fluid in the body. After 11 tough days, she was discharged on August 26. We still tried to live the dream of no dialysis, but I was quickly coming to the realization that dialysis would be the only salvation and only chance. We needed to settle into that reality. Discharge day meant ice cream day as we stopped by Dairy Queen to get our usual butterscotch dip cone.

On September 4, I had to call 911 again. The call was made at 12:59 AM. It was another middle-of-the-night panic call to me.

Sometimes, I would be in a sound sleep and abruptly awakened by the sound of the emergency button. I would scramble out of bed, losing my balance on my way to mom's apartment, occasionally tripping over dogs. Mom's poor body could not manage all the complicated health challenges without a lot of help. She needed to go back to the hospital and get her CHF and CKD under control.

When arriving at the emergency room at Mercy Gilbert Hospital, she had a bad infection once again that was driving other complications. Her electrolytes were abnormal, and she had excessive fluid retention. Her kidney function and hemoglobin were relatively stable. After a few days in the hospital, her mysterious ulcer was bleeding again, and it slowly eroded her hemoglobin down to the low 7 grams/deciliter.

Several times through the years, she had various scopes to determine where her bleeding was coming from by gastrointestinal specialists. It was finally determined that she most likely had a bleeding ulcer that was activated during times of bodily stress which, with mom, was often. The terrible result on mom's health, when her hemoglobin went too low, was chest pains. The chest pains were early indications of a pending cardiac event.

The doctors were wary of giving blood transfusions with her acute CHF and excessive water retention. Giving blood was adding more fluid to the body, so the two complications were competing. Generally, they would actively treat the CHF with intravenous diuretics first. This process would improve her breathing, but also systematically damage her kidney function. Once they removed enough fluids with diuretics, then they proceeded with a blood transfusion. She felt better once she had enough blood in her body and the chest pains and fear of cardiac arrest subsided.

This ongoing balancing act continued for 17 grueling days in the hospital. This came almost immediately after the 11-day hospitalization for the same problem just a few days separating the two long hospitalizations. By the end of her 17-day hospitalization, the diuretic treatment for her CHF had completely decimated her kidney function. She had the kidney dialysis catheter reinstalled into her jugular vein which enabled the needed dialysis.

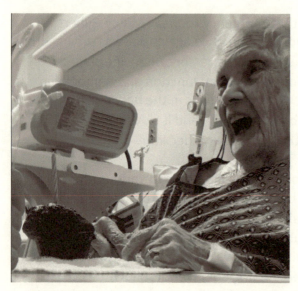

On September 20 (my birthday), I snuck in a cupcake, candle and matches into the hospital, so we could celebrate my birthday together. As soon as I blew out the candle, mom lit up and started singing me happy birthday like she always had done through the years.

On September 21, she was discharged from the hospital. It was such a difficult time. The wear and tear of the hospital, the IV diuretics, the blood transfusions, the fighting off infections, the kidney dialysis, the physical therapy, the on again off again dietary restrictions, the constant poking, prodding and disruptions throughout the day and night. The revolving door of specialists, hospitalists, nurses and therapists would come into her room. This difficult life went on every day for 28 out of the previous 35 days ending on September 21.

Going home was much more than just a cliché, it was life itself. It was a big win. It was a time to exhale for a little while, time to rejoice with our dogs, and time to celebrate with a DQ treat as our first objective. Deep down, we both knew it was just a temporary break from the rigors of poor health and hospital life, but we cherished every moment. A few days after the discharge, I tried my best to create some more memorable moments for mom. It was starting to become difficult to even go on car rides, but we persevered.

On September 25, we went on a wonderful car ride all the way to Coolidge, Arizona, and an ice cream shop on Main Street. Her health seemed so tenuous at the time, but I believed the rides were excellent therapy for her (and me). She was also experiencing  bowel and urinary incontinence more frequently. I had determined at the time to try and do a major road trip once a week. Coolidge was our first excursion.

On October 2, mom and I went on a long drive to my Phoenix Dog's location. She had never seen it before. I had opened it two years previously. While near the location, I was able to find a Dairy Queen so we could enjoy a dip cone as well.

At times, it was all too much for me, but there was no pause button I could push. All I could do was carefully manage my mental health to the best of my ability. My house on the other side of mom's door was my sanctuary. Leaving to go on a walk with Cha-Cha was my respite. It was my only solace in life to leave for an hour or so. Cha-Cha brought me joy and happiness. She also was getting older, but so far, she was holding up as mom's health was deteriorating. I was like a battery losing its charge every day. Whereas Cha-Cha was my battery charger. I felt better and stronger after some private time with her at a nature preserve.

When sitting with mom, we liked listening to an oldies country-western music station on TV. We still had our old favorites of the Food Network and all their interesting personalities. If not the Food Network, it was usually the Animal

Planet Network. I would usually take her three dogs for a walk at some point. Sakari was going to daycare regularly, so Bubba and Jonesey enjoyed the car ride to drop him off and pick him up each day. Mom would occasionally go along as well. Sakari was such a handful; it was a nice break for all when he was burning off all that puppy energy at daycare.

Then on October 14, there was the big irrigation scandal in mom's backyard. Sakari managed to find and dig up every irrigation tube connecting all the backyard irrigation system. He seemed to be proud of himself and couldn't understand my disappointment. He had found and destroyed all the "evil snakes" hiding underground in the backyard. He felt very accomplished.

After returning home from the month-long hospitalization, we were fully committed to kidney dialysis. Mom would attend treatment three times a week, on Monday, Wednesday and Friday. They were usually three hours per session. When calculating wait time, set up time and departure time, it was usually 4+ hours per day. The process was exhausting for everyone involved.

It was a strange environment—both boring and critically important. It was a room full of dialysis machines with all the patients hooked up getting their blood cleaned and vitals closely monitored. Half a dozen technicians and nurses patrolled the room. Occasionally, 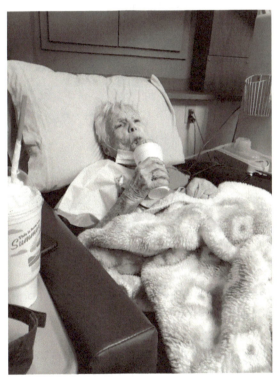 some sort of emergency would break out or a patient would crack under the process. At times, that person was mom. Getting her to and from the appointments was now our car ride. Getting dialysis would on occasion be dubious for mom, but the process was required if living was the goal. I tried to find ways to make the best of it. We celebrated the small victories. A treat after dialysis would be motivational. Invariably, the dialysis itself would make her feel better, but exhausted at the same time. Her mind would be sharp, but her body tired.

On October 16, I showed off my two wolves publicly at the  annual Barktoberfest Animal Rescue event in Gilbert. Sakari was almost as big as Cha-Cha now. Dogs 24/7 was the event sponsor for that year, a terrific way to give back to the rescue community.

On October 29, we celebrated another successful week of dialysis with a trip to the Dairy Queen. It was now clear her kidneys were almost gone, failing with little output or filtration. She was starting to urinate less and less.

Even on the days in between trips to dialysis, she slumped and didn't feel well. The weekends were especially hard as we had to wait three days for dialysis treatment.

Meanwhile, we started to play the game of blood pressure management before each dialysis. We would withhold important medications the day before treatment so her blood pressure would elevate. We wanted it nice and high before dialysis because dialysis would make blood pressure crash. Then, it would be back on the meds for a day and off again leading up to the next session. It was a difficult roller coaster ride for her body, not healthy, but it was the only way to get through dialysis.

If a technician cut her treatment short, I knew that would be detrimental to her making it safely to her next session. It might even require an emergency hospitalization. I would have discussions with the head nurse and administrators of the dialysis center about this topic all the time. We had to risk treatment at low blood pressure levels or else she would have a critical health event in between dialysis. It was a vicious cycle of dangerous options.

November 2 was a big day of celebration. It was mom's 85TH birthday. We started the day with our customary morning routine of a car ride with treats for all. We got her dressed in her favorite jeans and blouse. We reveled in her great milestone and discussed everything she had overcome to date—all the good times we'd had. There was NEVER  a discussion or desire to give up, to rest, to discontinue the race. It was full speed ahead, and we would deal with the problems as they arose. We would give it all we had on the hard days and celebrate the better days as small victories.

After the morning car ride on her birthday, we dropped the dogs off back at the house and decided to go to our favorite jewelry store, Jared's in Mesa. It was time to pick out some new jewelry. She loved her jewelry and loved to show it off. After a hospital discharge, we had a ritual of cutting off her hospital wristband, and putting on her bracelets, watch and rings. It was a return to normalcy in our minds. After picking out a beautiful gold necklace, we found a Dairy Queen to finish our celebration in town. At home, she blew out candles on her cake, and her children sang happy birthday to her by video conference.

On November 6, I went on a business trip to Washington, DC, and Hershey, Pennsylvania. It was the usual gathering of my industry. It was nice to get back to the meeting after missing it in 2020 due to Covid. My Vice President of Growth, Hannah Young, attended the Expo with me. We had a lot of good meetings with bankers ready to support our 2022 growth plans. I learned a lot at the expos every year and would make new, lasting friendships. As part of my small inner circle, Hannah and I had a good week. I am sure I wouldn't be where I am today without the daycare and boarding expos in Hershey and Burbank each year.

On November 15, I called 911 at 6:43 PM. The ambulance took mom to Mercy Gilbert Hospital. This was a rare case of more fear than substance. She stayed the night and was back home the next morning after observations. I would say for every hospitalization, there were 25 near misses that we were able to avoid the hospital and stabilize her condition at home either through calm talk, the BiPap, a breathing treatment, oxygen or a combination of these tools. The hospital could be unpredictable about how they would treat and handle a situation. I tried to avoid the hospital as much as possible. Hospitalizations were also hard on mom and only used as a last resort.

On November 25, we had Thanksgiving at Donna's house. We really let mom indulge, and yes, we paid for it with high blood sugar that night. I probably kept her up until midnight giving her insulin and stabilizing her blood sugar. We finally got it stable and were able to go to bed. By this time, I was sleeping on her side of the house every night, either on the floor near mom's bed with the dogs, or a hide-a-bed in the adjacent living room.

On December 15, I celebrated the anniversary of Joe, my Vice President of Operations. It was a nice gathering of several long-term employees. Doug attended; he was my first employee. Joe's sister Erica had been with me for over a decade. Carlos was an original employee dating back to 2011 and had a long history in the company. Joe and Erica's mom attended the special luncheon as well.

On December 19, we had a normal day. Mom got dressed up for our annual Christmas picture. We included our new baby Sakari. Christmas in 2021 was our 22nd year together since dad passed away.

Christmas #22
Together!

At 10:51 PM that night, I called 911 for mom. She was having a breathing/panic event. I was already asleep that night but was awoken by her panic device. Again, her status was not too bad. I tried to calm her and get her more stable, but fear was a powerful emotion these days. I ended up following through with the call after I assessed that her panic was not going to stabilize. Two days later, on December 21, she was discharged, and we had our customary celebration at Dairy Queen.

On December 25, all members of the car ride club went out for a Christmas Day car ride. It was foggy everywhere, so it was a nice white Christmas, Phoenix style. We sang Christmas carols as we drove around south Gilbert.

On December 27, I took mom into the emergency room. She wasn't feeling well. After taking labs and vitals, her hemoglobin was low, near 7.0. She needed a blood transfusion and got one. At this stage in her life, she was bleeding almost continuously. As mentioned previously, a low blood count puts tremendous pressure on her already weak heart causing her chest pains and a real fear of a serious cardiac arrest. She stayed in the hospital for 3 days to get stabilized. While in the hospital, she continued with the dialysis routine.

She was released from the hospital in time for the New Year on December 30. That was also the day Sakari had surgery to get neutered. The main problems with mom's health at this stage were the dual demons of infection and low hemoglobin. We had a good regimen to manage the kidneys. We had a good regimen to manage the nightly sleep apnea with the BiPap ventilator. We had the additional challenging variable of blood pressure management

during dialysis. The weekends were an especially big challenge as they required an extra day without dialysis. We occasionally were not able to make it to Monday and would need to go to the hospital due to the need for dialysis.

On December 31, I finished the year with a celebration of Saint. It was on this date I adopted him. We were celebrating 10 years together.

We had had a difficult year in 2021. Mom spent an amazing 77 days in the hospital. Five 911 calls, five paramedic visits and ambulance deliveries to the emergency room. Four of those trips to the ER resulted in transfers to the ICU. We were working hard to account for all her medical variables, but it was growing increasingly difficult.

CHAPTER 14
Conclusion
(2022)

"Be strong and courageous. Do not be afraid or terrified because of them, for the Lord your God goes with you; he will never leave you nor forsake you."

- *Deuteronomy 31:6*

On January 8, 2022, we celebrated a month of no hospital visits as I did a photo shoot of mom. We bought some new clothes and mom liked to show them off. She had a full-length mirror in her bedroom. I told her to look in the mirror on her way into the living room. She also had a couple of perfumes and loved it when I sprayed some on her first thing in the morning. On occasion, the male

nurses at dialysis would notice and compliment her on the classy outfit and perfume. Through all the struggle, through all the pain, she exuded class. Being helpless and having accidents was hard on her. I tried my best to help her live with dignity and class. Life is short and life is precious...live every day with a little bit of happiness.

On January 9, I announced the opening of my newest facility in Mesa. It replaced my Gilbert Dogs location. Our open house was a big success. Gilbert had been my original 24/7 location back in 2009. It was a little hard to give up on the name, but the new facility was technically in the city of Mesa, so it felt right to make the change in name. I wanted Doug and Joe to stand by my side during the ceremony to pay proper respect for their great contributions to the company.

I wished mom had been there for the big day. However, she was not feeling well, and it was most important to not push her stamina. I would have liked to talk about her in my ribbon-cutting speech with her in the audience. I would have liked to publicly tell her she was my hero. I did get a few opportunities to talk about mom at previous public gatherings. At my aunt and uncle's memorial services and my Chandler grand opening. I was glad she

heard me on those occasions. Yet, at the end of the day, none of my accomplishments were that important to her. She just loved me for who I was regardless of any successes.

On January 25, we celebrated the 11-year anniversary of Erica with Dogs 24/7. It was a touching ceremony as Erica teared up. We've had a lot of ups and downs through the years, but I adore Erica and think of her as family.

On January 29, it was car ride time for all and treats for all. Mom's entire crew of three big dogs were out on the ride—Bubba,

Jonesey and Sakari. You can't fake that smile on mom's face. The dogs all got a small bite of cheese and mom got one of her new favorites, a cone in a cup. Part of the trip was usually dropping off Sakari for a few hours of daycare.

On February 13, I took mom over to the emergency room. Her ongoing problem was hemoglobin combined with the challenges of CHF and CKD. Mom needed blood and eventually got a blood transfusion and needed her regular dialysis. At times, they were able to do both concurrently while in the hospital. It was really the best scenario to add fluids (blood transfusion) and clean and remove excess water with dialysis at the same time. Each dialysis visit would take about 5 pounds of water off (15-20 pounds per week). Every other day, it was relentless, we needed another 5 pounds taken off or her body would fail. On a social media post about this time, I said, *"In the end, we all succumb to our mortality, but not today!"* With mom giving the thumbs up after the doctors gave her no chance to make it during this recent hospital visit.

Also, during this hospital stay in mid-February, I asked the hospitalist if they could please assign a hematologist to mom's case. Hematologists specialize in blood. I asked the specialist if we could arrange a standing blood order with regular visits each week to get transfusions. It was a way potentially to bypass the emergency room visits that were invariably hemoglobin related. I was quite pleased the hematologist agreed and granted the transfusion standing order. The only problem with the blood transfusions was that the doctors usually resisted giving two units of blood, which is what she needed to get caught up and have a little bit of a margin for error. They resisted because of various protocols they had for giving blood and because of her CHF and the related fluid edema. She was quite often running short and needing more blood.

Mom's standing order for hematology was at Banner Baywood Hospital in their outpatient facility. Baywood was the location of many of mom's past medical treatments. Her open-heart surgery, post-op rehab, her stroke and stroke rehab were all at Baywood. It felt like we made a full circle.

We would visit twice a week to get her hemoglobin tested. If her hemoglobin was below the threshold of 8 grams/deciliter, then they would take her in for a blood transfusion the next day. The big problem during these days, or let me say several problems, was that first the threshold was too low, a threshold of 9 grams/deciliter would have been better. She was losing blood rapidly and by the time she was tested and scheduled for the transfusion, which usually took about two hours, her overall hemoglobin still was just above the threshold, and she was already needing more blood. The other big challenge was scheduling the blood transfusions with her already busy 3-days a week at kidney dialysis.

Traveling to outpatient facilities was a constant routine now. It was all very much required; every visit was essential. If she didn't get timely blood transfusions, she would have terrible chest pains as a prelude to a cardiac event. If she didn't get timely dialysis, she would swell up with fluid causing acute congestive heart failure and panic breathing problems. When the treatments were timely, she would feel good, but tired. The other added complication was that dialysis had to follow the blood transfusion soon thereafter or fluid overload/CHF would begin.

On March 6, my sweet Saint passed away. I wrote this poem to honor my boy.

Saint's Last Car Ride

You checked into Gilbert Dogs; I'll never forget.
You were the most beautiful dog I ever met.

Your parents told me your story, it was sad but true.
After boarding for two weeks, they planned to rehome you.

Their newborn was allergic, you could no longer stay.

I decided at that time, I would talk to them on pick up day.

They arrived and you were brought out.
I said, can I have him? I would love him without a doubt.

Your mom cried and your dad told me, He's an Akbash, never forget!
You were certainly the greatest and most majestic dog I had ever met.

You and Me, we lived an epic life - 11 wonderful years.
There were so many great memories and happy tears.

Smile on command, that was your special trick.
All those teeth would display fast and quick.

For so long, we ran every morning, oh what a sight.
You would run so fast; you almost took flight.

When you got older, your breathing was impaired.
For your safety, no more running, I declared.

We started to go for car rides, because you were a Good Boy.
It was mom, Sasha, You and Me—barking and singing with joy.

Today, I took you on your last car ride.
My sadness was great, I cried and cried.

You're a good boy, I whispered in your ear.
So sweet, so precious, so dear.

I was on a 48-hour trip to California when he died. Donna was staying with mom and looking after my dogs. He had been suffering from complications from steroid treatment. His death came suddenly and before I was able to drive home to see him. He died just a couple of hours before I arrived. It was a devastating blow to me. My trio of Fritz, Saint and Cha-Cha were my family, my fur children. They were also symbolic of my new life in the Culture of Dogs that I joined in 2009. Two of my three fur kids had now passed away. They both lived good lives into their teens. Especially Saint as a large breed, he lived a good life, but it's never enough for a dog parent.

On March 7th, the next day, mom needed to go to the emergency room. She was not feeling good. Fortunately, it was a quick turn around, and she was discharged the next day, on March 8. She received an iron infusion to help with her ongoing blood problems. It felt like a constant battle during these days, getting dialysis and getting blood transfusions. Always, checking the lab results. I had a phlebotomist coming once a week as well so I could stay on top of any trends—usually hemoglobin or an infection.

On March 21, I needed to take mom into the emergency room at Mercy Gilbert Hospital. She wasn't feeling well and was having chest pains. After getting evaluated, her hemoglobin was 7.8, and they gave her a blood transfusion. She was okay for discharge the next day, March 22.

Shortly after the New Year, I had hired a woman named Mandy Shalitis. Mandy had years of experience caretaking with the elderly. I had worked with two other ladies in 2021 who spent a few hours with mom during the day. Mandy was the right lady at the right time we needed in our life. She was sent from God to help mom and me. She was kind and loving to mom. She helped her with bowel and urine incontinence which had become a daily issue going into 2022. She helped us get through kidney dialysis and blood transfusion appointments.

One of Mandy's favorite memories during dialysis was when she brought a snack. Mom was usually a woman of few words. However, when Mandy gave her a bowl of popcorn, she handed it back empty and mom told Mandy, *"I thoroughly enjoyed that, is there anymore?"* She sat with mom during the outpatient appointments and kept her company and kept her spirits up.

Mandy was looking for full-time work. Almost immediately after hiring her, mom had multiple hospital visits, cutting Mandy's hours short. *"From the first meeting, I feared she would not live long, appearing so weak."* Mandy said. *"I had never actually seen anyone bounce back as many times as she did in her kind of shape and age. I would have to say one of my biggest memories of Shirley was her strength and resiliency."* Mandy just continued her care while mom was in the hospital, sitting with her while I took breaks. She was an absolute godsend, my appreciation to Mandy goes into a special category that will extend for the rest of my life. These times in winter and early spring of 2022 were the most difficult days in my life.

Typical Days & Nights

The last several months had almost broken me, every day was hard. I would wake up at 4:30 to 5:00 AM every morning and assess her vitals by webcam. It was all about the vitals. I didn't need to see her because I knew she was okay based on the readings. On a good day, if her oxygen and heart rate were stable, I would start preparing for the 6:00 AM wake-up. She had the BiPap on her face, the oxygen/heart rate monitor on her finger and the emergency panic button around her neck. I would walk into her house, turn on the lights, turn on the TV to the classic country music channel and get the place lively and happy. Occasionally mom would be sitting up on the bed waiting. Other times, I would wake her up. I would wish her a good morning and help her take the BiPap, o2/heart rate monitor and her panic device off. The first step would be to get her moved over to the bedside port-a-potty.

As for the many bad days in the morning, I would wake up to find mom already sitting on the potty because she had to go and wasn't able to make it. On some occasions, I found that she had fallen on the floor while trying to get to the potty, and every so often knocking the potty over—sometimes with it empty and occasionally with it full. On other occasions, she had unfortunately slipped and got wedged into the bed rail. If she had a potty accident, I would put a nose clip on and gloves as I tended to be gag-averse to the smell.

It was all delicate because the effort to maintain continence and/or the emotional impact of losing control would get her feeling bad, and on a few occasions, it led to breathing emergencies. Once on the potty, we would strip her down and change her adult briefs. If she had an accident, we would usually go straight to the shower and clean her off where she had a shower chair to sit in. We had to be careful not to get her kidney catheter port wet. It could lead to rapid infection and fast death as it was linked to her jugular vein. While in the bathroom, we would check her weight. At times, accidents happened while walking to the bathroom, which would often frustrate me and embarrass her.

After she was cleaned up, I would take her back to the bedroom where we would get a fresh brief and compression socks first. I helped her put her pants and blouse on and then finally her shoes. This process could take a few minutes to a few hours based on how she felt and based on any accidents she might have had. We would finish with perfume and maybe jewelry based on whether we were going out that day.

The next step would be to walk into the kitchen and sit down at the kitchenette bar. She would pause at the full-length mirror on the way to see how she looked. A cup of coffee was the number one goal to help her wake up and a routine she had been following all her adult life. I would check her blood sugar and vitals again as she had moved around a lot leading up to this stage and everything needed to be checked for stability. While she was having her coffee, I would generally go back to my house and monitor her by webcam and let her drink her coffee in peace and listen to the music. She would closely monitor as I fed the dogs. They would always hover close to her. I would get a washcloth and comb at this time to wash and wet her hair before finally combing it. I would leave and take a 10 to 15-minute break as she finished her coffee. This point in the day was a major milestone in getting her upright, dressed and stable.

After she finished her coffee, I would make her breakfast and give her many medications with apple sauce. Her port-a-potty was moved next to her in the kitchen. Coffee and breakfast would often lead to bowel movement or the need to urinate. She would have her panic button, and I would ask her to please push it if she needed to use the potty so I could make sure she got seated safely. It was right next to her bar stool, so occasionally she would do it on her own and usually did it successfully. Although there were a few times in which she slipped and fell in the kitchen while trying to navigate the potty. A few times were dire as the potty and bar stool would be turned over and a terrible mess on the floor. She usually was able to fall and not hurt herself, but the messes were a catastrophe.

It was during some of these times that I would be utterly broken as the cleanup was so difficult. I would implore her to please call me first, I could arrive in seconds. I imagine in her mind she was trying to maintain some independence and not burden me as much as possible. At times during these catastrophes, I would find myself completely broken on the floor. I would have to get her cleaned up, the room cleaned up and get her dressed all over again. The task would be overwhelming and on occasion, I just couldn't imagine how I was going to get everything fixed. Ultimately, there was no magic help button for me to push, so I had to get myself together and get everything in order.

After breakfast, she would be stable for the rest of the day sitting on the couch. Sitting upright was healthy and safe for her. Usually, the problems came when she was in the horizontal position in bed. Once she was on the couch, I would get her favorite shows on TV and one of the dogs would typically jump up on the couch and sit with her. The new puppy Sakari would lay underneath her walker.

It was at this point, I felt I could give a sigh of relief and go over to my house and relax for a few minutes. We would then get ready for the morning car ride. I would pack up the dogs into the Jeep. Then go over and get mom ready for the drive. I would set up her step ladder by the passenger door and guide her walker out to the Jeep. I put padding in her seat to protect her from accidents. In the back, I also had a blanket down for Sasha, who was also having frequent accidents as she was incontinent from her lower extremity paralysis that was setting in. From time to time, the act of getting up in the jeep would cause a bowel movement. We would have to go back into the house, remove all her clothes and get her cleaned up again. Once in the Jeep, we took our 30-minute drive around the neighborhood with stops at the mailbox and local convenience store.

Usually at 9:00 AM, Mandy would arrive and sit on the couch with her for several hours. I would drop mom off from our car ride. I finally had some time without responsibility as mom was safely in the hands of Mandy, and I could take Cha-Cha for a park trip of respite.

When returning an hour later, I would check on mom and Mandy and usually take Bubba and Jonesey for a walk or run. Then I would retire to my house and rest up. I trained Mandy on checking midday vitals and blood sugar before lunch.

On Monday, Wednesday and Friday, we would take mom to dialysis later in the afternoon. It was a lot of work to get her ready for the 3-hours sessions. We would keep a close eye on her blood pressure and heart rate as we needed it running high so she could get through the session of blood filtration and water removal. In the last few months, we also had to take her to Banner Baywood on Tuesdays and Thursdays to get her hemoglobin checked to possibly trigger a blood transfusion.

Mandy would accompany us to kidney dialysis and blood transfusions. I would get her set up with her entry weight and then help get her set up in the chair. I would share with Mandy how much water we needed to pull off that day and to make sure her dialysis continued without stopping or incident. On occasion there would be problems with blood pressure. It was really a catch-22. From time to time, mom would try to get out of dialysis by asking for a potty break in the middle of the treatment. If they cut off dialysis without taking enough water weight off, she would certainly not make it to her next outpatient dialysis in 2 days and we would have an emergency trip to the hospital that would be life-threatening. Mandy was an angel giving me a break from the treatments and sitting with mom and encouraging her.

Mandy recalled the car rides to and from the dialysis center with mom and me. *"I loved how you would play a song that would jingle her memory from long ago times, holidays or places. You*

274

would interject with related happenings to a song, and she would light up and seemingly recall a memory of said time or place, bringing her moments of joy, if only for a short time."

By the time we finished with treatment and got mom home, it was usually time for Mandy to leave for the day. Mom was invariably feeling much better but tired. We would get ready for dinner, dress for bed and take insulin and other medications. Mom loved her nightgowns and pajamas and always looked forward to the transition of clothing. Bedtime was usually 6:00 PM with a 6:00 AM wake up.

The next 12 hours were now the hardest times. The night routine would involve getting all hooked up with the BiPap ventilator, o2/heart rate monitor and the panic button around her neck. The webcam would be pointing to the o2/heart rate monitor. The night immediately after dialysis would usually be smooth as she had all the fluids removed, she was tired, and the night would typically go fine.

I slept lightly as I had rushed in to help her so many times through the years and subsequently called the paramedics. Every now and then, I would wake up in the night and look over at the webcam and see her sitting on a kitchenette barstool with the lights on. She would get confused with the time of the day and think it was morning and time to wake up, even though she had just gone to bed 1 or 2 hours earlier. I would come in to inform her she needed to go to bed, it was 8:00 PM and she would wake up at 6:00 AM. Nonetheless, it was amazing that she would get disconnected from the BiPap, get dressed and walk into the kitchen all on her own.

Often at night, her panic button would get pushed accidentally. I would hear it go off in my house and I would check the webcam on my iPad positioned by my bed. I could see her sleeping and her vitals stable. I would quietly go into her room and dislodge the panic device that was going off.

Other times, I would note her BiPap was not sealed properly on her face, and it wasn't functioning properly. I would have to wake her up, ask her to sit up and reapply her face mask for a proper seal. Some nights, I would note her heart rate was dangerously high, I would wake her up and give her a pill to help the high reading. Occasionally her o2/heart rate monitor would come off her finger or not be fastened properly. I would need to tape it to her fingers every night. Usually, I would be able to reapply it without waking her up.

During times when I was worried about her blood sugar getting too high, I would let her go to sleep, but come in periodically to check her blood sugar level with a prick of a finger and blood check, followed by an insulin injection.

There were a few times that I jumped out of bed after hearing the panic button, and I hurt myself as I would be disoriented and fall or trip on a dog in my haste to get into the other room. Before

I discontinued her "life alert" which would contact paramedics directly, I would be awakened by paramedics barging into the house. I would rush into mom's room in nothing but underwear only to find a room full of paramedics (both male and female).

One of the worst complications with mom's health was her need for blood thinners to counteract the threat of serious stroke. Blood thinners make the blood in the body flow more regularly. The problem with blood thinners was they were not permitted or advisable when the patient is actively bleeding. Mom was often actively bleeding from her stress-induced ulcer. She had a history now of a few strokes and was very much a candidate for another major stroke. Therefore, blood thinners were necessary, but ill-advised in the current environment of unknown bleeding. All the labs indicated elevated levels of blood coagulation, indicating stroke danger. I tried to learn the types of blood thinners and what might be allowable with mom's current health situation. We did what we could, including Plavix, under doctor's advisement from time to time.

On April 4 at 3:03 AM in the morning, I called 911. Mom had pressed the panic button that night because she was experiencing chest pains and breathing problems. After arriving in the emergency room at Mercy Gilbert Hospital, she had a high white blood cell count, indicating a bad infection. Her hemoglobin was 7.7 indicating a need for a blood transfusion. It was the Monday after the long weekend without dialysis, so she was in desperate need of her blood to be filtered and fluids removed. They got her stable and began the usual treatments needed. She was scheduled for dialysis and a transfusion. She stayed in the hospital for another 4 days to get stabilized with additional dialysis treatments. On April 8, she was discharged.

On Monday, April 11, mom, Mandy and I went out to a blood transfusion appointment at Banner Baywood. Mom got dressed up, and we stopped at a Dairy Queen before the appointment to

enjoy some food and snacks. Unfortunately, mom was close to the transfusion threshold, but missed it by .1 on her hemoglobin. I asked if they could please give it to her, or she would have to go inpatient to the hospital. The way her hemoglobin was dropping each day, I knew she would not make it to the next standing order appointment on Thursday.

On Tuesday, April 12 at 11:00 AM, as predicted, I needed to take mom to emergency. She was having chest pains and needed that blood transfusion badly. Once in the hospital, she was more irritable than usual and complained heavily about chest pains. The processing was especially slow that day and mom was in a lot of discomfort. They gave her Fentanyl for pain. This was the first time they gave her this drug; the usual was Morphine. We finally got mom stable in a hospital room away from the emergency room late in the evening.

On Wednesday, April 13 I drove to the hospital first thing in the morning as usual. I tried to time my visit just before they served breakfast so I could get her up and active. It was going to be a busy day as I knew she needed that blood transfusion as soon as possible to help with chest pains and she was due for dialysis as well. As I walked into the dark hospital room, I followed my familiar routine. I opened the drapes and turned on all the lights. As I was walking around, I was telling mom good morning. I said it a few more times, no movement and no answer. I came in a little closer and shook mom a couple of times and told her to wake up. She was not responding. I said it much louder as I shook her with panic. I yelled to the nurse, "My mom is not responding!" A nurse and a doctor came in, and we all tried to get a response. I was scared and angry. I told them, *"Does she not get checked in the night? How come no one had noticed her non-responsiveness?"* I had seen something similar once before when she had too many narcotics in her system. I told the hospitalist, *"It must be the Fentanyl they gave her yesterday. Why in the world did emergency give her a new stronger narcotic when she didn't have any history using it?"* For lack of a better answer, the hospitalist agreed with me that the Fentanyl was probably the reason why she was non-responsive. A CT scan was scheduled for the next day to check out her brain. I continued to plead with mom to wake up. I talked to her in her ear and played familiar music all day with no success.

On Thursday, April 14, the CT scan came back. The neurologist and the hospitalist both came to the room. They gave the family the shocking news that mom had had a massive stroke. Her chance for recovery was zero and she would never come out of her coma, the neurologist told me. He showed us the scans and said the stroke was caused by her constant rise and decline of blood pressure during the kidney dialysis process. I knew immediately in my heart that all paths forward were now gone.

I decided we would withhold dialysis and begin treating for comfort. They began morphine treatment. It was heart-breaking to see the fight leave the indomitable spirit inside mom. With every new dose of morphine, mom's rigid, fighting disposition slowly faded away. I could not bear it. She remained in the hospital another 3 days until April 17 when she was transported to a hospice facility for the last 12 hours. I accompanied her on the transport. My sisters stayed with her at the hospice. I could not bear to see her final moments. The ability to fight was taken away from her. It was for her own good, but I could not bear witness. It was just a matter of waiting, I went home and slept on the floor of her bedroom with Bubba and Jonesey, like I had done so many times before and waited for the call. On Monday, April 18, 2022, mom passed away.

On April 18, I said... *"Today, mom's inspirational fight against multiple illnesses came to an end. It's been 22 years since dad passed away in 2000. Shirley Ellen Biles was an angel living with us for a while and now returned to heaven."*

After turning 80 in 2016, she spent over 250 days in the hospital and always persevered on her way back home to her dogs. Let that sink in...250 DAYS IN THE HOSPITAL, dozens of 911 calls, weeks in the ER, and several weeks in the ICU. Every challenge put in front of her she overcame with grace, dignity, class and her signature smile. If there was a path forward, if there was any chance for success, we found it and fought for it. There had never been a stronger woman. When you eat ice cream, remember mom. When all the odds are against you and it seems impossible, remember mom's indomitable spirit! Today, remember my mom!

Legacy

I know mom touched a lot of people directly and indirectly throughout her life. She was a kind and gentle soul. You don't have to be a great athlete, actor, or businessperson to make a big impact in life. Mom was none of those things. She was a simple girl, born in rural America. She never had much money or great popularity. All she had was her inner strength, grace and kindness. That was more than enough.

Everybody has setbacks and everybody loses in life. However, the definition of indomitable is a person with a spirit that can't be beat. That was mom! She occasionally lost, she often had setbacks, but she could not be beaten.

None of us know how we will act when our time ends. I've seen some of the biggest, strongest men who became terrified with the prospects of death and often so paralyzed, they were unable or unwilling to fight for every day. I hope I will be like mom. She never stopped smiling and never stopped fighting. She had an inner grace that emanated from her like an aura.

What could be learned?

- When life was unkind, she found the silver lining.
- When adversity knocked on the door, she did not run and hide. She opened that door and confronted those demons.
- When presented with a monumental problem, she relished the small victories.
- She drew strength and love from dogs. All animals inherently knew her and loved her. They all could sense her kindness.

Life means different things to different people. As for mom, she loved petting a dog. She loved talking to family on the phone. She loved eating good Mexican food. She loved to go for rides in the car. She loved the spirit and camaraderie of water aerobics. She loved singing in church. She loved a good ice cream cone. Mom loved life. All the proof you ever needed of that statement could be seen in her beautiful smile.

EPILOGUE

"All his life he tried to be a good person. Many times, however, he failed. For after all, he was only human. He wasn't a dog."

- *Charles M. Schultz*

Returning home after mom passed away, I felt many emotions. I felt loss and I felt lost. I felt empty inside as I did not know quite how to navigate without caring for mom. I felt relief as the many tough years had taken their toll. I was always wondering if she was in pain, or even worse, if she was scared. Wondering if she was getting proper care, wondering if proper decisions were being made. I was now at the end of a journey that had lasted my whole life.

Over the past five years, there were 25 other occasions when she could have died. It was always through God's grace that she would make it home one more time. I would like to think God decided it was time, and he chose a gentle way for her to die, a stroke while she was sleeping and unconscious. Mom did not die in the way she and I had feared for so many years, by not being able to breathe. Just the thought of it terrified her and set her into a panic. I would like to think God was also being kind to me, and not having her die at home under my direct care.

One of the most memorable words from mom was when I was in the depths of my despair and filled with frustration. She told me, *"Stephen, I did the same for you growing up."* She was referring to the bathing, changing of briefs, cleaning up messes, and helping to feed me. She did this not only when I was a baby, but for years growing up, she had to help me dress because of my leg brace. It was a thoughtful reminder.

From 2000 to 2017, mom had made steady progress, improving and becoming more independent. When she started to decline from catastrophic illnesses related to metabolic syndrome, it was terribly disheartening. It was not in my DNA to accept the decline. In our years together, we conquered everything put in front of us, no matter how big or challenging. Mom tried so hard to make me happy, always trying her best. I was never able to accept fully the decline. I wish I would have reached out for professional help, I really needed guidance on how to accept decline. To this day, I am still disappointed with myself and sad I couldn't have been a more patient and accepting son.

I desperately needed a respite to keep my strength up. I rarely got it except for the short times to take my dogs for a walk and a few days a year to get out of town. The pressure and the responsibility were heavy. I learned to manage my mental health with the limited tools I had in my possession.

It was my dogs that helped me endure and help me maintain my mental health. It was the love and warmth from Bubba who would lay with me on the floor by mom's bed every night. It was the walks every day with Sasha that made me laugh and made me happy if only for an hour. My dogs were my support system that helped me make it.

It was so odd to go to bed at night and to go to sleep. The relief of sleeping and not worrying about missing something important for mom's health was a strange experience. At times after she passed, I would wake up in the night thinking I had heard the panic button only to be dreaming I heard it.

I visited grocery stores every week for 22 years with the primary objective of buying healthy but delicious food for mom, most of those 22 years with her alongside. It is quite a life adjustment when I go into a grocery store now. Those grocery store aisles that were the centerpiece of my diet plans and my health objectives for mom, I now just skip them, as I have no reason to go down those aisles, carefully reading label after label on the food products. It was more than a trip to the store; it was a major part of our life. It's one of the many missing voids today.

I started to check on my own health as I had neglected it for many years. I had an eye exam for the first time in 20 years. I got a colonoscopy for the first time in my life. I got a sore shoulder checked out that hurt for years. I wore the Invisalign treys to correct some teeth that weren't straight. I had a physical with a doctor.

Mom and I maintained two households of dogs for over 15 years. For the first time, I combined both groups in my house. Bubba, Jonesey and Sakari joined my darling Cha-Cha Fancy. Many years ago, Bubba was afraid of a young Cha-Cha. In contrast, now they were both over 13 years old, and they got along fine. Cha-Cha still tried to tease and posture with Bubba, but it was just friendly banter.

As I no longer had mom to care for, I now had Cha-Cha to care for. She was suffering from degenerative myelopathy. It is a disease that causes the nerves in the lower spine to stop working properly. It causes weakness, paralysis in the back legs, and incontinence (both urinary and fecal), all of which would get worse over time. She was stubborn with where she lay down in the house even though she had great difficulty standing up on tile. In the night, she couldn't stand up and would urinate where she lay and then would cry as she was not able to stand up. It felt like déjà vu as I would wake up in the night hearing her cries and rush to wherever she was in the house to help her stand up. For the last few months and for the rest of her life, she did all her urinating in the house. I had a routine where I would mop the entire house every morning. I did this for many months.

Cha-Cha was also not eating much. She had been extremely finicky, but now it was bad. She weighed under 30 pounds. We still went on walks every day, and she would magically transform during the walks and have a bounce in her step. I would usually resort to force feeding if she wouldn't eat on her own. I tried everything possible when it came to food. It was a constant worry of mine.

In the summer of 2022, my longtime groomer and employee Melissa informed me of a lump she found in Bubba's throat. She was concerned but tried not to worry me too much. She told me I needed to go to the vet right away. I scheduled an appointment with my vet, and after seeing Bubba, she called me in to talk. I was not expecting what she told me; Bubba had lymphoma and only had a couple of months to live. She told me that oncology was an alternative, but she did not recommend it as she tried it with her own dog and felt it was a mistake as his final days were bad days from oncology treatments.

This made me very sad. I was looking forward to spending considerable quality time with Bubba during his final years. He was such a good boy. There was a certain poetry to his end coming after a lifetime of service to mom. I was selfish and wanted more time with him, like we all do.

When I got the news, I immediately planned a trip up in the mountains while Bubba was still in good condition. I think Bubba really enjoyed the trip. He waded out in the water and was still the most daring of the dogs maneuvering in the river.

Back home, Bubba seemed to be doing all the things he liked to do. He ate all his food. He still liked to play with toys. He went on car rides, and he closed his eyes with enjoyment from the breeze coming from the windows.

As I was approaching my first birthday without mom, the only person I had ever celebrated with, Bubba wouldn't get up. It was September 18, 2022. He wouldn't eat; he wouldn't move. It had been over two months since the diagnosis of lymphoma cancer. I knew the day was coming soon, and that day I dreaded had finally arrived. Just like with mom, I knew the end had arrived, and I had to make the decision to end a great life. I was fortunate to know it was coming, and I made every one of those last days memorable and loving for him.

I called a mobile vet to come to the house and put him to sleep with me loving him as his final experience. The vet left me alone with him after his heart stopped. My sweet Bubba boy was gone. The vet knocked on the door a few minutes later, as it was late on a Sunday night, and they had made a special house call. I finally let the vet take him away to be cremated.

My birthday two days later on September 20th was somber and sad. I had now lost mom and two of my long-time companions in Saint and Bubba, all in the same year. As usual, Sasha helped me with my grief as we went on walks.

Then on September 25, exactly a week after Bubba died, Sasha was having a terrible problem as she was falling and losing her balance in my bedroom. It was terrible, I was crying and trying to help her stand. She fell again, and I loved her on the floor, and unlike her normal disposition, she allowed love and affection. I didn't know what was happening. I thought it might be a stroke or seizure or something very bad. After we laid on the floor together for quite a while, I got my composure, and it seemed as if she was better. I helped her up and tried to walk her, and she was able to walk to the Jeep. I lifted her up. It was late, near midnight. We got to the emergency vet, and I carried her inside. They took her back for emergency triage.

I went home as the vet office was still following Covid protocols and was not allowing people to stay in the lobby. I got a call in the morning from the vet. She told me Sasha had problems with her heart rhythm. The vet was optimistic that medication might help. I got optimistic news I wasn't expecting.

However, just one hour later, I knew it couldn't be good, the vet called again. She told me Sasha had died; I was devastated. I couldn't believe it; I told her you just called me and said she was better, and you were optimistic. But then, what more could I do or say, I told her I would come right over. I immediately started crying inconsolably. It wasn't fair, my heart and soul had died. I was crying so much; it was hard for me to drive safely. I arrived at the vet hospital and told the front desk I had arrived. They prepared Sasha in a private room for me to see her one last time. It gave me overwhelming grief to see her dead. I hugged her face and cried non-stop for at least 30 minutes. My tears were falling on her beautiful husky coat. I finally had to leave her as they needed the room. I packed up my two remaining dogs, Jonesey and Sakari, and left town that day and drove up to the mountains to contemplate my future.

The death of Bubba and Sasha brought closure to mom's life, and it all hit me at once. They were the last connections to mom and my personal struggles of care for five years. They were my everything and I owed them everything.

I have experienced sudden deaths, and I have experienced long goodbyes. It is without question to me; sudden deaths are the worst. Sasha's death coming just 1 week after Bubba was a tough time for me, a time of great grief and contemplation.

At the end of September 2022, I booked a trip to Istanbul, Turkey, for October. I had the trip scheduled during my birthday that I ended up cancelling because of Bubba's health. It was a trip I had wanted to go on for well over a decade but was never able to because of mom's health and the risk of traveling to Turkey. While I was in Istanbul, I gave a lot of thought to my life and what I wanted to do.

I knew I wanted to travel a lot, by myself. I like to solo travel to many of my favorite places of history in the world. I wanted to focus more on my personal life for the first time in a long time. Finally, I wanted to work harder on my business, now that I could focus on it.

288

After Istanbul, the former capital of the Roman Empire, I next went on a cruise down the Danube River in Central Europe—from Budapest, Hungary to Passau, Germany. Next, I traveled to Israel and Jordan in the Middle East. I finished 2023 with a trip to Paris, Berlin and Warsaw to visit significant places from World War II. In early 2024, I visited Brazil. I made a lot of friends during those four major trips and hope to make several more in the future.

With business, I acquired four new locations in 2022 and 2023. I have nine total locations with two in Seattle, Washington, one in Santa Fe, New Mexico and six in the Phoenix area. Our best year was 2023 as our workforce was nearing 200 employees. I am frequently approached by private equity firms wanting to buy my business or use it as a platform for further acquisitions, making me the CEO of a much larger consolidating company. So far, I have declined all offers, keeping 100% ownership. Someday, I will probably sell, but I don't believe it makes sense right now. Plus, I'm good at this business and wanting to see how far I can take it on my own.

On the morning of June 7, 2023, I got the communication I had been fearing for a long time. People in the company were trying to reach Doug by phone and email and he was not responsive during his shift. It had been a couple of hours, and completely out of character for Doug. I was in Santa Fe at the time and would be flying back later that morning. I immediately made a call to the local police department and contacted his brother and sister. Members of my staff, police and his siblings all arrived at his apartment. They finally got a key from the apartment management, and they discovered Doug was non-responsive but alive on the floor near his computer. He had had a massive stroke and died later that day in the hospital. I got the news that he was brain-dead just before I lost reception on the plane heading back to Phoenix. I quietly sobbed in my window seat for the entire flight back to Phoenix.

Once again, I believe God intervened, sparing me a very personal and traumatic experience. If I had been home instead of Santa Fe, I would have been the first responder on the scene. Who knows what I would have done; I might have broken the window to his apartment. Regardless, it would have been exponentially harder on me and even more heartbreaking to find Doug in a non-responsive state.

Later in the day on June 7, I wrote an article about Doug...

Today, we lost a giant of a man— Doug Underwood. It was the love affair of the ages that launched Dogs 24/7. Doug was the first employee back in 2009. I specifically wanted to start a business that could accommodate Doug's need to be with his blind and deaf great dane, Roxy, the love of his life. Doug had battled drug addictions for most of his life. It wasn't until Roxy came along that he kicked his bad habits. He loved her dearly; it was their love that helped launch this company.

For 14 years, Doug created relationships in and out of the company. His last position was Vice President. Everybody loved Doug, and everybody will miss Doug. We had an amazing journey together; I will dearly miss my cousin. The company will never be the same. The great legacy of this company will be that it was formed based on a special love affair—Doug and Roxy. They are now together again.

Doug was the smartest of all our cousins. He was never trying to set the world on fire. He just enjoyed the journey day by day, person by person he would encounter. Doug and I had a close connection. We were extremely competitive with each other! Doug was a special man, and he was a tremendous loss. The void he's leaving in my life is irreplaceable.

In the spring of 2023, I had a local artist paint giant murals of my two babies—Bubba and Cha-Cha on the front wall of my Phoenix-based facility. The two of them were such important parts of my life; I am forever grateful to them. I found a wonderful way to honor their memory with these beautiful murals to share with the world.

It was around this time that I began to see a big, white dog receiving walks in my neighborhood. This dog had a remarkably close resemblance to my deceased dog, Saint. As I got to know the owner, I found out that his dog was born at the same time that my Saint passed away, a little over a year ago. When I would see this big, handsome dog, he would often stop and look at me with the greatest look of familiarity. After reading the masterpiece novel by W. Bruce

Cameron, _A Dog's Purpose_, I had always been a believer of his premise—after dogs die, their spirit lives on in a new dog and that sometimes that dog will follow the path of their previous owners to check in on them. When I see that big, white dog around my neighborhood, and he stops and looks at me across a lake or across a field, I feel like it is Saint checking in on me and making sure I'm okay. I whisper to him, "Hello son".

In my search to find mom's psychiatric records, I reached out to her former psychiatrist in Tucson on January 11, 2024. He did not have any records, but I had a pleasant conversation with Dr. Daniel Fredman, her psychiatrist for almost 20 years—from 1983 to 2002. Dr. Fredman retired after practicing psychiatry for over 40+ years. He remembered mom and dad very well and we had a pleasant 20-minute conversation. He was happy to hear she lived her final 20 years without any bipolar episodes and rarely any symptoms. We continued to keep in touch, and Dr. Fredman was one of the first to read my book and graciously wrote the foreword.

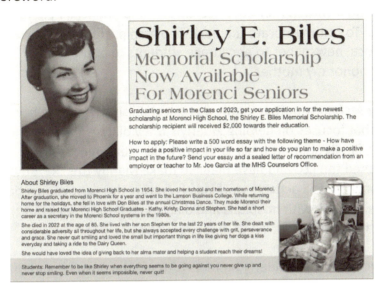

As a final tribute to mom, I wanted to do three things in her honor. The easiest was to establish a scholarship at our high school alma mater, Morenci High School. The new scholarship is called the Shirley E. Biles Memorial Scholarship.

In May of 2023, I spoke to the students and parents about mom and the new scholarship at the Morenci High School Award Ceremony. I then had the honor to name the three recipients I had picked and awarded them their certificate and financial help for college. To commemorate the new scholarship, I ran the below ad in the local newspaper to encourage students to apply and to further honor my mother.

My second tribute to mom was to establish a charity in her honor that focuses on helping elderly kidney dialysis patients without family support make it through the treatment sessions. I established the LLC and have plans to make Mandy the Executive Director. I am still actively working on getting the right connections in place to work with hospitals and dialysis centers to seek out the people that need help.

I would witness elderly patients often in the hospital and the kidney centers who never had family to help them. I felt mom was fortunate as she really needed the support and was able to get it from me. Many seniors are not that fortunate. I have put a lot of effort into this endeavor, but it's still not a reality. I will keep working on this charity until I get it established.

Finally, I wanted to author a book in honor of mom and our amazing life together. It was a biography and an autobiography all rolled into one, our shared life. It was the story of how she made me into the person I am today, and the person that helped her overcome her greatest life challenges—Like Mother, Like Son. I believe she was a uniquely inspiring person who overcame much. My intention is to give help and hope to people in similar circumstances.

It started with my childhood leg disease, and how mom helped me endure with patience and perseverance and never allowed me to feel sorry for myself. I took that education with me all my life and reapplied it to her life as she endured years of mental illness and then the end-of-life battles with metabolic syndrome. I trusted her implicitly growing up, and she trusted me implicitly as she endured her difficult health conditions, Like Mother, Like Son. In the end, I fell short of being as good of a person as she was. Life is a journey, and I still have time to become a better person.

During my years of working for Phelps Dodge, I had made a nice acquaintance with a man named Miguel Espinoza. He worked at a copper mine in Peru. Over the years, we worked together and had some time of leisure and fun. He asked me one day, *"Is it true that in America when your parents get old, you send them to places where other people take care of them?"* I laughed and told him, *"Yes, it is sadly quite popular."* He shook his head in disbelief as he couldn't understand why anyone would do that to their family. I told him, *"My mom lives with me, and she will remain with me if she is able, I will figure it out. She likes to be home with her dogs."* I honored that pledge to mom until the end, for over 22 years.

From 2000 to 2022, I had a terrible dichotomy of loving to be a caretaker and loving all the ways I improved her quality of life. At the same time, I was angry that this responsibility took too much of my life. In the end, I would not have done anything differently, except that I would have tried even harder to improve her quality of life when her health was so good.

Shirley Ellen Biles lived a good life! She had a meaningful life and an inspirational life. I have also lived a good life because I got to spend so much of it with her. I got to see mom every day during her last 22 years. That was a rare gift, a one in a million gift. I know she is looking down on me and remains my biggest fan. I continue to live my life trying to make her proud. I still have a lot of work to do.

Afterword

I would have to say that when I think of Shirley and Stephen, I think of a relationship between a mother and a son unlike any that I've ever personally seen or witnessed.

Stephen absolutely and unselfishly devoted his life and time to understanding how to help, encourage and heal his mom. I could tell that respect and love were mutual. It was incredibly special to witness. I would often secretly run down through all my boys, wondering which one would ever truly do this for me? I had realized that Stephen had devoted his whole entire adult life to helping, encouraging and being a great companion / care giver to his mother.

Stephen was a walking encyclopedia of anything that his mother suffered from or was inflicted with and ensured that they did what was needed to help her. I witnessed him strongly advocating with a few nurses & doctors, knowing his mom and many of her idiosyncrasies and her health were accurately represented. Stephen was not afraid to stand up and speak as he would educate himself well on each topic.

His mother adored him and there is no doubt in my mind that her life had been enriched and prolonged because of the love and care he gave to her. What a haven of comfort he gave his mom by having her back and being there for her every step of the way. What a true blessing he was to her, and she was to him.

Mandy Shalitis
Long-time caretaker for the elderly

Made in United States
Troutdale, OR
04/18/2024

19272408R00181